Invisible Roots

How Healing Past Life Trauma Can Liberate Your Present

by Barbara Stone

Energy Psychology Press
Santa Rosa, CA 95403
www.energypsychologypress.com

Cataloging-in-Publication Data

Stone, Barbara, 1948–
Invisible roots : how healing past life trauma can liberate your present / Barbara Stone.
— 1st ed.
    p. cm.
Includes bibliographical references and index.
ISBN 978-1-60415-017-9
    1. Energy psychology. 2. Psychic trauma—Treatment. 3. Post-traumatic stress disorder—
Treatment. 4. Mind and body therapies. I. Title.
RC489.E53S76 2008
616.89—dc22

Cover design by Karen Kane, www.CuriousSky.com
Photos by Barbara Stone unless otherwise stated
Typesetting by Karin Kinsey
Editing by Stephanie Marohn
Typeset in Ex Ponto MM and Bernhard Modern Std
Printed in USA
First Edition

10 9 8 7 6 5 4 3 2 1

This book is dedicated to Dr. Elisabeth Rüf,
my beloved analyst at the C. G. Jung Institute in Zürich
who helped me understand myself.

*When you eventually see through the veils to how things really are, you will keep
saying again and again, "This is certainly not like we thought it was."*

–Rumi

Praise for Invisible Roots:

Fascinating reading...whether you believe in past lives or not, this book offers new understandings of subtle energies and effective ways of relieving human suffering.

—Dorothea Hover-Kramer, EdD, DCEP
Cofounder of the Association for Comprehensive Energy Psychology and
Author of *Second Chance at Your Dream*, her sixth book about human energies

Dr. Stone bravely walks with her clients into the territory of the soul to find the Invisible Roots of the traumas held in their bodies, chakras, and biofields. Reading these true stories makes the linear mind want to know more, satisfies the dream-time mind, and provides the reader with a basket of sacred tools for dramatic and lasting healing.

—Mary Hammond, MA, LPC, DCEP
Author of Living Your Soul's Purpose

Contents

Section III: Root Cause

Appendices

Foreword

We all need to open to and accept our experiences rather than close our minds to what we do not or cannot believe. Medical training focuses on diagnoses and leaves out important aspects of healing such as teaching physicians self-care and how to listen to the experiences of their patients. Due to this deficiency, many doctors close their minds and reject ideas that do not fit into their framework of reality. Quantum physicists accept the reality they see before them, even if they cannot explain how or understand why it is the way it is. I encourage everyone to be open-minded and do the same.

As a physician, my life changed when a patient asked me to help her to live between office visits. Seeking answers for how to live, early in my career, I sought out other open-minded physicians who practiced holistic medicine. I also found many poets and authors who wrote about their direct experience and awareness of the true nature of life.

Years ago, many doctors criticized me for asking patients who developed cancer and other illnesses what had happened in their lives prior to the onset of the disease. This was before research revealed that loneliness lowers immune function, while laughter improves survival statistics. Decades ago in W. H. Auden's poem "Miss Gee," a doctor points to the origin of cancer by saying:

> Childless women get it,
> And men when they retire;
> It's as if there had to be some outlet
> For their foiled creative fire.

In the early 1900s, Jungian therapist Elida Evans wrote that cancer is growth gone wrong and a message to take a new road in your life. Other doctors said I was creating guilt and blaming the patient; however, I was brought up believing that God redirected us at times and that the curse of a life-threatening illness could become a blessing.

Barbara Stone is a prime example of turning a diagnosis of cancer (in 1991) into a challenge to live life more fully and to heal the past. As part of this process, she followed the turn her psychotherapy practice took as her clients began to bring past life trauma and earthbound spirits into the therapy room.

Today, I see how much people benefit physically from creating a new life. Taking a medical history focuses more on what is wrong with a person than on what is happening in that person's life, dreams, and experiences. Health professionals need to open to what is right with people and become the midwives of life's labor pains to produce a new person! Stories contain the truth. When people know you are open-minded and can accept and listen to their experiences, they will share their stories with you without fearing criticism and rejection.

For many years now, I have known Dr. Ray Moody, the author of *Life After Life,* and Dr. Brian Weiss, the author of *Many Lives, Many Masters.* I talked to Brian about a problem I saw in the theory of reincarnation. Parents would tell me stories about a deceased child returning years later in some visible and/or spiritual context. At the time, my reaction was, "Your kid is a bum. He should be reincarnated by now, in a new body and in school."

But Brian explained to me, "There is no time when you are out of your body."

Gradually, my mind opened to new frameworks of reality. Though I did not seek paranormal experiences, many of them came into my life and opened my mind to realms beyond the physical. I will share some of these stories with you, starting with one from my childhood.

Near-Death Experience

One day when I was four years old, I was home in bed with one of my frequent ear infections. I took apart my toy telephone by unscrewing the dial, then put all the pieces in my mouth as I had seen carpenters do while working with nails. Before I could take the pieces back out, I aspirated them and went into laryngospasm. As I write this account, I can still feel my intercostal muscles and diaphragm forcefully trying to suck air into my lungs. My mother was in the kitchen, but because my larynx was totally obstructed, I was unable to make any sounds to attract her attention. Then I was not struggling anymore and was above the head of the bed, perfectly comfortable as I watched the boy on the bed die.

As a four-year-old, I found being free of my body a fascinating blessing. I never stopped to think about how I could still see while out of my body. People born blind are also able to see when they have near-death experiences. The book *Mindsight: Near-Death and Out-of-Body Experiences in the Blind*, by Kenneth Ring and Sharon Cooper, discusses these cases. I agree with the words of author William Saroyan who described a dying young man in one of his stories as becoming "dreamless, unalive, perfect." The drawings of patients tell me the same thing. When people with disfigured bodies, amputations, and colostomies suddenly draw themselves as whole and perfect again, I realize they are telling me they are going to die and be perfect again, free of their bodies.

Although I felt sorry that my mother would find me dead, I preferred my new state and intellectually chose death over life. Then the boy on the bed began some agonal vomiting, which had the same effect as a Heimlich maneuver, and all the toy parts came flying out. As he began to breathe again, I felt very angry. Against my will, I found myself back in my body. I can still remember yelling, "Who did that?" My four-year-old thought was that God had a schedule and had made the decision that I was not supposed to die yet. Apparently, an angel did the Heimlich maneuver on me.

More Miraculous Interventions

Twice people driving through red lights have totaled my car. Once I fell off our roof when the top rung on my wooden ladder snapped off. None of these accidents resulted in any significant injury to my body. After mentioning these and other near-disasters in a lecture, a man in the audience told me I had an angel, and he knew his name.

When I asked for my angel's name, the man inquired, "What did you say when the ladder broke?"

I responded, "I yelled, 'Oh, shit!'"

He told me, "That's his name."

I will add that my angel always shows up when I call him in an impassioned way. Quantum physics teaches us that desire and intention alter the physical world, changing the outcome of events. Now, when I have an accident, I call my angel's name and start laughing so that I am relaxed when I hit the ground—as after skidding on the ice while riding my bike—and I don't sustain any injuries.

Spiritual Energy Healing

My next experience was with the healer Olga Worrall. I had injured my leg training for a marathon, and the pain was not responding to rest or therapy. Olga was a guest speaker at an American Holistic Medical Association

Norman Shealy, MD, lecturing on spiritual healers Ambrose and Olga Worrall at the Toronto Energy Psychology Conference "Lighting the Way to Wholeness," November 11, 2006. Note the orbs of light in the photo: Over Norm's head is an orb that may represent his spirit guide. Over the head of the woman in the front row, second from the left, is an extremely bright orb. Several orbs of different sizes appear near the ceiling. On the screen is a beautiful orb of light between Ambrose and Olga.

conference. My wife encouraged me to ask her to heal me, but I was too embarrassed to ask and very frankly was a non-believer. Nevertheless, my wife pushed me forward. Olga sat me down in a chair and placed both of her hands on my leg. The heat from her hands was incredible. When Olga finished the healing, I stood up and was completely healed. The pain was gone, and I could walk normally. I became a believer!

Spirit Guides

A few years later, Olga and I attended the funeral of a mutual friend. Afterward, as we were standing in a deserted hallway, Olga asked me if I am Jewish. I inquired, "Why are you asking?"

Olga responded, "Because two rabbis are standing next to you." She went on to tell me their names and describe their garments, which included their prayer shawls and caps. Her description of them was exactly what I had seen in previous meditation and imagery sessions when I had met these figures.

While giving a lecture one evening, I could not follow my notes. I felt like someone else was giving the talk, and I was simply verbalizing it for him. Since his talk seemed better than mine, I just let it happen.

A woman came up to me after the lecture and reported, "I've heard you before. That was better than usual, and standing in front of you for the entire lecture was a man. I drew his picture."

Again, she drew the exact face and features of my inner guide. I have the picture hanging in our home.

Messages from Beyond

One of my patients revealed to me that she was a medium who communicated with the dead, and since she knew I wasn't a normal doctor, she felt she could talk to me about the messages she had received for me. At various times, she gave me messages from people who had died. She named the people and spoke with words and expressions that sounded like them.

One unforgettable message was from a doctor named Frank, a deceased member of our cancer support group. Frank communicated, "Bernie, if I had known it was this easy, I would have bought the package a long time ago and not have resisted death so much."

When I relayed this message to his wife, she exclaimed, "Oh, my God! That's what he would say every time we left your group—'I can't buy the package.'"

More recently, this medium called me after my mother died. The medium lives far from my mother and me and had no conscious way of knowing about my mother's death.

She told me, "Your mom and dad are together and are happy and proud of you. They are being shown around by a woman who likes cigarettes and chocolate. Do you know who that is?"

Since I told her I didn't, she continued, "Oh, it's Elisabeth Kübler-Ross. She's showing your folks around."

This fit, as Elisabeth liked the items mentioned and was my dear friend and teacher before her death in 2004.

Synchronicities and Appearances

During one group therapy meeting, a woman was talking about the murder of her daughter. During her other daughter's outdoor wedding, a bird interrupted the ceremony with an incredible amount of noise. Since the deceased daughter had loved birds, everyone felt that her spirit was in this winged one. As the mother told the story, a bird flew into our therapy room through the open window—the only time in all the years we used that room that a bird ever entered. Of course, we all thought, "It's your daughter saying hello again."

I look for pennies from heaven to tell me I am on the right path. When my mom died, we found more than three dozen pennies in and around the house, with no explanation for how they got there. I would pick them up walking to the mailbox, then find more on the way back to the house—pennies that were not there on my trip out!

Telepathic Communication and Nonlocal Consciousness

I totally believe that consciousness is nonlocal and not limited to the body. A few years ago, one of our son's indoor cats disappeared when a door was left open. After several weeks with no sign of her, I was sure she had been killed by a predator. I pestered a friend of mine, Amelia Kinkade, who is an animal intuitive in Los Angeles, to tell me the whereabouts of the cat. We live in Connecticut, and Amelia has never been to our home or our son's nearby home.

One day I received an e-mail from Amelia, saying, "The cat is alive because I can see the moon through her eyes." She detailed the other animals and people who were presently involved with the cat. She also described our son's house and yard in exact detail. Amelia reported the cat was under the house, which made no sense since the house had a foundation with no open space under it. Nevertheless, the following day, I stood in my son's yard calling the cat's name and finally heard her cry from under an outdoor stairway with sides that came down to the ground. She had been hiding there to protect herself from the aggressive cats that lived in the yard.

I now talk to our animals. Recently, when I stopped for gas, an abused dog I had just adopted jumped out of my car and ran out into the street. When I got home, I asked him nonverbally, but consciously, why he did that. The dog communicated that his former owner was an abusive alcoholic. He would tell his wife he was going to take the dog for a walk, then go to a bar to drink and lock the dog in the car. Now the dog does not jump out of the car, even if I leave the car door open.

Past Life Memory

My next experience came during a phone call. I was telling a friend how busy I was, and she inquired, "Why are you living this life?" Her intention was to get me to slow down and travel less, but her question sent me into a trance. I immediately saw myself with a sword in my hand, killing people. My first thought was that I had become a surgeon in this life to use a knife to heal rather than to kill.

A few days later, while looking out an airplane window, I went spontaneously into trance again and saw a past life that felt like it happened in Ireland. The experience was like watching a movie in which I was acting. I was a knight, and the lord of my castle was angry at a neighboring lord for continuously infringing upon his land and not abiding by their property boundaries. My lord summoned me and ordered me to kill the other lord's daughter in retribution. I suggested he kill the neighboring lord instead of his daughter and inquired what would happen if I refused. He asserted, "Then I shall kill you." Well, my fear and survival instinct led me to consent, and off I went to the neighboring castle.

I told the inhabitants I was traveling through and asked to rest there awhile. They welcomed me in. I avoided the young woman to minimize my emotional involvement and learned the location of her room. I befriended her dog with treats so he would not be aggressive toward me. Then one evening, I quietly made my way up the stairs to her room and opened the door. I wanted to kill her while she slept so she would have as little pain as possible. As I opened the door, her dog came forward. I offered him a treat, but he sensed my intention and growled. I brought my sword down on his skull, killing him. The sound disturbed the young woman, and I turned quickly to kill her before she awakened, but I was too late. As she turned and looked at me, I saw the face of my wife in this lifetime and knew they were incarnations of the same soul. Nevertheless, I proceeded to chop her head off.

This past life memory devastated me. I sobbed for hours afterward and intermittently for days. At the same time, I realized why my wife's face has always had a hypnotic effect on me and why I am so involved in rescuing animals. Our home has always been a shelter for a multitude of animals of every species, and I keep rescuing more animals at our local animal shelter. No matter how upset or angry I feel with my wife, when she looks at me, the negative feelings evaporate. We met while working as counselors at a children's day camp and have been married for almost fifty-four years as I write this.

When I presented the young woman's head to my lord and asked him if it made him happy, he replied, "You did it, not me. If you had faith in me, the outcome would have been very different."

His response confused me and tore me up inside. How could I place my faith in someone who would make this kind of demand on me? My heart was heavy with sorrow and regret for what I had done to the woman and her dog, yet my only other choice had been my own death. This past life memory made trusting in my faith and decisions extremely difficult.

I remained very distressed until I was reading some of James Hillman's work, and his name appeared three times in articles I was reading. I called him, and he invited me to come and talk. Dr. Hillman is a Jungian analyst, and I learned later that he did a process with me that Carl Jung developed called "active imagination," in which one sets up a conscious dialogue with a figure from disturbing material. This interaction completes unresolved trauma and can lead to a breakthrough in consciousness. Hillman encouraged me to relive the experience to see what I could learn and to realize I was talking about my true Lord and not just the lord of a castle.

I went back into a trance, saw the memory in my mind's eye, and created a new dialogue. I said yes to my lord's request, with no hesitation. This shift in my attitude altered the interaction profoundly, and I realized that I had said yes to my true Divine Lord, as Abraham had, not just to the earthly lord of the castle. My true Lord put his hand on my shoulder and said, "Wait, my son."

I replied, "I am not your son. Why do you call me your son?"

My Lord assured me, "When you have faith in me, you are my son. Now go and bring the young woman and her father here to talk to me. I promise no harm will come to them."

I went back to the young woman and convinced her that I would give my life to protect her and her father. They agreed to come with me. When we stood before my Lord, he inquired, "Why are you standing in front of them?"

I responded, "To shield them from harm." He reassured me that no harm would come to them.

Then he said, "I can see you and the young woman have affection for each other. So I suggest that you two marry and that the land we are talking about becomes your wedding present. Then we will become one family with no boundaries to fight over."

Ultimately, this experience taught me to have faith in the true Lord. Like Abraham, Jesus, Moses, Noah, and others, I understand that what our true Lord asks of us is always for the greater good. And in this lifetime, I did marry the young woman and became one family!

I know that my wife and I have had several lives together, and I still feel the need to care for her and make up for what I did to her out of fear in that knightly lifetime. We have five children who may also have shared the past with us. After realizing that my choice to become a surgeon correlated to my desire to use a knife to heal rather than to kill, and then moving into an area of therapy where my spoken and written words became my instruments of healing, I was stunned by an art project our son Stephen did in school. He filled a canvas with the word "words" repeated over the entire area:

wordswordswordswordswords

In the center he wrote, "wurdz saying nothing." This project hangs on the wall in our home, because it brought awareness that the letters can become:

swordswordswordswordswords

and that I, and doctors in general, can kill or cure with words or…swords.

Conclusion

I believe we bring unconscious awareness of the events of our past lives with us throughout our life experience. I believe that when the body dies, consciousness continues to exist and relocates or reincarnates into a new body in a circle of life. Just as a graduation is also a commencement, so death is also the beginning of a new cycle of life. Because of the brain wave patterns of a child, a parent's words have a hypnotic effect on the child up until the age of six. Likewise, our past lives have this same unspoken, hypnotic effect, which we each bring with us at birth. The choices we then make are related to our past lives, even when we are not consciously aware of why we do things the way we do. Thus, the more we heal from our past life trauma, the better the future will be—our future incarnations and the future of society and our planet as a whole.

I encourage everyone to read *Invisible Roots* with an open mind, even when the experiences of Dr. Stone's clients take you beyond your current belief systems, to see how the healing knowledge in this book can help you liberate yourself from the wounds of your past and step into the presence of your true, authentic self.

Bernie Siegel, MD

April 2008

Acknowledgments

Many contributed to the research and writing of this book and I am grateful to them all. Though space does not permit thanking all of the family members, friends, colleagues, teachers, mentors, analysts, health care practitioners, and authors who have opened my understanding, I will name a few.

First, I thank all of my clients and consultees for their courage in exploring the depths of their beings. I have learned so much from each one of you! Special gratitude goes to those who gave permission for me to share their stories in this book.

Next, I thank my partner, Bert Fellows, for his expert advice as a psychologist in shaping the manuscript, his editing skill, his wisdom during difficult moments, and most of all, for his loving support and patience while my attention was focused on writing this book!

I am grateful to my older sister, Johanna Mary Stone, for her influence on my life and especially for the increase in spiritual activity in my practice as she transitioned from her physical body into the Light. I also thank my mother, Rosa Stone, for her love of books, for supporting my education throughout my life, for introducing me to Jungian psychology, and for editing the earliest version of this manuscript and guiding the process with her broad knowledge of psychology.

I thank the many others who gave feedback and helped bring the manuscript to clarity: Dorothea Hover-Kramer, Greg Nicosia, Cindy Robinett, Sarah Courtemanche, Leonard Kilmer, Michele Seay, Evy Fellows, Mary Hammond, Diane Eyer, and Jane Beard.

I am deeply grateful to Dawson Church for believing in this book and guiding the publication process, and especially for his outstanding dedication to the whole field of energy psychology. I also thank my wonderful editor, Stephanie Marohn of Angel Editing Services, for her skill and appreciative engagement with my book. Heartfelt thanks also go to Bernie Siegel, MD, for his enthusiasm for this project and his willingness to step beyond his medical training into the fullness of human experience.

Gratitude also goes to my mentor and teacher Greg Nicosia for introducing me to energy psychology and for inviting me to serve a term as a board member of the Association for Comprehensive Energy Psychology (ACEP) and to all the ACEP members and teachers who joyfully spread their knowledge of the power of energy psychology to relieve human suffering around the globe.

And finally, I am grateful to all the Beings of Light who guide my path.

Introduction

The research for this book took my soul into places far outside my comfort zone. Past lives, discarnate spirits, hidden childhood trauma—neither my upbringing in a traditional Protestant church nor my professional education had prepared me for the emotional impact these volatile discoveries held as I searched with my clients for a path to true and deep soul healing.

The method we used was phenomenological research, which captures the richness of individual experience, then examines the essence of how this experience presents itself in consciousness to find its underlying principles. The ideas in this book will be new for some people and may seem initially threatening to others. Theories of healing outside of the current paradigm often trigger criticism.

In mid-nineteenth-century Vienna, physician Dr. Ignatz Semmelweiss met with opposition when he proposed that an infectious agent was responsible for the 16 percent death rate from puerperal fever, commonly called "childbed fever," among women who gave birth in his hospital. Dr. Semmelweiss noticed that women who delivered their babies at home with midwives had a much lower death rate from puerperal fever. He postulated that the culprit was a tiny infectious agent, too small to see with the naked eye, present in the hospital.

People have a hard time believing in the existence of things they cannot see, and the colleagues of Dr. Semmelweiss ridiculed his theory. Later, when the microscope was perfected, we could see these tiny organisms. Now the existence of bacteria is commonly accepted, and we can defend ourselves from their harmful effects by washing with antiseptic solutions and using antibiotics.

Many people likewise do not believe in discarnate spirits because they cannot see them; however, we now have a technology that can photograph fields of energy invisible to the naked eye, called Polycontrast Interference Photography (PIP), invented by Dr. Harry Oldfield. A healer invited Dr. Oldfield to photograph her while she worked, explaining that her spirit guides had invited him to take their picture. In the digital image on his PIP camera, Oldfield saw a nun and the face of a boy with red hair. Maintaining scientific skepticism, he inquired what her guides looked like. The healer responded, "I have a young nun who died when she was a novice, so she wears the white habit still, and a young boy who died in the nineteenth century on the wagon trains to California. He is a precocious youth with red hair."[*]

Just as knowing about bacteria helped us protect ourselves from bacterial infection, examining the dynamics of past life trauma, earthbound spirits, and other issues that bind our life energy can help us protect ourselves from their detrimental effects.

Heresy!

Like the colleagues of Dr. Semmelweiss reacting to his hypothesis, I approached the theory of reincarnation kicking and screaming that it was an outrageous heresy! I grew up with the dualistic belief that after death a soul went to a resting place to await the final judgment, when good people went to heaven and bad people went to hell. When my younger sister started believing in reincarnation, I thought she was terribly mistaken and was pretty sure she was headed for the hot place!

As I did my own work in therapy, however, and searched the subconscious mind to find and release the structures that held trauma for my clients, I had to change my belief system to incorporate what I found. This detective work for the soul indicates that people behave as if the theory of the soul having multiple incarnations is true and as if consciousness survives after the soul is no longer connected to a physical body. Whether these paranormal ideas have objective truth or not, they are effective therapeutic tools.

Catalysts for Healing

Sometimes certain details from my clients' past life memories do not quite match what history books say happened at that time. Sometimes the

---

[*]Oldfield, H. (2006). The human energy field and the invisible universe. *Subtle Energies & Energy Medicine* 17(2), 102.

names that souls ask us to call them do not sound like names from the cultural setting of the past life. Yet the stories that pour forth from the souls of my clients carry tremendous emotional impact and act as powerful catalysts for healing present life issues.

In essence, I assume that what my clients tell me is absolutely true metaphorically, whether or not it has any objective, historical accuracy. We work to detect the structure of the emotional impairment that has brought the person into therapy and the soul story that needs to be treated to bring healing to the wound. Belief in the theory is optional.

Captain Robert Snow, a highly respected officer in the Indianapolis Police Department, was totally dedicated to rational thinking. At a party, he accepted a dare to be hypnotized just to debunk hypnosis. To his amazement, under hypnosis, he had vivid memories from the life of a little-known painter named Carroll Beckwith. Because he did not believe in reincarnation, Detective Snow launched an intensive two-year investigation aimed at finding some alternative explanation for how he knew so much about Beckwith. He even wrote a book about it, called *Looking for Carroll Beckwith*. In the end, the evidence for Beckwith being his previous incarnation was so overwhelming that Detective Snow had to revise his belief system.

Prevalence of Belief in Reincarnation

A Gallup survey from 2005 reported that about 75 percent of Americans hold some paranormal beliefs from a list that includes reincarnation, extrasensory perception (ESP), communicating with the dead, haunted houses, ghosts, and mental telepathy.[†] More specifically, Gallup indicated that 20 percent of all adults in the United States believe in reincarnation. Among U.S. Christians, 25 percent believe in reincarnation, including 10 percent of all born-again Christians.[‡]

[†]The Gallup Organization, website at www.gallup.com, survey from June 16, 2005.

[‡]Philips, M. (2007, August 20–27). Belief Watch: Reincarnate. *Newsweek*. The survey of U.S. Christians was done by the Barna Group, a Christian nonprofit organization on the web at www.barna.org.

The doctrine of reincarnation was a central tenet in most ancient religions and is widely accepted in most countries other than the United States. The following statement about reincarnation is so ludicrous, humorous, and shocking that I quote it directly from its source in *Newsweek:* "In one of history's more absurd acts of totalitarianism, China has banned Buddhist monks in Tibet from reincarnating without government permission." This law went into effect in September of 2007 and is aimed at letting the Chinese authorities choose the next Dalai Lama, whose soul is continually reborn to continue the work of relieving suffering in the world.[8]

Alternative Explanations

- Following are some possible alternative explanations (not involving belief in reincarnation) as to why past life therapy works:

- Jesus often taught in parables, telling a story that taught a spiritual truth. Past lives could be considered metaphors, stories that come forth as parables, setting the stage for the emotions that need to be healed in the current life.

- Sometimes a life problem that shows up as a traumatic past life issue may actually come from the life of a forefather—a life in one's genetic history. These ancestral memories of trauma may be imprinted into the DNA and passed from generation to generation, consistent with the biblical teaching that the sins of the parents fall on their children up to the third and fourth generations.

- Swiss psychiatrist Carl Jung theorized that every person who has ever lived is connected to the matrix of the web of human life through what he termed "the collective unconscious." Every action taken by any one person resonates through the whole of humanity, whether for healing as with Mother Teresa, or for wounding as with Adolph Hitler. Everyone is linked into this collective pool of life experience. At times, pieces of this web may surface as archetypal patterns and feel as if they are "past lives" of an individual's soul.

---

[8]Ibid.

- Reincarnation may simply be "Archetypal Synchronistic Resonance," a term coined by author Jeffrey Mishlove, PhD, to explain the synchronicities that lead people to the conclusion that their soul may have had a past life. The term neither accepts nor rejects the theory of reincarnation; however, it does say that at times a powerful bond exists between a current life and the life of someone from the past.

Dream Scribe

In my thirties, I went into Jungian analysis and began keeping a dream journal. In one dream, a scribe read me a list of people I had been in other incarnations. I did not believe in reincarnation at the time and vehemently resisted this idea. One of the people on the list was Simone de Beauvoir, a French author born in 1908. Since she was still living at the time of my dream, I decided my dream scribe had to be mistaken. How could Simone be my past life when she was still living? The concept of a soul being able to have simultaneous incarnations (as discussed in *Seth Speaks: The Eternal Validity of the Soul*, by Jane Roberts and Robert F. Butts) was even more foreign to me than the theory of sequential incarnations. Trying to find an alternative explanation, I reasoned that perhaps someone else in history had carried the name of Simone de Beauvoir before this well-known author. After all, my health insurance company had seven people named Barbara Stone in their system. I was not an author at the time of the scribe dream; however, I had always felt a burning desire to write a book.

Though I still have difficulty believing that Simone de Beauvoir was an incarnation of my soul, I see from my current perspective that issues in my own life resonate with threads in hers. Writing was the way she communicated, and her ideas broke new ground. Before her death in 1986, she wrote on politics, ethics, and feminism, including a landmark book about the status of women, *The Second Sex*.

The dream also seemed particularly ludicrous to me because one of the people on the list was King Henry VI of England. To prove this theory of reincarnation wrong, I set out to study the life of Henry VI. To my chagrin,

I found that I do carry an "Archetypal Synchronistic Resonance" to issues Henry faced. His parents placed Henry in a monastery as a boy because they were too poor to maintain the servants necessary to run the castle. Henry grew up so pious in his devotion to God that he would not fight on Sunday. During his reign, the French, under the leadership of Joan of Arc, easily defeated the English in many battles on Sundays. Henry was not a very good king and lost all the English territory his father Henry V had gained. Henry became mentally ill and had catatonic spells. He lost the throne and was exiled, fleeing for his life. His wife managed to get him reinstated eventually, but shortly thereafter, he was murdered in the Tower of London, stabbed in the back while praying. After his death, he was made a saint, and healing miracles happened when invoking his name.

How does Henry's life resonate to my life issues?

- **Mental illness.** I truly love finding out how mental disorders work and how to turn suffering into healing, and I have a special place in my heart for those suffering from schizophrenia.
- **Devotion to God.** This drive runs my life.
- **Healing miracles.** The new field of energy psychology[1] has made possible rapid, deep, lasting healing for my clients, and each session feels like a miracle.

I remain with some challenges Henry faced and failed:

- How to live a spiritual life in a secular world.
- How to claim my power without misusing it.
- How to hold on to my sanity when the world seems to be falling apart around me.

God's Will

Being diagnosed with breast cancer in 1991 was a turning point in my life. My first book, *Cancer As Initiation: Surviving the Fire* (1994), is the autobiographical account of the holistic approach I used, including surgery,

---

[1]For more information, see the website of the Association for Comprehensive Energy Psychology at www.energypsych.org.

radiation, and chemotherapy as well as acupuncture, meditation, and a host of other complementary therapies. After I recovered, I dedicated my life to God, asking to be used according to God's will, not mine. Working with ghosts was not on my list of things I most wanted to do—but God had other plans!

Discarnate spirits started coming to therapy via attachment to my clients, and I had to figure out how to deal with this situation. When a spirit was present, I noticed that the room got very cold, my clients suddenly seemed to take on someone else's problems, and their level of physical energy dropped extremely low, as if two people were running on a battery that had enough power for only one. I also had to figure out how to approach this subject without sounding like I had lost my mind. This challenge birthed the Soul Detective protocols presented in section III of this book.

Powerful Therapeutic Tools

The crucial and important lesson I learned from my clinical experience is that whether the stories my clients tell of past lives, spirit attachments, and childhood trauma have any historical accuracy or not, working *as if* they are true releases the trauma and helps people to heal.

A more complete list of theories as to why spirits remain earthbound appears in that section, but several major reasons seem to be the following:

- Being unable to let go of emotional attachments on Earth.
- Having strong negative feelings at the moment of a traumatic death.
- Fearing retribution for misdeeds.

In addition, people are sometimes so confused or disoriented at the moment of death that they do not realize the spirit has left the body. Consciousness remains after death, and a person can see and hear everything. Author Gary Leon Hill quips on the back cover of his book *People Who Don't Know They're Dead*: "Being dead is so much like being alive that many people die without realizing their condition." So if you ever find that everyone stops talking to you, acts as if you are not there, and that people walk right through you, consider the possibility that your spirit is no longer in your body—and look for the Light!

Book Preview

The first section of this book consists of ten chapters, each with a case history in which an earthbound spirit was the root cause of the client's emotional disturbance. In the case histories in the ten chapters of the second section, the root cause of the emotional blockage was past life trauma. These detailed case histories show the varieties of human experience, both incarnate and discarnate, in this lifetime and throughout history.

The third section of the book outlines my method, which integrates and synthesizes the work of many other energy psychology teachers and healers. I call my form of therapy "Soul Detective" because it uses the client's own energy system to detect how a targeted problem is encoded in the client's soul, then systematically unlocks and removes each barrier to healing.

I began this journey of working with discarnate spirits with fear in my heart. Frankly, I was afraid of people without bodies! But as I have drawn on help from the spiritual world, the angels of healing have made this journey of working with past lives and rescuing earthbound spirits and helping them cross into the Light one of the greatest joys of my life. The following chapters tell some of the heartwarming stories of this journey. (Names and identifying details have been changed to protect confidentiality. All stories are used with permission.)

SECTION I

Earthbound Spirits

CHAPTER ONE

Mary's Trip to School

"Something is not right," Margaret asserted over the phone. Her voice was urgent as she continued: "All of a sudden, for the past three days, I have had no energy, can't think straight, have no appetite, can't sleep, feel totally exhausted, and my voice is hoarse. I'm supposed to start my new job teaching first grade in a couple of days. Can I come see you for a psychotherapy session?"

Margaret and I had worked together for several years on family issues, and these symptoms sounded nothing like the well-organized, highly intelligent schoolteacher I knew. I wondered what on earth could be going on and responded, "I'll get you into my schedule right away."

One session of delving into the invisible roots of these symptoms surprised and amazed us both. The process stretched Margaret's belief system and led us outside the commonly accepted framework of reality—and our work also helped a little girl named Mary even more than it helped Margaret.

Detecting Root Cause

Currently in her late forties, Margaret had suffered from a long history of Crohn's disease. She had taken a leave of absence from teaching the previous year while attending to her mother's final year of life. After her mother's death, Margaret had gradually rebuilt her energy and was very happy to land this new teaching job. She feared her symptoms might be another episode of Crohn's disease.

Margaret sensed that her energy field was not centered, because she could not think straight. When we checked the perimeters of the energy field around her body with dowsing rods (see appendices B and C), we found that her energy field had shifted backward, a condition consistent with feeling exhausted. We began with a quick centering exercise.

Then we set our intention to find and treat the root cause of Margaret's disturbances. To access the wisdom of her subconscious mind, we used a form of clinical kinesiology called "muscle testing," described in detail in appendix D. The basic premise of muscle testing is simple: A muscle tests strong to a true statement and weaker to a false statement. Muscle testing indicated that the best place to start therapy for these strange symptoms was an intervention to increase her vitality via a modality called NeuroModulation Technique (NMT; see appendix F). We further muscle tested that a major source draining her vitality was an earthbound spirit.

Naturally, Margaret wanted to know how an earthbound spirit worked and whether it was the same as a ghost or being possessed. Every time this issue comes up in therapy, I cringe inside as the thought flits through my head that my client might think that I have dissociated from reality. After all, I hold a doctorate in clinical psychology and am about to tell my client that to get better we need to do therapy with a deceased person whose energy field is attached to hers. Even though I have done soul rescue many times with very good results, the scientist within me still holds the whole phenomenon of earthbound spirit attachment in the light of examination until I see positive results in my client's emotional life. Yet to uphold my dedication to providing client-centered psychotherapy, I need to address the problem the way the client's subconscious mind tells me it is configured, laying aside judgment on whether the situation has objective truth.

I explained to Margaret that some people die confused, afraid, or disoriented and do not know what has happened. Consciousness remains, so the person can see and hear everything. Not realizing death has come, the spirit might not follow the Light to reconnect with Source energy. These spirits who are bound to the Earth plane often wind up feeling very depressed and lonely since hardly anyone will talk to them. To add to their isolation, when they try to get someone's attention, the person just walks right through them. They cannot figure out what is wrong. Since the human body generates energy, and since the earthbound spirit no longer has its own power source, the attachment of the earthbound spirit to a living person will drain the life energy of the host.

This situation is different from a possession, in which a spirit takes control of the mind and body of someone else. An analogy is that an earthbound spirit is like a passenger on the back of someone's bicycle, increasing the load for the person pushing the pedals. In spirit possession, a discarnate being takes over the handlebars. I explained to Margaret that her sudden unusual disturbances might come from the feelings of an earthbound spirit who had attached to her energy field. Also, this situation is different from loved ones who die, go into the Light, and then return in their new spiritual bodies to help people on Earth. Since these heavenly spirits have reconnected with Source energy, their presence is warm and comforting, like the presence of angels, Beings of Light who were never in human form.

Soul Detectives at Work

To find out more about Margaret's earthbound spirit, we followed the Soul Detective protocol I developed, explained in detail in section III, which uses muscle testing rather than hypnosis to access the contents of the subconscious mind.

First, we muscle tested the statement "This spirit is male." The muscle went weak, indicating that statement was false. Next, we tested "This spirit is female." This time the muscle stayed strong, indicating the statement was true. Muscle testing further indicated that this spirit had been with Margaret for about three days.

Margaret wanted to know if the spirit was her mother, an appropriate question since her mother had recently died. Muscle testing indicated this spirit was not her mother and instead was a seven-year-old child who had died from an illness. Our hearts melted for this poor little girl who wanted us to call her Mary. Margaret had picked up Mary's spirit at the new school three days earlier, which was exactly when all of her symptoms had started.

I asked Margaret to tell Mary that we had some good news for her. She was going to get a brand new body! Margaret's heart opened up to this little girl, and she immediately made an intuitive connection with Mary. From here on, we no longer needed to use muscle testing to get information about Mary. Since Mary's energy field was attached to Margaret, their mental fields were like two computers that were networked. Margaret could "open Mary's file" and sense what was going on with her through mental telepathy.

Margaret reported that Mary did not know she was dead and insisted she was still in her body. We asked if she remembered being sick, and Mary did not remember any illness. But she did know that she was with Margaret. Although Mary's responses did not match Margaret's muscle testing that Mary had died from an illness, we went ahead with our Soul Detective work.

We next had Margaret look in the mirror to show Mary the body she was in. Margaret laughed and exclaimed Mary's thought, "The body I'm supposed to have is not this old lady's body!" We explained to Mary that since she did not have a physical body to generate energy anymore, her attachment to Margaret was draining Margaret's life energy. Furthermore, she was missing out on getting her new spiritual body. Then Mary got scared, as she realized she was dead and could no longer stay with the nice lady Margaret.

Since Mary felt frightened, we offered to help her feel better by tapping on a series of acupressure points (see appendix E) to relieve fear, calling it a "Tapping Game." Mary consented, so Margaret tapped the points on her body to show Mary where to tap and then visualized Mary tapping on herself. Even though Mary did not have a physical body, since she was attached to Margaret's energy field, she got the benefit of Margaret's tapping.

Meridian Tapping

Everyone knows that fear makes the stomach knot up. Tapping under the eye, which is the acupressure point at the top end of the Stomach meridian (energy channel, according to traditional Chinese medicine), unlocks this fear by bringing the line of life energy to the stomach into balance. See appendix E for more detail on the development of this new form of rapid release of emotional disturbances and a chart of the correspondence of treatment points to meridians and emotions.

We first had Mary tap under her lip to release the shame that was blocking her healing. Then we tapped under the eyes, arms, and collarbone to clear the fear from her Stomach, Spleen, and Kidney meridians. Mary felt calm after this tapping game. Now we were ready to help Mary find a guide to get back home to God. Since Mary did not know anyone deceased, we called an angel to help her get her new body.

Mary wanted to know, "Where are my parents?" We explained that since Mary was not in her body anymore, her parents had buried her body, stopped talking to her, and thought she was dead. Mary insisted she wanted them to know they could still talk to her. We asked for the names of her parents, hoping to locate them and fulfill this request. Mary replied, "Mommy and Daddy." At seven, she did not remember their given names.

After a moment of disappointment, we scrambled to figure out how we could grant Mary's wish, and an idea arose. Margaret and I prayed for Mary's guardian angel to talk with the guardian angels of her parents and to send them a dream with three messages:

- Mary was all right.
- She was going to heaven to get a new body.
- They could talk with her anytime they wanted.

After this prayer, Mary felt ready to go to heaven. To help with this important passage, we called an angel of protection, Archangel Michael, and also all of the guardian angels for Mary, Margaret, and me. When angelic presence is invoked, the quality of light in the room changes, becoming both brighter and softer at the same time. Radiant joy was present in the room as we invited Mary to take the hand of an angel and go home to God. Tears welled up in our eyes at this numinous moment. As Margaret felt Mary's spirit detach from her and go upward, Margaret felt lighter and more energetic.

I asked Margaret to check inside whether she needed to know anything else about the situation. Margaret saw an intuitive flash of Mary being hit by a vehicle on the way to school. Not realizing she was dead, Mary had just gone where she was supposed to go—to school. We muscle tested that this accident happened ten years earlier. Since this cause of death differed from our muscle test that Mary died from an illness, we retested her cause of death. Again, the muscle held strong for dying from an illness, but it also held strong for dying from an accident.

Puzzled by this contradiction, Margaret did some internal intuitive detective work to figure out how both of these statements could be true. Margaret then relayed her sense that nobody knew this child's vitality had been compromised by an underlying illness in her blood. The accident would not have killed a healthy child, but because of Mary's weakened condition, it was fatal. Though her parents must have deeply grieved her death, if they had not lost Mary from this accident, they would have had to watch her die a slow and painful death, perhaps from leukemia. Their suffering would have been increased. We wished we could have comforted the parents with this insight and hope they will find this book.

Results

At the end of the session, we dowsed Margaret's energy field again and found it was totally centered and much larger than its original size. Although she still felt tired—she had been working with very difficult emotions—she no longer felt the exhaustion she had arrived with nor any of the other presenting problems. Margaret realized that much of what she had been feeling would be the way a seven-year-old might feel in Mary's situation. The confusion could have come from head trauma in the accident. The poor appetite and insomnia could have been signs of depression from feeling abandoned by her parents—an emotional issue that resonated with Margaret, who had been adopted. After the session, Margaret's skin tone took on a rosy color, and she looked refreshed, vital, and joyful. Her heart was filled with peace, knowing that she had helped this child even more than she had helped herself.

The next day, Margaret e-mailed: "I went to my classroom today with a friend to get things in order, and we accomplished a tremendous amount in an hour and a half. I did not get to rest, and I am still going at around 10:30 tonight! Thank you for all your work!"

Further Questions

This whole process brings up some important questions:

- How many people remain earthbound when they die?
- Why don't they all go back home?
- Why did Mary attach to Margaret and not to someone else?
- Will Margaret pick up other spirits?

Although some of these questions may always remain a mystery, the experiences that came through this pioneer work with my clients have led me to forge theories about what might be happening.

Doing classical scientific research on these questions would be difficult, as most of the data would have to be gathered from the deceased, and the scientific model usually excludes the concept of life after death. Here are some theories that grew out of my review of the literature and my own phenomenological research:

- Sometimes a person is not able to let go of someone who dies, such as a parent, partner, or child, so the deceased person remains earthbound to try to comfort the one who is grieving.

- People who come to Earth to be of service to others sometimes broadcast this intention on the spiritual level, and spirits who are in need take them up on their offer. Margaret is a very compassionate woman and loves children. Her heart goes out to these little ones who are suffering, and she wants to help them. But helpers will burn out if their own life force is drained by "hitchhikers."

- The person who picks up a spirit attachment usually carries an emotional wound similar to that of the spirit. This wound in the host may be the portal through which the spirit enters. Margaret was adopted, and many children who are put up for adoption carry deep emotional wounds from not knowing why their birth parents gave them up. Likewise, Mary did not know why her parents had stopped talking to her, so she too carried feelings of parental abandonment. The web of life connects all beings in the Universe, and each person's healing affects us all, making the healing process easier for everyone else with a similar problem. Mary's healing helped heal Margaret's heart.

- A person who dies may not realize what has happened. They cannot figure out why people stop talking to them and walk right through them.

- Psychiatrist George Ritchie's pioneering book *Return from Tomorrow* (1987) is a fascinating account of his death in an army hospital at age twenty and his return to life nine minutes later. While dead, heartrending loneliness set in as he realized other people could neither see nor hear him. His subsequent encounter with the Son of God and travel through other dimensions of time and space transformed his awareness. Raymond Moody heard Dr. Ritchie's remarkable story in 1965 when Moody was an undergraduate philosophy student. Coming from a well-respected physician, the account had credibility. Later, Dr. Moody began investigating near-death experiences. His book *Life After Life* (first published in 1975) contains over a hundred case studies of near-death experiences. The fact that this book has sold over thirteen million copies indicates people's hunger to know what happens after we die.

Invisible Roots continues in the next chapters with more examples of healing that came through releasing spirit attachments. Readers, please feel free to form your own theories of what might be going on in these true case histories.

CHAPTER TWO

Guardians Galore

*T*om, an electrician, came to therapy in his late thirties for bipolar disorder, chronic pain, and a sleep disorder consisting of frequent awakening at two o'clock in the morning. He had been hospitalized twice for manic episodes. He instinctively felt that something more than a biochemical imbalance was involved in his mental state, and he wanted to get to the bottom of what was going on. A natural student, he loved learning and wanted to use energy psychology to figure out how many of his unusual experiences came from mental illness and how many came from spiritual phenomena—an important distinction.

Earlier, a Reiki practitioner had pulled the energetic imprint of a spiked mallet out of his side, a past life wound. She also advised him that an ancestor named Aunt Bea had distress that was still registering in the family soul.

Tom had been seeing a frightening shadow in his room since he was eighteen. Another therapist taught him how to invoke protection and then dialogue with the shadow. This interaction ensued:

Tom: May I ask your name?

Shadow: Yeah, my name is Michael.

Tom: You have changed. (Instead of looking like a shadow, Michael was now appearing in a clear form that looked like Darth Vader in a black shawl with no face.)

Michael: Yeah, you did this to me.

Tom: Maybe we did this to each other.

Michael

The work with this shadow named Michael did not feel finished for Tom, so we invoked the presence of our guardian angels and got permission through muscle testing to do a Soul Detective session with Michael. Muscle testing indicated that the cause of death was an automobile accident. Tom was highly intuitive and already had a strong telepathic connection with Michael, so I requested Tom to ask Michael if he had a body.

Tom reported that Michael started screaming, freaking out that he could not find his body. I realized my approach was not therapeutic and decided to be more tactful in the future! We told Michael the good news that a new spiritual body was waiting for him and that we would help him get to it.

The last thing Michael remembered was going to a big party and drinking. He was twenty-five years old when he was killed in the car crash, which had occurred at two in the morning, the time Tom had been awakening. Michael was still in a lot of pain and consented to therapy.

After making a customized meridian tapping sequence (see appendix E) to release his shame, rage, fear, and sadness, Michael was calm and quiet. He wanted his sister Andrea to come for him. They went to the Light in peace.

We ended with a prayer of healing for Tom's etheric field, to cleanse the vicarious trauma he had experienced as a result of Michael's attachment. Tom also learned to quickly center his energy field with an intervention from educational kinesiology called the "Over-Energy Correction" (see appendix C).

Aunt Bea

At his next session, Tom felt more relaxed and was holding his center. He felt Michael's spirit had crossed and reported that his own physical pain had eased. He felt his body was healing and was ready to address Aunt Bea's distress.

Tom quickly made an intuitive connection to Aunt Bea and sensed that she had conceived a child from a rape. Unable to bear the shame of the pregnancy, she killed herself. She was still earthbound, screaming, "I want him to pay!"

We first let Bea know that we totally understood her rage at being violated and impregnated against her will. Then we gently inquired who was paying—who was suffering at the moment for this transgression? She realized she was. We made a customized meridian tapping sequence to release the pain in her heart, her shame, and rage. Then sadness flooded in, and Bea wanted to see her baby, who had gone back to the Light immediately, being totally innocent. Bea decided to let go of her rage so her heart could come to rest at last, and we asked the angels to take her to the other side to see her baby. Peace flooded the room as Bea's spirit crossed to the Light. Tom's rational mind could not make sense of why his chest felt so much better after helping Aunt Bea heal and go back to God.

Todd

After a month of smooth sailing, Tom caught a bad cold and felt off track in his physical health, his career, and his close relationships. Muscle testing indicated the invisible root of this disturbance was attachment by another spirit, Todd. Tom was angry that someone else had hijacked his energy field. He yelled at Todd, "How about if I set you on fire? Pouf!"

I first helped Tom calm down from his emotional upset over this situation. Then we went back to Todd, a young man of twenty-one. Todd did not know that he had died in a one-car, one-person crash. He felt sad and could see the blood on the tree where his car had hit the trunk. Once he realized what happened, Todd was ready to cross over and went quickly. After Todd's spirit detached, Tom felt that he got himself back.

Fred

At the next session two weeks later, Tom once again felt that aspects of his life were in chaos. He felt the presence of an earthbound spirit on his right side. Furious at yet another invasion, Tom angrily threatened the spirit, "What if I stab you in the heart?"

Once again, I first treated Tom for his fury at these hitchhikers. When we got back to the spirit, he refused to tell us his name. In fact, he was so afraid of Tom's anger and aggression that he would not talk with Tom at all. He did not trust him and did not want Tom to know his business. Not realizing he was already dead, he was afraid that Tom would hurt him by stabbing him in the heart! He was willing to talk with me, however. To ease his paranoia, I asked him to make up an alias name so I could call him something as we worked together. He asked us to call him "Fred." After some energy tapping to calm down from his altercation with Tom, Fred went to the Light.

Hiatus

Tom was unwilling to continue having his energy field commandeered by discarnate spirits. Praying for spiritual guidance, I felt the presence of Jesus clarifying that Tom needed one year of healing and stabilization with no earthbound spirit attachments. After that time, he could consciously decide whether he wanted to continue his pattern of being a spiritual EMT. We prayed to Jesus to have the gatekeepers put a one-year block on letting any discarnate spirits come Tom's way. This intervention brought great calm to Tom.

At the following session, Tom felt tired physically but better emotionally. He reported some significant changes. Formerly, when he saw the figures of discarnate spirits, they were always in black, dressed in regular, business-type clothing. During the past week, he had seen a protective figure robed in white watching him and his wife.

To increase awareness of his spiritual protection, we next did a Theta Healing (see appendix F) intervention to connect with his guardians and guardian angels. In the model of Theta Healing, each person has two to four spiritual helpers comprised of ancestors, spiritual figures, and angels. A guardian may be a beloved ancestor such as a grandparent or a spiritual figure such as Jesus or Krishna. Everyone has at least one guardian angel.

To our amazement, four archangels surrounded Tom with the following messages:

- Archangel Michael stood in front for protection. His message to Tom was "Be strong. You're fine."

- Archangel Gabriel stood behind for direction. Message: "You're OK. You're fine."

- Archangel Ariel was on his left for healing and was present to make him feel good, loved, and protected. Ariel gave Tom an angelic hug. Message: "You're going to be OK."

- Archangel Raphael was on the right for strength and also spanned his entire energy field. Message: "We are healing you."

At termination the following month, Tom felt stable. For Lent, he did a forty-day practice of prayer and the Over-Energy Correction. He had been centering himself physically, emotionally, mentally, and spiritually and also connected with his inner physician, named George.

Tom knew that I was writing a book. Because of all the paranoia that had come up in our work together, I assured him that I would never consider writing about our sessions. To my surprise, Tom wanted me to share his story with others—a sign of how deeply he had healed.

Follow-up

Tom got his full year with no spirit attachments. After that, he decided not to do any more soul rescue work and instead to focus on building internal cohesion. He identified and worked with different parts of himself: his inner child, his feminine side, and his shadow. A new part was emerging: his Higher Self. This calming voice came through with strength and power and kept asking Tom, "So what do you want to do?"

Eighteen months after we completed our work, Tom was doing well. He still heard voices, but he did not move into fear when he noticed them. He often recognized the voices as inner parts of himself. He could still see visions of people in the shadows, but he felt no encroachment from them. He sensed they knew he could see and hear them, but Tom chose not to engage with them.

Tom reflected that having spirit attachments was a problem he could not handle on his own. Before treatment, he had been hearing an intrusive, hateful voice viciously criticizing others (this was Todd), and Tom had known these weren't his thoughts. He had also known his moods were not right and had felt as though he were pushing a big rock up a hill. He had been eating well and not abusing any substances, so his situation made no sense to him. Now, none of these symptoms of spirit attachment were present. Tom had moved to a higher level of awareness and realized that he could choose how to use his psychic gifts.

CHAPTER THREE

Waiting for Onalea

*T*he following case is the first time an earthbound spirit was someone known to my client. Timari frequently came to a therapy
session right after going to the nursing home to visit her elderly
mother, who had gone downhill rapidly after losing her husband the previous
year. Her mother had lost the ability to speak coherently and to recognize
people. Her mind was pretty well gone, various body systems were beginning
to fail, and she was in hospice care.

My hands felt very cold during our session. I tried to get them warm by
burying them in the folds of my shawl, but they refused to warm up. I turned
up the heat, but my hands were still ice cold. I also noticed fatigue setting in
during our session, so I excused myself to get a caffeinated drink to keep me
awake. Falling asleep during a session would be very embarrassing!

Timari was taking painkillers for severe pain in her left cheek, located
right at the seventh point on the Stomach meridian. While her father was
ill, Timari had experienced numbness in her left arm, a symptom linked to
heart problems. She never went to a doctor for the issue, and the moment
that her father died from congestive heart failure, the numbness disappeared.
She suspected that she was having "sympathy pains," imprinting to the health
problems of her parents, and that the current jaw pain might have come from
her mother's problems.

Fear rides on the Stomach meridian, and Timari intuitively sensed that her mother was afraid to go into the next world—perhaps because Timari did not have a man in her life to take care of her. Timari's father had always protected and sheltered her mother.

Ancestors

As we did energy work to release the imprint of her jaw pain, Timari felt the presence of her grandmother, an independent woman who had survived three husbands and was able to manifest for herself and invest well. After we did a NeuroModulation Technique (NMT) protocol to release fear from all of Timari's female ancestors, my hands were still ice cold. Suspecting a discarnate spirit was present, I checked whether this grandmother was on the other side. Muscle testing indicated that Grandmother was in heaven, but a male earthbound spirit—someone she knew—was attached to Timari.

Father

Timari thought for a couple of seconds and then piped up, "Well, then, if it is a male I know, it has to be my dad. All of us in the family feel that he never left. We feel he is still here."

I inquired, "Where do you feel his presence in the room?"

She pointed to the place where she had just been getting her NMT treatment.

I asked permission to check the area with a small device called a Gauss meter, which measures an electromagnetic field in units of milligauss.

Everywhere else in the room the meter read half a milligauss. But in the area where she felt her father's presence, the meter registered over two milligauss. Timari and I both saw the readings on the meter. Now I knew why my hands were so cold and why the waves of fatigue had hit me.

We talked with Timari's father through a combination of muscle testing and Timari's intuitive connection with her dad. He knew he was deceased and was just waiting for his wife, Onalea. He had promised to help her when her transition time came.

We explained to him that he no longer had a body and was draining Timari's energy. We told him he needed to cross over. He did not understand and was convinced he was supposed to wait for his wife.

Stymied, we tried another angle. We asked if he had noticed anyone else there with him. He responded that someone was babbling (likely his spirit guide), but he was not paying any attention.

"Just like him," Timari noted.

So I presented the situation to her father. If he did not cross over, when Onalea died, the two of them would both wander around in the dark in confusion.

Timari added, "And where would they park their energy fields? Whose battery would they drain? *Mine!*"

I unplugged the little lamp in my room, explaining, "When the spirit incarnates into a body, the body is like this little lamp." Then I plugged in the lamp and added, "And the spirit is the light that comes out of the lamp." I continued, "Then at death, the spirit is unplugged from the body." I unplugged the lamp, and the light went out. I explained that the physical body takes in energy from the air we breathe and the food we eat. Since he no longer had a physical body, he no longer had a way to generate energy on his own. He was plugged into Timari's energy field and was draining her life energy. He needed to go to the Light to reconnect to Source energy.

Since he would be outside of time—in the eternal now—when he went back, the time between the day of this session and the day when Onalea was ready to cross would be, to him, like the blink of an eye. He could also be of infinitely greater service to Onalea by going to the Light and getting oriented there so he could help her cross into the next world when she was finished with this one.

We also explained that his parents and all of his loved ones were waiting for him on the other side, and they had big plans for him there—a welcome back party for him and a lot of fun. He was starting to catch on, and he was willing to go where his ancestors were.

We called Archangel Michael to give him safe passage and wept with emotion at feeling the sacredness of this moment. Timari sent love to her dad for the journey, and we felt him cross. Suddenly, my hands were warm and I felt wide-awake. Joy filled the room, and we were both amazed.

When we finished, I got out my EMF Gauss meter and checked the spot where Timari's father had been. The whole room now measured only half a milligauss. We were two very happy Soul Detectives!

Timari reflected that she had always hoped to help her parents with all the holistic methods she had learned. Although they were open to complementary healing methods, they had never taken her interests seriously. She suddenly realized that she did help her parents with her holistic knowledge by helping her father cross safely into the next world so he could help her mother when the time came for her to go.

Two days later, Timari sent me the following e-mail: "My jaw pain is almost totally cured! It has felt better each day. You are the supreme Ghost buster!!!!!"

Six months later, Onalea made her transition from this world into the next. Both Timari and her brother felt their mother's soul energy really left. While their Dad had needed our help to cross, when Onalea left her physical body, her husband was present to receive her in a joyful reunion and to guide her home.

CHAPTER FOUR

Goodbye, Grandma

One of my energy psychology students went through a series of unusual events that changed her life forever. The story of Kelly's interaction with her narcissistic grandmother is so unusual and powerful that I asked her to tell it herself. The following is her first-hand account:

"On a cold day in March, at 3:30 a.m., my husband sat up abruptly in bed. An old woman's face appeared to him and telepathically communicated the message, 'You will be widowed soon. Go back to college, have a novel made into a movie, and remarry.'

"He did not tell me the whole message immediately, since it predicted my death—just that he had a strange dream. By eight o'clock that morning, we learned my grandmother had died around midnight. David had a sinking feeling that Grandma had contacted him, and he was afraid of losing me.

"My grandmother had been an unhappy woman and was often unpleasant. She was not affectionate and seemed to deny aging and afterlife concerns. Sometimes she even seemed to resent the vitality and youthfulness of her own grandchildren.

"David felt she was influencing our lives from 'the other side.' This idea sounded crazy to me, and I felt he was overreacting. I began to feel angry at his behavior. He also felt guilty, frightened, and confused over the message Grandma had given him. He sought help and made an appointment with Dr.

Rosa Stone, a wise counselor with a specialty in dreamwork and mentoring spiritual transformation.

"Two weeks after Grandma's death, as I sat in the rocking chair of our living room, my husband looked startled as he gazed at me. David saw a gray outline around my body that kept moving out and then snapping back. At the same time, my left arm was very tingly, and I felt anxious, unsettled, and scared. That night, David woke up and found me moving fitfully, as if I were struggling to push someone from my chest and face. My arms and hands trembled, and then went limp. Watching me struggle was so upsetting that David left the room.

"The next day he told me what he had seen. Anger arose within me. Why would Grandma do this to me? I did not know what to do with my internal sense of weakness and emptiness. My neighbor noticed an unusual darkness and coldness about me as she made eye contact. I became really frightened as I felt death trying to creep up on me!

"During the following weeks, David and I both noticed the staleness of my breath and the way my lips, hand, and fingers felt unfamiliar at times and the erotic but unsettling manner in which intimacy also seemed to be unfamiliar at moments. Our home environment had the same quality of feeling invaded. We had moments of waking up in bed with both of us shivering from bone-chilling cold, or reading or sitting in the living room and having the temperature instantly become bitterly cold.

"David came down with a very bad kidney infection. Two weeks later, I also began to urinate blood. These infections frightened us. Looking back, the kidney infections make perfect sense. The root chakra governs the kidneys, and the negative emotion attached to the root chakra is fear. We were both scared to death over what was happening!

"Dr. Stone told David he had nothing to feel shame or guilt about and that these phenomena were not coming from him. She asked to see me, as I was the target of this discarnate spirit.

"I needed to do something to save my life, so I contacted Dr. Stone. She gave me her copy of *The Unquiet Dead,* by Dr. Edith Fiore. I stayed up all night reading the book, fascinated by the stories of others in similar circumstances. This whole situation was foreign to me. My belief system as a fundamentalist Christian had no place to put these events. But I knew some force was trying to take over my body, so I had to change my belief system!

"I began to tell Grandma that I was not going with her, that she was not welcome in my home, and that she was dead and needed to go to the other side. I made a cassette tape with these messages, just as the book suggested, and began my work with spirit releasement. I played the tape daily in our home while I was at work, and I smudged the house every day with incense to cleanse the atmosphere.

"One Sunday, I couldn't get myself settled down after church. My anxiety level was sky high. Dr. Stone had invited me to call her daughter Barbara, who held a doctorate in clinical psychology and had experience working with earthbound spirits. Finally, I called the other Dr. Stone, who assisted me with a technique called Thought Field Therapy (TFT) that calmed me down and gave me a real sense of ease and safety.

"Soon, my symptoms became more physical, including chest and arm pain. I went for a complete physical exam and also saw an acupuncturist, a chiropractor, and a physical therapist for a spinal problem. Blood work also revealed a high CA-125 count, the marker for ovarian cancer. Topical and vaginal ultrasounds revealed enlarged ovaries loaded with cysts.

"I desperately wanted to live, but David was convinced I was dying. He became distant, not wanting to go through the agony of my death. Dr. Stone continued to work with him, and he also saw a healer who had trained with a spiritual healer and energy consciousness pioneer named Barbara Brennan. Both of these sage and wonderful women helped him discover the innumerable mythopoetic meanings of death. Meanwhile, I applied myself to getting my life back.

"I continued to tell Grandma she had to leave our house and our bodies and that she was not welcome here and that I was not going with her! I donated everything in our home that had belonged to Grandma to a local charity. This action felt very cleansing to me. I continued to pray and meditate, because I knew my life depended on it.

"I dedicated myself to learning a healing art to offer my service to others some day. That night I had a visitation from an angel—my angel! Her figure was small at first, but when I recognized her presence and asked why she came and what she wanted to tell me, she became life-size. She put her arms around my husband and me. She put her hand on my stomach, looked gently and compassionately into my eyes, and smiled. That look was the most soothing experience I have ever felt. From that point on, I knew I was going to be okay! The next day, our home felt very different. I knew that no matter where Grandma was, she could no longer harm me, because a force of good was surrounding us!"

Grandma and My Sister

"Years passed, and I got well and became a foot reflexologist. I believed that Grandma had crossed over into heaven. But on a weekend retreat with my sisters, my oldest sister woke up and announced, 'I just had the weirdest dream about Grandma. And when I woke up, I swear I thought Grandma was here!'

"My first reaction was panic, then anger, then sadness. I realized that when I ordered Grandma to leave my house, she just moved in with my sister! For the next several weeks, I did not know what to do. I could not talk with my sister about Grandma actually being around her, as she already thought I was pretty kooky. I began to hold my sister in white light, praying for her protection.

"Over a year earlier, I had signed up to take my final energy psychology workshop with Dr. Barbara Stone. When class enrollment was not high enough to run the workshop, I felt very disappointed; however, looking back, I see that postponing this workshop for a year brought it to me when I needed it most—right when I was wondering how to help my sister! Near the end of the workshop, we were all trying to hone making customized meridian tapping sequences. I felt so serene that I had trouble coming up with another practice issue. But when we muscle tested what to work on, to my chagrin, I found that Grandma's presence was with me at the workshop, asking for my help! I struggled with resenting Grandma's interference in my life and my sister's life, then decided the only way for us all to be safe was to help her spirit come to peace and get Grandma back to her true home.

"As we began, I inquired why she had stayed earthbound so long. She reported she had been confused and afraid. She thought she would be going to hell if she left the Earth plane. We made a customized meridian tapping sequence to ease her fears about her future.

"I assured her that she was not going to go to hell and that crossing over to be with her friends and family that had gone on before her was safe. I coached her, 'Just let go, Grandma. There is no life left here for you anymore.' Finally, to my great relief, Grandma was ready to cross over to the other side.

"She wanted her father to come for her, and a beautiful glow surrounded their reunion embrace. Finally, Grandma, my husband and I, and my sisters were all safe and at peace.

"After this work, my energy was completely spent! Still, I felt a tremendous sense of accomplishment about getting Grandma to heaven. Dr. Stone asked me if I would consider helping others that have been in my shoes. I quickly replied, 'No! I cannot do this work—it is too hard and draining! I prefer to assist people who are alive to find healing for themselves. Maybe that attitude is selfish on my part, but for now, I choose to stick to the living!'

"This experience changed my life forever. The past three years are a blur in some ways and very vivid in others. Before this drama, my life was stale and suffocated because I was not fully embracing my soul's purpose. Today, I am grateful for my life and for the love my husband and I share. This process propelled David into his own transformation, and he indeed went back to school and wrote a novel; however, he did not need to find a new wife since I am still here and healthy! I have a new awareness of strength and assuredness with me now, and I know it will always be present. I allow my mind and spirit to be open and expansive, and I have a new trust in life and living. Hallelujah!"

CHAPTER FIVE

Sinking in Ice Water

Usually, the problem of an earthbound spirit comes to awareness through physical symptoms that develop in the person carrying the attachment. In the case in this chapter, however, the deceased person was the brother of the client and was not carried as an earthbound spirit attachment, just as a close emotional connection. Fred's brother reached out to him for help in a dream, knowing he would be talking with me that day. This dream outlined both the departed person's situation and the treatment plan.

Fred, a competent and caring counselor in his early sixties, had just gone through a series of deaths in his family. Seven years earlier, his only brother fell very ill. Fred drove across the country to attend to his brother, Phil. He advocated for Phil with the doctors for further tests to find out what was wrong. Finally, they reached a diagnosis: brain cancer. After brain surgery, Phil went into a coma and then died. Fred took leave from his job and stayed by his brother's bedside during those final two weeks of Phil's life.

Brokenhearted from this loss, their mother died two years later. Still grieving over the loss of his wife and his son, their father died a few years after their mother passed. Fred brought the following dream to therapy, which clearly outlines his brother Phil's need for help, the mental confusion of the deceased, and Fred's starring role in helping Phil's energy field:

Phil and I are playing baseball, but there are just two of us and perhaps a third person. Phil is the pitcher, and I am the batter. I am at bat first and feel like there is a catcher as well—but I seem to be the catcher as well as the batter. We are in this huge field of some- thing—it doesn't look like a baseball field—and it has a huge pit for the pitcher's mound.

On hearing about the huge field, I immediately thought of the huge human energy field.

It seems like kind of an odd situation, but Phil finally pitches to me, and I hit the ball and it goes way out, but I'm pretty sure I am put out. He catches the ball, and it is his turn to bat.

So Phil goes to bat, and I have to trade places—I am the pitcher. When I get out to the mound, it is like a huge pit, and I can just barely see out.

I keep telling him there is no way I can pitch to him from there, that it is too deep, and it is too far, and I am going to have to throw a huge curve ball to get in from where I am, and I can't throw a huge curve ball and can't even get it there.

I interpreted this part of the dream as indicating that communicating with his departed brother's soul was not currently in Fred's belief system— it was too "far out." Fred felt that the distance between his consciousness and his brother's consciousness was just too great, and he did not feel he could reach his brother's energy field. Still, the dream suggested that a huge curve ball, perhaps a bending of his belief of what was possible, might enable contact.

Phil just keeps telling me, "Oh, don't worry about it, just throw it!"

So finally I throw the ball, and he hits it a good whack. Then suddenly he's flying through the air, and he's got a suit on like a scuba diver and also has skis on. He lands right on the pitcher's mound, but now the whole field has changed into ice and snow.

In the middle is an open place of ice with an area of ice-cold water in the center, about half the size of a swimming pool. He plunges right into this place and immediately goes under.

I can see the look on his face and can tell he is afraid as he goes down. I start to go over there, because I know I am going to have to rescue him. I get a little closer, and he comes up for air.

I can see the terrified look on his face, and only then do I realize he has skis on and is really burdened down by all the clothing and this wet suit and is not able to pull himself up. So he goes down under again with this horrible look on his face, the look like he had right before his brain surgery. He is scared.

I am getting closer, and I feel I am definitely going to get there in time. I think he comes up again, but I'm not close enough to reach him, and he goes down again. Then I am just right there at the edge, and if he comes up again, I can easily grab hold of his hand or one of the skis and pull him out.

But I wake up, so I don't actually get to save him.

The dream carried such a strong emotional charge that it awakened Fred. We often have to wake up right during a dream to remember it. What was happening to Phil in the dream did not sound like heaven. He was weighed down and terrified—an excellent description of the trauma people go through when they die and are bound to Earth's gravitational field by the heaviness of their emotions. Phil's personal hell, however, was not hot; it was ice-cold. In the dream, Fred clearly was the one who needed to rescue Phil, and he was very close to saving him.

Muscle testing indicated that Phil's spirit was, indeed, still earthbound. I asked Fred if he wanted to do some work to help his brother, since the dream showed that Phil was in distress and gave a clear and direct call for Fred to help him. Fred did not really believe that people could wander around without a body, and the concept of doing psychotherapy with a ghost felt really weird to him. He had assumed that his brother's soul would be in heaven and had trouble accepting the theory that Phil's spirit was still bound to Earth seven years after his death.

This session was in person, not over the telephone, so once again we muscle tested the statement, "Phil's spirit is still earthbound," and Fred's muscle response was strong. Even though the concept of working with an earthbound spirit was completely outside his belief system, Fred loved his brother so much that he was willing to give this highly unusual therapy a try. He could see that his dream was calling him to do some extraordinary rescue work with Phil, even though the dream also showed Fred's initial doubts about his ability to connect.

Getting Free

We set up a sacred healing space by invoking a pyramid of light, anchored into time and space by the archangels, a technique from Psychoenergetic Healing (PEH). We called for the presence of all the guardians and guardian angels for Phil, Fred, me, their parents, and all the other deceased family members that Phil had known. Fred felt the sense of family inside this pyramid.

Muscle testing indicated that Phil was the only family member who was still earthbound, and he did not realize that he had passed out of his body. His cognitive process had been impaired by the brain tumors, and he had been in a coma right before he died.

When Fred broke the news to Phil that he was no longer in his body, Phil was a little puzzled and asked for a chance to think. Then Phil telepathically communicated to Fred, "Well, I was trying to figure out what was going on, and I couldn't figure it out." He had not been ready to die and did not know what death was.

I asked Fred to inquire of Phil what year he thought it was. Since he had been outside time for awhile, Phil thought the year was five years previous to the actual date. He did not know that their parents had died or that Uncle

Milt had also passed. Phil agreed to do a little bit of work with us to help him feel better about this transition he was going through—as long as it was work and not therapy!

We first did a Thymus Thump (see appendix D) to help Phil clear up his mind. Right then, a hummingbird buzzed into the feeder outside my office window. Fred felt that the hummingbird was a sign of Phil's presence and reported that Phil would think this whole process was silly. I laughed, "Yes, and it's going to get sillier. If you thought that was ridiculous, you should see what is coming next!"

We made a customized meridian tapping sequence to help Phil clear his shame over what had happened to him, his fears about what death is like, and the feeling of having wasted his whole life. Fred sensed that Phil was catching on and starting to feel better, so we continued with tapping the Thought Field Therapy (TFT; see appendix E) trauma algorithm (sequence of tapping points) to release the trauma of the changes in his body when he got cancer, being unable to work, hiding his disease from his family in shame, and hating the doctor who missed the diagnosis.

As we tapped the trauma-release points, we added the affirmations, "It's over now. The cancer is over. I'm going to go get a new body! A healthy body! A very healthy body!"

After this treatment, Phil felt a lot better. Fred sensed that Phil wanted to reincarnate, to start in the uterus and do the whole thing over again. Fred brought him up to date on the events in the family for the previous five years:

> After you left, Phil, Mom grieved until she died, basically. But the first couple of years were the worst. She just couldn't get over your dying and her guilt over not being able to be with you at the end. She also felt guilty for all the bad things that happened to you down through the years and for all the dysfunction within our family.
>
> Then finally she died suddenly—she didn't suffer. She went real quickly. They took her to the hospital, but she was already gone.

We had a nice gathering of the family to say good-bye to her. She was cremated. Her ashes sat next to your ashes on the table in Dad's living room until he died. Aunt Lucy was there. We had another nice family gathering for the ceremony of saying good-bye to Dad. He was cremated, and now our sister has all of your ashes together. I don't know where she put them, but they're probably in the living room someplace. So you're all together.

Last year, Aunt Lucy died too. She always thought a whole lot of you, and you know that. Down through the years, she was always very generous with you. She helped you a lot. She never ever said anything about that. She always held you in high esteem. Uncle Milt was always very fond of you too. Uncle Milt's gone, and his youngest daughter, Kathy, also died, from cancer. That kind of brings you up to date.

Phil felt a sense of resolution about his situation and was happy to know other loved ones were awaiting him in the next world. To check for any unresolved feelings between the brothers, I asked if Phil wanted to say anything to Fred before he crossed. Fred wept deeply as he reported:

I think he always loved me. He just always wanted to be the older brother. He wanted to be more like me and have a family. But he also wanted to be free, didn't want to be tied down. So he sort of lived his family life through me. He felt inferior in a sense, but he didn't want me to know that.

As I was inquiring if Phil wanted to add anything else, Fred interrupted, "Phil says, 'Get me out of this damn cold water! I'm ready to move on!'"

Laughing, I responded, "He's ready, and we're just dallying around here. And do you want to say anything to him?"

Fred's final good-bye to his brother was very moving:

I just want to say I always loved you, and I always hated the distance and the separation we had, how different our lives were. Our interests never seemed to be on the same wavelength, but we always tried. I just want to say good-bye [weeping]. I'm real glad I had the chance to be with you toward the end. Those last few weeks were probably the best two weeks that we ever had. I felt a shift between us—it was just us. I just wish I could have taken you home and kept you with me, but I couldn't. You were too sick already. So maybe you can come back as one of my grandchildren. Now I'm ready to get you out of the cold water!

We asked Phil who he wanted to come for him. When he responded that he wanted his father to come, we both cried, very moved to realize that although Phil and his father had been estranged for many decades, he longed for his father's presence. The following dialogue ensued:

Fred: So now, Dad, it's time to patch up all those differences and reconcile all those forty-five years of separation from real connection with Phil, and all the heartaches it caused in our family, especially for Mom. So just—

Dr. Stone (interrupting): So Dad, do your Dad thing! Get your son. Get him out of that cold water!

Fred: Yeah, get him out of that cold water! Yeah, that's right. You do it. Don't make me do it. It's your job!

Dr. Stone: Just reach a hand down. And, Phil, just take Dad's hand.

We both wept from a combination of joy and sorrow in this moving, numinous moment. When I make an empathic connection to a client, my energy field attunes to the client's energy field, locking into emotional and sometimes physical resonance with the client's system. I watch for "clues" of physical sensations in my body that come as I am mirroring the client's process. Often I feel in my emotional body the same feelings the client is experiencing, especially intense sorrow and joy. Likewise, the client locks into emotional resonance with the earthbound spirit.

Fred: And I know Dad would. He loved Phil, even though he never really showed it. He would definitely dive right in the water, even if it meant his death—he would do it. I know he would. He would do it for any of us.

Dr. Stone: We call the angels to surround the spirit of your dad to come get his son. In your mind's eye, just see how it is. Is he there yet? Do you see him?

Fred: Yeah, Phil sees a picture of himself when he was about four or five with our dad holding his hand. Dad had on his naval uniform, and Phil is looking up, and Dad is looking down toward him. That's when they were still connected. That's the way he's feeling now. They are back holding hands, looking at each other, feeling love between them.

Dr. Stone (amazed at the beauty of this image of reunion): There's a big trip ahead. And whenever they're ready, we just ask Archangel Michael to wrap his beautiful loving wings around both of them [voice trembling, crying] and take them home, take Phil home to get his new body. Send all your love with Phil.

Fred: OK, Phil, I'm sending all my love.

Dr. Stone: Have a great trip. Fred, tell Phil, "I'll be there later. I'm coming, but I need some time here first. I will come too; I'll be there later. You go first."*

Fred (after repeating the message): Go ahead. Dad's with you now, Fred. He'll take you up with the rest of the family. There's going to be a big party.

Dr. Stone: Yes, a welcome home party!

Fred: Uncle Milt will be there, and Kathy, and Grandma and Grandpa, Aunt Lucy, Aunt Martha, they will all be there. [Long silence.] Hmm...I just saw them passing to the other side.

Dr. Stone (jubilantly): Hallelujah! Hallelujah! I want you to ask one more thing before we finish: Who sent you the dream? [Soul Detective at work!]

---

*One of the tenets of the family constellation work of Bert Hellinger is that when significant others die, the principle of "I follow you" pulls others close to them into death, just like Phil's death pulled his mother toward death, and then his mother's death pulled his father toward death. To cancel the pull on Fred to follow all of these family members into death, the person who still has a body tells the departed ones, "I'm coming too. But I'm not done here yet. I need some more time here first." Since a person steps outside time at death, a decade or even a century passes by in the blink of an eye to those on the other side. They can wait!

Fred (after some reflection): My mother sent me the dream. She said, "Hey, Fred, I've got a job for you to do. Help your brother!" All right!

Fred pointed out that we did this work on the day before the five-year anniversary of his mother's death. From heaven's point of view, Phil, his parents, and other deceased family members were all together again.

Fred reminisced that wherever Phil worked, he had always given one hundred percent. All the people he ever worked for had loved him. Speaking to me, Fred said, "You were perceptive enough to see that this dream held great spiritual meaning and a message that Phil was lost out there. This dream was the signal that he was waiting for someone to come pull him out of that cold water, that limbo, that bardo, whatever it's called. I never would have figured that out, so thank you!"

We ended by giving thanks to the angels, who had done the really hard part of connecting our awareness to Phil, facilitating the therapy, and transporting his spirit to the other side. We just watched. We also thanked all the family members who were there to help in this process.

Fred laughed and added, "And the angels thank us too, because they were on the unemployment line waiting for a job, getting bored—but we'll dream up some more stuff for the angels to do!"

We ended with both of us exclaiming, "Hallelujah, amen!"

CHAPTER SIX

Friends Forever

L ike the previous chapter, the person coming for therapy in this example carried the earthbound spirit as a close emotional connection, but not as a spirit attachment. Once again, a dream pointed to the issues we needed to address.

Skye came for energy psychology because years of talk therapy had not stopped the nightmares that had plagued her for most of her life. She wanted to work at a deeper level to get to the invisible roots of her inner turmoil. Six weeks before her initial appointment, Skye had tried to end her life by overdosing on her medications and shutting herself up in her room. Somehow, even though she was in a drug stupor, her body got up and walked out into the hall, where her son found her. Skye believed that the spirit of her dear friend Pearl, who had been murdered eighteen months earlier, had prodded her to get up—an act that saved her life. After a short stay in a psychiatric hospital, Skye came out feeling like a new person. She also joined Alcoholics Anonymous and kicked her dependence on alcohol, but the nightmares continued.

In her first session, Skye reported the following nightmare:

> I am trying to find work, dressed in a business suit from the 1970s. A friend sets up a job interview for me. The man in charge looks all right on the outside, but I sense he is evil. He is into big money. I can see he has been throwing good people out the window.

Broken glass, gore, and guts are strewn all over. This man fooled my friend, but I can see through him. In the dream, I escape with only getting my business suit slashed. I wake up watching the face of the man switching back and forth from devil to businessman.

We did a therapy called Eye Movement Desensitization and Reprocessing (EMDR; see appendix F) on the nightmare, desensitizing the trauma of the businessman's betrayal and the wormy feeling like maggots in her belly. At the end of the session, as she felt her fear release, a flock of birds flew up in front of my office window. Skye felt this synchronicity was a sign that her terror had lifted. Then the businessman-devil in the dream no longer scared her. In fact, he looked kind of funny to her.

In the second session, Skye reported feeling much better and noticed that her intuition was getting very sharp and clear. Her nightmares had stopped. She was getting along with people better and had accepted a dinner date. She had visited Pearl's daughter and was concerned because this sixteen-year-old was anorexic. As Skye related the story of Pearl's murder, I understood why her daughter did not trust men and did not ever want to have a boyfriend.

Background on Pearl

Pearl's parents had many miscarriages, trying very hard to bring a child into this world. With the birth of Pearl, their fondest wish finally became a reality. They treasured this one and only child and were extremely protective of her. Skye's mother and Pearl's mother were best friends, and Skye was two years old when Pearl entered this world. The children played together, and Skye's job was looking out for Pearl.

When Skye was seven, her mother died from cancer. From then on, Pearl's mother took Skye under her wing, and she spent more time with Pearl's family than with her own.

In junior high, Pearl and Skye drifted apart as Skye got interested in boys before Pearl did. Pearl then spent more time with another neighborhood girl named Cindy. One winter day, while they were ice-skating, Cindy tripped and fell on a stick that perforated her perineum. Cindy just pulled out the stick and made Pearl swear not to tell anyone, because the injury was "down there," and in those days, private parts were unmentionable. When Cindy got septicemia and died from the infection, Pearl felt terrible that she had kept her promise not to tell a grown-up.

After Cindy died, however, her spirit remained in contact with Pearl. Often Pearl's mother would find Pearl chatting away by herself. When questioned, Pearl reported that she was just talking with her friend Cindy. Since her parents got so upset at this explanation, Pearl eventually stopped talking about Cindy. Still, many paranormal events happened in their household. Sometimes handprints appeared between two panes of glass where nobody could reach.

Soon after Pearl got her driver's license, she was driving down the coast with another girlfriend. The car went off the road and wrecked on a high cliff overlooking the ocean. Pearl claimed Cindy told her to grab her hand and also her passenger's hand, and Cindy led them out of the car. The rescue people said their escape was miraculous, because anyone stepping out of that car would have upset the balance and plunged the car over the cliff. When cleaning her up after the accident, Pearl's mother found glass embedded everywhere except her face. Her mother asked, "Pearl, how did you manage not to get a single cut on your face?"

When Pearl replied, "Cindy stuck her fat ass in my face," her mother became a believer.

Later in life, Pearl moved away, married, and had two children. When she divorced her first husband and moved back home, her friendship with Skye picked up right where they had left off. By this time, Pearl's parents had become very wealthy and Pearl was the sole heir to their fortune.

Pearl married again, this time to Peter, a man she had dated in high school. Although others liked Peter, Skye did not trust him and never warmed up to him. Peter was very controlling. He would not let Pearl out of his sight when he was around and made her fix his dinner the way his Italian mother had done, making everything from scratch. When Pearl's father became seriously ill, Peter rejoiced, thinking the inheritance was getting closer to him. Pearl was horrified by her husband's reaction, feeling that he valued money over her parents' well-being. Peter was also unkind to her children, the final straw that made Pearl decide to leave the marriage.

She separated from Peter and set out to make a new life for herself. Peter refused to accept her decision and begged her to return, saying he could not live without her. He threatened to kill himself if he lost her. Pearl feared him and was under so much stress that she checked herself into a psychiatric hospital to treat her anxiety attacks.

After Pearl got out of the hospital, she had lunch with Skye, celebrating a future with the freedom to have fun together and do all the things they had missed because of Peter's strict control. The divorce was in process, and Pearl had never looked more radiant. Skye and Pearl decided that when they retired, they would move to Miami Beach, lie out in the sun every day, get skin like leather, and do away with all men!

That Saturday night, Peter came to try to win Pearl back. Out of guilt, she spent the night with him. But she went forward with the divorce proceedings.

Two days later, he called, saying he had papers for her to sign, and came over to the house. During this encounter, he became enraged and grabbed her by the neck. Pearl fought very hard to get his hands off her throat, gouging her own neck in the process and breaking several of her fingernails. But Peter was stronger than she was, and he strangled her to death. After weeping over her body for a long time, he hid her corpse in the closet. That afternoon, Peter killed himself with carbon monoxide poisoning in his garage.

Skye's Grief and Guilt

No words exist to describe the depth of grief and loss Skye felt over the death of her beloved friend. When she first heard that Peter had murdered Pearl, she wanted to go kill him. But she could not, because he had already ended his own life.

Skye's job had always been watching out for Pearl, and she felt very guilty that she had not taught Pearl more basics of self-defense and survival, even simple precautions such as "Never turn your back on a hostile partner" and "Never let him get between you and the door." Skye knew what she was talking about because her ex-husband had been mentally imbalanced and had tried to kill her. Skye felt she had not done her job of protecting Pearl well enough.

In the next session, we made a customized meridian tapping sequence to treat Skye's shame, sadness, and rage over Pearl's death. During the session, I sensed that Skye was feeling Pearl's presence. As she had already informed me that her intuition was getting razor-sharp, I asked Skye to inquire of Pearl why this murder had happened.

Skye instantly locked into resonance with Pearl's emotions and responded, "It was her time. She had to go ahead of me this time. She is mad at Peter and doesn't know he is dead. She says that her body was just too damaged to sustain life anymore."

I asked Skye to tell Pearl about Peter's death, and she laughed, really enjoying this assignment.

Spirits

Pearl's spirit was still earthbound though she understood that she was dead. I had Skye inquire when Pearl had realized that Peter was going to kill her. Pearl knew when she saw his face change to an enraged demon-mask while she was at the sink. She tried to get out the front door, but he blocked her. Pearl felt frantic. She still had so much to do—seeing her children grow up, a promotion at work, and a trip to Paris. We did energy tapping to desensitize Pearl's shame and terror, and she quickly calmed down.

Since Pearl's death, her daughter and her parents had been seeing her face on the wall at their home almost every night. We explained that without her physical body, when her spirit was present with her loved ones, she drained their energy. Pearl reflected that she had put a lot of money into that physical body!

Skye told Pearl that her daughter looked like frozen marble, and that even though her intentions were good, her presence with them was hurting them. We told her she could cross through the veil and go get a new body, a spiritual body. Then she could come back and look in on her family any time, and when she did, her presence would be warm and nurturing.

Pearl trusted Skye and listened to her. We called in angels to take Pearl back home to God. But wait—Skye noticed that Pearl was not alone. Her deceased friend Cindy was with her! We had them hold hands and asked Archangel Michael to take them home. We sang "Sing Me Home" (from Damaris Drewry's album *Through the Shaman's Door*) to them to use the power of sound to help them on their way, and they took off for heaven. We both wept.

Skye reported, "Pearl sees trees, and she is finally WARM! She has been cold for a long time. She says, 'It's better here than on the beach in Miami!'" Skye also reported Pearl's warm thanks to both of us.

Skye felt radiant that she had finally been able to do her job of taking care of Pearl, helping her in this one last final, very important technicality of getting her home to the Light—or at least that's what we thought we did.

Chained to Earth

Skye looked terrific at her next session. Her energy level was much better, and she had started a new job. She felt clear of the emotional disturbance around Pearl's death. She also put her love for Pearl into action by organizing a fundraiser for domestic violence in Pearl's honor.

We both thought that Pearl had crossed into the Light and was enjoying the Miami Beach section of heaven. Skye spoke with Pearl's parents, however, and found out that they had continued to see Pearl often. They reported she came with people who were horribly disfigured and that Pearl was angry. Her mother knew Pearl was present when the lights flickered, and she could see Pearl's mouth moving on the photograph of Pearl on the wall. Her demeanor varied. Sometimes her mother saw Pearl with her hair up and sometimes down.

At this point, I did not know whether Pearl had not gone all the way to heaven but had come back because of unfinished business or whether she had already crossed and her mother was hallucinating these events.

We called in Skye's guardian angel, Gillian, to help us solve this mystery. I warned Skye that if we were going to run into any work with Peter's soul, we would need to approach him from the energy of unconditional love and forgiveness. Skye knew this spiritual attitude was the only way anything could really heal, including her own heart, and she agreed to stay focused on forgiveness.

With Gillian's help, Skye again connected to the essence of her friend Pearl and intuited that she had come back to get Peter. She could not go all the way home without him. Skye reported, "She did love him and still loves him and regrets that they could not work things out in their relationship. She feels enraged that she was plucked from her prime. But still, she has pity for Peter."

Through her telepathic connection with Pearl, Skye reported that while Pearl was in the warm place, she had felt a heavy feeling inside of her—grief and a tremendous amount of sorrow that so many people felt so bad that she was gone. Pearl was a person who always helped anyone she could, and her heart was heavy because so many people were hurt by her death.

We asked what Pearl's soul needed to be able to have real rest on the other side. She sent Skye a mental picture of an angel being held earthbound by chains. We inquired what the biggest chain was, besides Skye's grief. Pearl felt equal grief about Peter, her children, and her parents.

Peter

We started with her husband. Skye felt that Peter had been possessed at the moment that he murdered Pearl. After she was dead, Peter wept over her body for a long time. The evidence showed that the tears that soaked Pearl's camisole contained his DNA. A chill ran up Skye's spine as Pearl reported that Peter was in Saint Teresa's graveyard, face down in the mud, all cold and wet. Pearl was crying from not wanting their relationship to turn out the way it did for both of them.

We asked if Pearl felt she had made any mistakes. She blamed herself for being greedy and grasping and going out with rich men. She felt pain that she had made Peter feel inferior. We did some positive affirmations with Pearl, including "I totally forgive myself for all the mistakes I made with Peter" and "I release all grabbing and grasping for wealth from my soul forever."

Next we inquired what Pearl had learned from this experience. She responded that she had always tried to live up to the expectations of others. Her parents had really liked Peter, especially since their mothers were good friends, and Pearl was a people-pleaser. Peter was invested in enjoying the benefits of affluence, and Pearl also wanted to "live the good life" that money could buy. When her father became seriously ill, Pearl suddenly realized that in order to get her parents' money, they would have to die. She valued their well-being far above the inheritance she would receive when they were gone. She resented Peter's control, but she tried very hard to please him. Eventually, nothing she did made him happy.

Pearl realized she could have disengaged more gently. She regretted that she had not followed the advice of her parents to separate for awhile and not move so quickly toward a final divorce.

We asked if Pearl wished she had done anything differently on the last day of her life. She regretted venting her anger on Peter that day. She had not realized how close he was to his breaking point when she told him, "You're not the kind of man who can get me where I want to go. You won't leave the house, and this other man I am dating will take me to Paris." She insulted his mispronunciation of English words and humiliated him.

The point at which Peter switched to the demon-like energy was when she told him, "No, this is final, and I want you to give me my half and go away. Just sign and go away."

Then she belittled his performance in the bedroom two nights earlier and said she was just pretending to enjoy sex so he would sign the papers.

We inquired whether she recognized the dark energy that had come out of Peter. Pearl had experienced that same energy in her deceased mother-in-law, Lilly, who had been wickedly manipulative. Lilly had imposed great guilt on Peter and his brothers. Lilly would whine to Peter, "You will do that for Pearl, why not for your own mother?" Peter lost his grip on reality when Lilly died. He was the youngest son, and his mother had her claws into him very deeply.

Next we inquired whose energy had been present when Peter strangled Pearl—his or Lilly's? Skye reported, "He switched, and Lilly's spirit possessed him and got rid of her number one rival."

As awareness of what happened dawned, Pearl lamented, "Poor Peter. He didn't have a chance under her thumb. Peter's whole family hated me. His mother wanted a huge wedding, and we just sneaked off."

At this point, Pearl gave Peter a heartfelt apology for her part in this tragedy. She had felt his sorrow when he was crying over her body and forgave him. Peter was as shocked as anybody to find his hands around Pearl's throat and wanted so badly to undo it. He could not believe he had killed her. After Pearl was gone, he did not want to live anymore.

We asked Peter if he remembered strangling Pearl. He did not. He remembered her standing by the sink, but then he blanked out. When he came to, she was dead on the floor. He wanted Pearl to know that he did not just dump her body in the closet; he placed her in there very gently and covered her with clothes so her daughter would not see her dead body.

Peter felt betrayed and shocked that his mother hated Pearl that much. He was sorry now that he had sided with his mother instead of protecting Pearl. He regretted that he was not able to stand on his own two feet as a man. He knew his mother's control of him hurt Pearl, and he apologized deeply. Pearl had wanted to hear that apology for a long time.

Skye noted, "They are saying such intimate things to each other that I feel like an intruder, overhearing them."

Peter told Pearl, "I was protective of my mother and should have been protective of you."

Pearl responded, "I wanted you to be a man and stand on your own."

They were both like little lost kids with overprotective parents—so alike, fighting off parental control. Neither of them knew how to stand on their own. Peter promised not to call her "fat ass" and not to be so critical. Pearl told him, "I tried to tell you it was your mother all along!" Then they walked off together toward the Light.

Lilly

The therapy hour was drawing to a close, but I felt we really needed to do some Soul Detective work with Peter's mother, who was the new culprit. Skye was wearing a huge ring made of diamond, pearl, and sapphire that had belonged to Lilly. Pearl wore this ring to Lilly's funeral and joked that Skye could have it after the funeral—and Skye got it after Pearl's funeral. The essence of a person imprints into semiprecious stones, and I could feel the resonance of Lilly's presence in this ring.

Skye inquired how Lilly was feeling. Lilly was all alone, and she missed being the center of a big family with pots of spaghetti and children all around. She was a devout Catholic and blamed herself for her sin of jealousy. She would not let Pearl in because Pearl's being tall with blonde hair and blue eyes just did not fit into their family of short, dark, wide Italians. Pearl was like a swan among ducks.

We inquired what had happened to Lilly after she killed Pearl. Lilly reflected that she got just the opposite of what she had wanted, and now her son would not talk with her at all. She had hoped she could be closer to Peter if she got rid of Pearl. "I don't know what I was thinking!" she exclaimed.

Lilly had taken many beatings to protect Peter from his alcoholic father and did not want to see her boy hurt. She had just wanted to rescue her boy, to protect him. She knew she went about it the wrong way and blamed a mother's instinct. Lilly felt she always knew Pearl would hurt Peter's feelings. She felt Pearl was too difficult and did not understand her. Lilly had had little education, spoke in broken English, and had had few opportunities in life.

Skye assured Lilly that she was not judging her in any way. We asked what Lilly had learned from this experience. Lilly rambled on about sin and how she should have just loved Pearl. But she was too afraid of losing her son, and that is exactly what happened. What she feared, she made happen.

Knowing Lilly was Catholic, we asked what form of God Lilly felt most connected to—the Blessed Virgin? Jesus? Heavenly Father? Lilly had had to fight for everything in her life, so she felt most connected to Archangel Michael, the warrior angel of protection. Referring to herself, she exclaimed, "She fight!"

I inquired whether Lilly wanted to ask forgiveness for what she had done, reminding her of the Catholic rule that if she confessed her sins and asked for forgiveness, God would forgive her. Lilly dug in her heels and refused to ask forgiveness. I realized she had free will, in or out of her body, and this decision was her choice. So I inquired whether she knew what to do if she ever wanted to ask for forgiveness. She showed Skye her medallion of Jesus with the sacred burning heart and let her know she knew exactly what to do.

Lilly told us she would go when she was ready. She wanted Pearl and Peter to have some time alone before she got to the other side, pointing to them and saying, "Honeymoon!" Lilly knew that All Saint's Day was coming up soon and planned to go then, on the Hallowed Eve, October 31, at midnight, when the veil between the worlds is at its thinnest.

Follow-up

After this healing work, Pearl's parents put a memorial for Pearl in the local newspaper on her birthday. Skye felt this action was a sign of emotional healing for them, signifying a deeper level of acceptance of their only child's death.

Skye's nightmares never returned, as the trauma of their invisible roots had been eradicated from Skye's emotional system. Her presenting dream mirrored the energy she had sensed in Peter. Though he had looked good on the outside, his love of money had made him rejoice when Pearl's father got seriously ill, thinking Pearl's inheritance was getting closer. Skye had sensed the danger of his love of money and responded with fear, which felt like wormy maggots in her belly. As she faced and released her fear of evil through her EMDR session, courage and strength filled in the blank spots where the fear had been.

Two years later, Skye was working full time in a rewarding job, and her relationship with the man in her life continued to blossom and to be a source of great joy for them both. Skye sent me this e-mail: "I am flabbergasted each day at how great my life is now! I told God that I've let him off the hook for all the bad things that happened to me when I was young!"

CHAPTER SEVEN

The Bridge

Martha, a compassionate massage therapist and energy healer, came for a Soul Detective session to deal with multiple physical problems that started right after she went to a workshop on journeying out of the body.

During the workshop she had an out-of-body experience. Afterward, Martha was diagnosed with a malignant nodule on her pancreas and told that she had only a couple of years left to live. During the surgery to remove this tumor, she had another out-of-body experience and went to "the other side." She passed through a barrier, went across a bridge, and had a delightful time running free with a group of children. Beings of Light there told her that between lives she is a "holder" to keep negative energy away from the positive energy. They also encouraged her to hold healing space but not try to fix everything.

After this operation, the pathology report on the section of her pancreas that had been removed came back negative for cancer. She felt relieved that she did not have cancer but also somewhat disturbed about the misdiagnosis. She questioned whether or not she had really needed the operation. Since the surgery, Martha had been having trouble with her lymph system. The left side of her face was puffy, and her neck was visibly swollen from lack of lymph drainage. She had recently attended a workshop on the lymphatics of the brain. During that course, a student who was practicing their new technique on Martha spotted an energetic void on the left side of her brain.

Martha had not felt well since the out-of-body workshop. I inquired what she had done while she was out of her body. She replied that she held out her arms and offered to be of healing service to whoever needed her. She noted that she had a tendency in life to help others a lot and to give of her healing energy bountifully, sometimes to the point that she did not have enough energy left for herself.

Energy Collapse

We started the assessment by dowsing the edges of Martha's etheric body (see glossary). Ideally, a person's physical body will be centered in the middle of the etheric body, but often the etheric biofield will be shifted on the front-back axis and/or the left-right axis. Martha had a highly unusual pattern with about four feet of energy on the front, back, and right side, but only about an inch of etheric field on her left side. Usually, when one side has less energy, the opposite side has more energy because the field has shifted; however, Martha's pattern showed a collapse of the biofield on the left side of her body. She noted that all of her health problems had come on her left side, which is where the pancreas is located.

We muscle tested that the invisible roots of her physical difficulties originated from an earthbound spirit attachment that she had picked up at her out-of-body workshop—a four-year-old girl named Melanie. We both wept with compassion for this poor child. Since Melanie had lost her means of getting energy on her own, she had attached to Martha's energy. Now we knew why Martha's energy field showed a collapse on the left side: Melanie was hanging on to her in that exact spot!

"Everyone Left"

Martha immediately made a telepathic connection with Melanie, who did not understand what had happened. Frightened, Melanie lamented, "I was sick, and then all of a sudden, everyone left." She had been very lonely and did not understand that she had died. She had been in a dark, frightening place, but then Martha came along and offered to help. Martha was the friendliest one there, and Melanie was delighted she had found somebody. She felt safe with Martha and did not want to leave.

To help Melanie calm down, we asked if she would like to play a tapping game. Melanie was all for it! So we made a customized meridian tapping sequence to clear Melanie's limiting belief that getting well was impossible and then her trauma. She repeated, "I am safe and calm" as she tapped the energy points. Melanie cooperated fully, since she trusted Martha. Melanie told her affectionately, "I knew you were the right one!"

But when we completed the "tapping game" and talked to Melanie about leaving, she began to cry. She did not want to leave her friend Martha and felt hurt and rejected. We explained that she had lost her body and needed to go get a new body. Melanie did not buy that story, even when we explained that her presence was draining Martha's energy and making her sick.

As I was wondering what to do next, Martha stepped in as a co-therapist for Melanie and assured her she would always be her buddy and that she could come visit anytime once she got her spiritual body. Still, Melanie was not budging. When Martha told her about all the kids to play with in heaven, however, Melanie perked up and was ready to go have some fun.

Playmates at Last

Martha connected energetically with the group of kids she had seen in her out-of-body experience during surgery and showed Melanie the bridge to get there. Melanie wanted an angel to take her, so we called her guardian angels to stand beside her, holding her hands, and we asked Archangel Michael to take Melanie safely home to heaven.

The pack of kids came across the bridge to get Melanie, and to Martha's amazement, her granddaughter was the leader of this pack. Martha wondered out loud, "How could that be? My granddaughter is still alive."

I explained Michael Newton's concept from *Destiny of Souls* that the soul brings only part of its energy into an incarnation, maybe 25 percent or 50 percent or even 75 percent for a really challenging life, and that the soul always leaves part of itself on the other side to continue learning and growing.

So off Melanie went, toward the Light and the bridge to the other world, to the kids waiting to play with her. Tears flowed for both of us with the emotional impact of this sacred moment. Martha felt great love and compassion for this little one who had been with her for the past year and wondered how she had died. We muscle tested that the cause of death was asthma, swelling of the bronchial tubes. Martha exclaimed, "I've been having trouble with my bronchial tubes!" I inquired how long this problem had been going on, and she replied with a look of amazement, "Ever since the out-of-body workshop."

Soul Purpose

At a class in Integrated Energy Therapy (IET; see appendix F) in Boulder, Colorado, Martha had discovered that one purpose of her soul was to be a "hall monitor for ascension." This term had not made sense to her at the time, but after our session, she realized that a hall is a passageway to get a student from one classroom to another. A hall monitor makes sure each student gets to the intended destination. So a "hall monitor for ascension" would mean helping souls find their way from their Earth school classroom up the passageway of ascension, returning to Source.

To complete the treatment, I inquired whether Martha would like to take along some guardian angels to rescue the spirits of lost children the next time she goes out of body. She liked that idea. Since the angels have a rule that they cannot interfere with the free will that is our divine right as humans, they cannot help unless they are asked. I call it the "polite" rule. So Martha prayed out loud, invoking the help of the angels throughout her life and in any future trips to the other side, asking them to scoop up the spirits of any lost children she finds and to take these little spirits directly home across the bridge to join the pack of kids having fun on the other side.

Follow-up

At her second session, five weeks later, Martha reported that the puffiness in her neck started to go down right after our first session—without any further treatment. The left side of her face was no longer puffy, and the swelling in her neck was down to half of what it had been while Melanie was still hanging onto her neck. Martha was very pleased that she had been able to help this precious little girl get to heaven, and the healing effect on Martha's body was a visible sign that our work had been successful.

CHAPTER EIGHT

No More Taxi!

Sprite, a psychotherapist in her fifties, was extremely sensitive to energy of all kinds. Her stress load was huge with all the demands of work, household repairs, parenting a special-needs child, and coping with an illness. She had struggled with depression off and on ever since her childhood and wanted to get to the root cause of this emotional dysregulation.

Two previous sessions had worked with aspects of her depression. In one, Sprite gained some temporary relief after doing a NeuroModulation Technique intervention to program into her system a decrease in the "worry" neurotransmitters epinephrine and norepinephrine and to increase the "feel good" neurotransmitter serotonin. Discouragement and heaviness soon returned, however. In another session, she complained of feeling an "energetic implant" pushing against her foot, a very uncomfortable and negative feeling. At that time, we did a Theta Healing session to release the negativity and to program in the belief "I am impervious to evil." Again she got temporary relief, but the feeling of an energetic presence being attached to her foot returned. For three days leading up to this session, Sprite had been curled up on her bed, crying profusely, feeling lost and depressed.

Because Sprite was so sensitive, the crosses along the road marking automobile deaths bothered her every time she drove to my office for therapy. Muscle testing indicated that the invisible root of her current depression was an earthbound spirit attachment. As we worked, I felt the bone-chilling waft of energy in the room that I associate with a discarnate spirit, a ghost.

Sprite really wanted to get to the bottom of her pain and to get free from the aggravation of being stuck with someone else's problem.

We started with prayer, calling forth the presence of the guardians and guardian angels for both of us and also those of the discarnate spirit. Sprite focused her energy on connecting with the person whose energy was attached to her to help this soul cross over to the Light.

Malcolm

The irritation we initially felt at the psychic interference in Sprite's life melted as muscle testing indicated the attachment was a four-year-old boy who had been killed in one of the car accidents that the crosses along the road marked. We both wept when we connected with the sadness of this child, who was feeling lost and separated from his mother. Sprite made a strong telepathic connection with this little boy and reported that his name was Malcolm. He remembered the accident but had blacked out after the crash and did not know he was dead. Muscle testing further indicated that the accident had happened twenty-five months earlier, and his spirit had been attached to Sprite for over a year. She had been trying to shake him off and had been surrounding herself with angelic protection, but Malcolm grabbed hold of her leg and would not let go! She had been experiencing his sadness during the past three days that she had been in bed sobbing.

Sprite talked with Malcolm and told him about a beautiful place that was waiting for him where he could be with his loved ones again and with his mother. But when we checked to be sure his mother was really in heaven, we muscle tested that she had also been killed in the accident and had not yet crossed to the other side. She was still searching for her little boy! Malcolm was very upset, so we made a customized meridian sequence for him to tap to calm him down and release the trauma of the accident. Once he had quieted, we sent out an angelic spiritual search party to find and bring in his mother. Within half a minute, Malcolm could see her walking toward him. We were all moved to tears as they embraced.

Malcolm's mother believed in God, so we told her it was time to go back home, back to God and to her loved ones. She missed her own mama, who had crossed already. We then called for Malcolm's grandma to reach a hand down through the veil to her daughter, who was holding Malcolm, and asked Archangel Michael to wrap his wings around all three generations and carry them back home to God. We cried again as they left, heavenward bound.

I joked with Sprite that I had a new song, "Om is Home." We chanted these words to use the power of the sound of God's name to speed Malcolm and his mother back home. Later I named my e-mail newsletter "Om Is Home."*

Why Me?

Sprite felt the heaviness lift, but then she exclaimed, "Why do all these spirits keep coming to me?" We next did a Theta Healing intervention to investigate the root cause of her propensity for picking up discarnate spirits. What came to light was that Sprite's soul had originated in another realm, a place ruled by love, creativity, and balance. She had come to Earth on a mission to help make the planet better, but the violence in this realm jarred her sensitive emotional field, and the depression from the terrible things people on this planet do to each other had penetrated her soul. Through the Law of Attraction, the depression in her core drew others suffering from depression, like poor little Malcolm. We did a Theta Healing to lift this depression from her soul and to impregnate every cell in her body with love and light from the Devic realm (see glossary), her true spiritual home.

Taxi No More

At her next session, Sprite reported that all the emotional disturbances she had experienced from Malcolm's clinging had lifted. She felt he had gone to the Light; however, Sprite felt distress at her energy field being used as a "taxi" for lost souls when she needed all of her energy to heal her own body.

---

*For a free e-mail subscription to this quarterly newsletter, sign up on my website at www. SoulDetective.net.

The clawing at her foot had really frightened her before she knew it was just a four-year-old child.

Sprite felt adamant that these lower astral attachments (see glossary) had been too hard for her to handle. Because the person with the spirit attachment feels the impact of the emotions of the deceased person, this attachment can make the host act differently and can alter one's personality. Sprite exclaimed, "People need to take this problem seriously. People reading this book need to know what these attachments can do to their relationships, the way they perceive themselves, and the way others perceive them."

Malcolm's attachment had caused a personality change in her, and she made a conscious choice not to continue this taxi service for lost souls to get to heaven. Sprite needed to focus her energy on her own healing and on finding joy for herself. Furthermore, she wanted to release the fear of driving to therapy because of sensing the spirits of so many deceased people hanging out on the road between her home and my office. Sprite also felt that these souls could be helped to get back to their Source from a higher vibrational plane. She decided to just say to them, "Go to the Light. Your loved ones are waiting."

Etheric Break

Sprite asked to work on releasing her vulnerability to picking up any more lower astral energy forms. Muscle testing showed that Sprite had a break in her etheric body in the area around the pineal gland. The emotion that accompanied this situation was fear. We then found six inner children who were soul fragments from Sprite's past lives. Scared and depressed, they were still carrying emotional disturbance over the way they had died. One was male, and the other five were female.

One of these inner children wanted therapy all by herself, so we let her go first. The customized meridian tapping sequence we made for her treated shame, distrust that healing was possible, guilt, and rage. The customized sequences for the other five inner children first released their limiting belief that healing was not possible and then treated their fear. Sprite called on the energy of courage to help clear these phobias. Afterward, we installed the positive statement, "I am fulfilled, affectionate, and invigorated."

At the end of the session, Sprite muscle tested that the energy of her pineal gland had been restored and that she no longer carried the vulnerability to picking up any more spirit attachments from the lower astral plane. She left the session able to focus fully on strengthening herself in positive ways. She vowed to help others from the higher plane in the future, not the lower one. Since Sprite was a writer and a therapist, I asked her to share her perspective on the work we did together. The following are her reflections.

Dark Night of the Soul

"As we evolve, personal trials and tests of greater spiritual magnitude come our way. Life may appear to get harder rather than easier. When Malcolm and other attachments happened, I was having what I believe Saint John of the Cross labeled a 'Dark Night of the Soul.' In *Secrets of the Lost Mode of Prayer*, Gregg Braden writes about how just as things seem to be falling into place, instead, everything falls apart. I was going through a time when I felt like I had lost all I loved and cherished. I perceived myself as helpless, hopeless, and stuck—no way out. These feelings came totally unanticipated, without warning, at one of the happiest moments in my life. We had just purchased my dream vacation beach condo, and I had just finished decorating it and making it my own. My dream of creating a private retreat from life's stresses grew fainter and fainter as, instead, I withdrew inward with my shadow and began an intensive healing journey.

"Having graduated from several of Dr. Stone's wonderful trainings, I decided to hook up with her for counsel. I had also read her book *Cancer as Initiation: Surviving the Fire*, the autobiography of her journey through illness. So I knew she was deeply spiritual, like me. Best of all, I felt safe in her warm, compassionate presence. Her pure intentions and kindness as a therapist are outstanding.

"As I drove to my weekly therapy and healing sessions, I noticed the numerous white crosses that decorated both sides of the busy highway that connected our homes. Many of the crosses had flowers and other artifacts for the deceased. When I see these crosses, I often send a loving prayer to the soul that transitioned so tragically. Only in retrospect did I realize that this prayer was perhaps sending out sparklers to the astrals, lighting a path for them to find me. The problem was that the date was not the Fourth of July, and I never pick up hitchhikers—or so I thought! Yet if you were lost in the dark, scared and afraid and lonely, wouldn't you try to get help, especially from someone kind enough to actually recognize you? Astrals frequently try, but they are ignored since most people don't sense or see them. I, however, seemed to be a taxi service for them. Perhaps my vulnerabilities, the inner work, openness, sensitivities, and lack of protection all contributed.

"Previous to Malcolm's rescue, Barbara had helped me remove an astral that accelerated my gas pedal while driving to her house. Fortunately, I still had control of my car, as the maneuver seemed to be mainly an attempt to get attention. This episode forced me to have another unplanned but terribly necessary astral rescue/removal session with Barbara. My other agendas were put on hold as my sessions became no longer my issues, but those of the astrals. This situation frustrated me and felt harmful, as I badly needed the sessions for myself.

"Another time, I felt an astral presence that had hitched a ride home with me. One night I was reading one of my many spiritual books about how God does not judge, but is all love and how life is a journey to be experienced. Suddenly, this astral presence left of its own accord. Perhaps the person had feared condemnation and felt free to enter the Light after reading about the true nature of God. I wondered whether I could have been his spiritual teacher.

"The little boy Malcolm, however, was the one who captured my heart and Barbara's and brought us both to tears. Many soul threads may have contributed to attracting him to me. Perhaps the pink in my aura reminded him of his mother's love, coupled with some dark areas from my dark night encounters that may have been similar to his own mother's period of despair. Coming with me may have given him a degree of extra comfort and safety, considering the extreme trauma he was in at the time. His presence was so strong that I could easily feel him as he clung to my leg. Going about my daily business, I told a healer I knew to feel the area, and she too was alarmed at feeling the presence of this energetic attachment that turned out to be a ghost.

"I often remind myself that life has no accidents, and everything happens for a higher reason as part of this divine drama we call reality. I know I incarnated at a most challenging planetary time. I have always had a deep sense that I am here to help others, but initially I overlooked the finer print involved with assisting my fellow man! Just as marriage vows include 'in sickness and in health,' helping humans includes incarnate and discarnate. Perhaps we could make a new bumper sticker, 'Aid an Astral Today'— just kidding!

"Most important of all, I remember Barbara and I feeling extraordinarily grateful for God's presence enabling us to reunite Malcolm with his mother. At the time, doing this soul rescue felt like the most extraordinary thing a person could ever do. Despite the fact that this work can bring tremendous personal satisfaction, it needs to be undertaken seriously, with a pure heart and intention. Soul rescue is not a game, nor for curiosity seekers who want an astral experience. Rather, it is the emergency room of the astral world. Just as you would want a doctor present in an ER, specialists are also required in this work. If you decide to become a Soul Detective, train well, because you never know who or what situation you might encounter. Get the help you need to feel spiritually protected as you doctor these souls."

Peace and Blessings to All,

Sprite

CHAPTER NINE

Vow of Poverty

A t a professional conference, I had lunch with a hardworking colleague. He had just decided to rearrange his work life to spend more time with his wife and delightful little daughter instead of working long hours six days per week to make ends meet. He had just cleared his limiting beliefs around letting in abundance at an Emotional Freedom Techniques (EFT; see appendix F) class and noticed how good this new attitude felt. He was exploring developing multiple streams of income and ways to shift his caseload so he could bring in more money without working more hours.

Earlier in his life, he had felt a call from God to serve in the clergy as a Catholic priest. However, before taking his final vows, he left his order to become a psychotherapist. Over lunch, I mentioned to him the work I had done in a Theta Healing class to release myself from the vows of poverty I had taken in my past lives as a nun. I explained that the vows one takes in a past life are written on the soul. If one has embraced poverty as a path to God, to preserve integrity, the energy field will conspire to block abundance so that the soul's commitment to poverty will stay intact.

I offered to check whether he had any vows of poverty still written on his soul, and muscle testing indicated that he did. He was very pleased when I offered a three-minute Theta Healing intervention to release those vows from his system at four levels: the Core Belief Level, the Genetic Level, the

History Level (which includes past life memories and collective consciousness experiences), and the Soul Level. He intuitively understood the problem and was eager to release this barricade to prosperity.

After this quick intervention, we did a "blind" muscle test to find out whether the poverty vows were erased. So I could not influence his answer, I asked him to think the statement "I have released all vows of poverty" or the statement "I have not yet released all vows of poverty," but not to tell me which one he was thinking. Then I muscle tested the strength of his arm.

Muscle testing indicated that the poverty vows were still present. Surprised, I did what any energy psychotherapist might do when one intervention does not solve the problem: I added another method focused on the same issue. Since Theta Healing is done in silence, I asked him to add a release technique of repeating out loud, "I, John, release from my soul the vows of poverty I took."

He repeated, "I, Joseph, release from my soul the vows of poverty I took."

I felt quite embarrassed to find out that I had been using the wrong name for him the whole time. I figured my mistake might have had an influence on our not getting the desired results.

Joseph next added more comprehensive wording, releasing his poverty vows from all parts of himself: the inner child, the inner priest, the adult, the inner wise man, and so on. I also quickly repeated the Theta Healing using the proper name. We then created an affirmation to replace the vow of poverty with accepting joy, gratitude, and abundance in all areas, including financial abundance.

Joseph felt a deeper release after this affirmation, but our blind muscle test indicated that the vow was still there. Then he insightfully added, "Well, I took a vow of poverty in this life when I entered training for the priesthood." We discussed his reasons for this vow, based on the belief that suffering brings one closer to God and that poverty enhances spirituality. I inquired whether Joseph wanted his daughter to suffer to get closer to him. He found the idea preposterous and wanted only good things for his little girl. Then Joseph released himself from viewing God as a father figure who actually wants his children to suffer and embraced an all-loving God.

Next we repeated the release statements for the vows he had taken in this life, but they still did not lift. Puzzled, we wondered what could be blocking the process. The only thing Joseph could identify was that he had felt a distinct calling from God to be a priest. I asked him to go inside to find what God was calling him to do right now, this year. A huge smile came over his face as he realized that he has always wanted to do humanitarian work, to go to a country where people are in great need and do energy psychology healing with the poor. Doing this humanitarian work would be much easier if he did not have to worry about money. After clearing a deeper level of his guilt around leaving this call to the priesthood, he once again tried to release his vows of poverty. Still, they would not go. What I thought would be a simple three-minute intervention was turning out to be a much more complicated issue.

Invisible Roots

We finally muscle tested for the root cause of the blockage in this process. The interfering culprit was an earthbound spirit! Surprised, Joseph further muscle tested that the spirit was male, known, and a family member—his father, Robert, who had died twenty-five years earlier. Robert had suffered from depression and had self-medicated with alcohol to try to numb his pain. His connection with Joseph had been tenuous.

Robert did not know he was no longer in his body. He was afraid to cross over because, as a Catholic, he knew he was due for a long stay in purgatory due to the way he had let his family down with his alcoholism. We made a customized meridian tapping sequence to ease Robert's fear. I explained to Robert my belief system that:

- Alcoholism is a disease.
- God does not send people with diseases to hell because they are sick.
- Robert was doing the best he could.

But these were my beliefs and we needed to work with Robert's belief system that he was supposed to be punished in purgatory for his sins. We made a therapeutic intervention of asking whether he would let himself count his suffering of the past twenty-five years as an earthbound spirit—alone, frightened, and tormented—as sufficient punishment for what he felt he deserved. Upon reflection, Robert made the spiritual decision that he had indeed suffered enough to pay the price for what he had done and was willing to let himself move on to a better place.

Robert wanted Jesus himself to come get him and take him home. So we called in the Lord Jesus Christ, and tears flowed from both of us as we felt Jesus come, gather Robert up in his arms, and take him home to heaven.

Joy flooded Joseph's heart as he felt the lifting of the vicarious depression he had been carrying from contact with his father's earthbound spirit. He felt so happy that his father had crossed home to God and had finally found peace.

Release at Last

Once more, Joseph repeated the release of his vows of poverty, and this time they cleared. Joseph reflected, "It's so amazing that things I didn't even realize were happening have had such a powerful effect on me."

Two months later, I received the following e-mail from Joseph:

> My life is going great. I feel completely free to pursue my goal of being financially independent so that I can work with people from disadvantaged countries. I am presently developing one network marketing business and just signed up for a second. Last month I attended a seminar called "The Science of Getting Rich" and signed up for a financial coaching program by a coach that has helped hundreds of people become millionaires. This month I fly to Las Vegas for a seminar in getting organized for wealth creation, and next month I will attend a seminar on real estate in New York. As you can tell, I am serious about becoming financially independent. Thanks for your help in freeing me up.

CHAPTER TEN

I Can Only Imagine

Lucy, an energetic, vivacious woman in her early fifties, noticed that she had been suffering from a drop in energy for many months. She came to therapy to find the root cause of this energy loss.

In the first session, muscle testing indicated that the problem originated from an unresolved past life issue (the topic of section II of this book). Further muscle testing showed that Lucy had been a male born around 1650 in Italy and had died at thirty-three years old from an illness, leaving a wife and two children. We did not have time to do any further work on this issue during the initial session.

At the following session, Lucy asked to be checked for a spirit attachment. A close friend named Grace had died a year earlier at the nursing home where Lucy worked. She suspected that Grace might be earthbound and attached to her. These two women had loved each other deeply and had been singing together in a choir for decades before Grace had a stroke and came to the nursing home. Grace gradually declined from the vibrant, dynamic woman she had been to a vegetative state in which she could not even indicate she recognized her husband and family when they visited. Watching her deterioration had been heartbreaking for Lucy and devastating for her family.

When muscle testing indicated that Grace's spirit was attached to Lucy, she began to weep from grief. The day that Grace died, Lucy had gone into her room to sing to her, not knowing that she had passed. When she realized her room to sing to her, not knowing that she had passed. When she realized that death had finally come for Grace, Lucy had stayed in the room talking with Grace's spirit and expressing her deep love for this wonderful friend.

The family asked Lucy to sing "I Can Only Imagine" at Grace's funeral because the two of them were so close. Little did anyone imagine just how close they were!

Grace's Secret

Muscle testing indicated that Grace did not know she was deceased. Lucy loved Grace so deeply that she easily attuned to her feelings. She reported that Grace felt very alone, as nobody had talked with her for quite some time. She missed Ralph, her husband of sixty years. We made a customized meridian tapping sequence for Grace to treat the barrier of shame that was holding in her rage, anger, sadness, and trauma. Grace felt angry with Ralph for deserting her. When she first went into the nursing home, he had visited her every day. As she deteriorated and was no longer able to give any indication that she recognized him or even knew he was there, the frequency of his visits decreased to once per week, then stopped altogether.

Ralph had been ill too and gradually lost his strength and his ability to get out. He could not bear the pain of having no communication with Grace even though her body was present. Heartbroken, he had told Lucy, "That is not my wife!"

When Ralph died, Grace's cognitive abilities were so impaired that she did not know that he had stopped visiting because he was deceased.

Sadness filled the air as Lucy explained the situation to Grace. Her anger and rage began to melt. "I miss Ralph," Grace lamented. "And I don't want to leave my children."

Lucy and I had a long talk with Grace, breaking the news to her that she no longer had a body and that her children did not even know she was still on the Earth plane. They were not getting any benefit from her staying here. Lucy let her know the time had come to move on.

Grace was a Christian and wanted to see Jesus, her Savior, but immobilizing fear came up at the thought of going to meet her maker. She froze. I could not understand this stance, given her religious faith. We did some detective work to find out what was at the bottom of this fear. Since trauma had been at the core of her customized treatment sequence, I asked Lucy to inquire of Grace what trauma was beneath her shame, rage, anger, and sadness.

Through the tears, Grace told us that she had gotten pregnant out of wedlock as a teenager and given the baby up for adoption. This event happened before she ever met her husband. She felt such shame over this transgression of her Christian standards that she never told Ralph or her other children what had happened. She had never divulged this information to anyone, including Lucy.

Grace did not even know the sex of the baby, but her soul longed for connection with this child, whom she prayed for daily. Because of her lifelong guilt and shame over this pregnancy, Grace feared God would not let her into heaven. No wonder she attached to her friend Lucy, given the alternative destination she imagined for herself.

Soul Lesson

We then asked Grace what she felt her soul's lesson had been this lifetime. Grace was clear her lesson had been to learn forgiveness. She had been angry with Ralph for deserting her, just as she had felt remorse for deserting her firstborn child. She was so angry with Ralph for the decrease in the frequency of his visits that she could not even reach out and acknowledge his presence when he did come. At last, Grace was able to forgive Ralph and to forgive herself for the devastation of her illness.

Guilt results when a person violates his or her own value system. This guilt makes a person lose power. Human nature demands some form of suffering to "pay the price" to release this guilt and stop the power loss. Locked in agony, Grace imagined that the price of her transgression of loving outside of wedlock was that she would be excluded from heaven.

Knowing her guilt was holding her back from being reunited with God, I gently suggested that perhaps she had suffered long enough for what she had done. I reminded her that some women in her situation would have chosen to abort the pregnancy so nobody would ever have known; however, she chose to give her baby life and to bear the stigma of being an unwed mother back in the thirties. Finally, after much internal deliberation, Grace agreed that she had suffered enough and was finally able to forgive herself. We made a customized treatment sequence to desensitize her fear that God would not let her into heaven. Then Grace gave herself permission to move on.

Lucy then called the presence of Jesus, Ralph, and all the departed loved ones of both Grace and Lucy to help Grace on her journey toward heaven. Since Grace had been an avid musician, we played "Sing Me Home" to help her cross. When the music began, Lucy sensed Grace felt empty, afraid, hopeless, and utterly alone, with no connection to anything—like falling into a bottomless hole.

Then we felt Grace move through her fear toward the joy of being with Ralph again. Lucy did not feel present with Grace as she crossed and was not sure whether Grace made it. I had a very strong sense of absolute joy as Grace came out of the bottomless hole she had been trapped in and reconnected to God's love and her beloved husband's love. The quality of peace present in the room convinced me beyond a doubt that Grace was on her way to heaven, holding Ralph's hand.

Karmic Connection

Putting together the pieces of our previous session, Lucy muscle tested that Grace had been part of her incarnation in Italy around 1650 and was one of the two children this man had left, leaving a hole in his soul at the disconnection from his loved ones. These two women had loved each other greatly in this life, and the reconnection and healing work Lucy did with Grace helped Lucy's soul repay the debt she felt from dying so young in their former life together.

After this work, Lucy was radiant. She felt a huge burden lift from her heart, and her level of physical energy returned to normal. Shortly after the session, the song "I Can Only Imagine" came on the radio—the first time Lucy had heard it since the funeral a year earlier. She felt this synchronicity was a sign that Grace had indeed made the journey back home and at last was reunited with her beloved Ralph.

I Can Only Imagine

Surrounded by your glory, what will my heart feel?

Will I dance for you, Jesus, or in awe of you be still?

When I stand in your presence, on my knees will I fall,

Will I sing alleluia, will I be able to speak at all?

I can only imagine, I can only imagine.

SECTION II

Past Life Trauma

The ten chapters in this section are devoted to case examples in which the root cause of an emotional and sometimes physical disturbance muscle tested as unresolved trauma in a past life. Whether these accounts have historical accuracy or whether they are parables demonstrating the exact emotional structure of the current issues causing emotional distress, working with them as if they were true led to rapid and permanent resolution of current problems.

The discoveries of quantum physics are changing our view of the nature of reality. Time and space are actually much more fluid than we once thought. The soul seems to operate outside of time and space so that feelings work as if all time is now. Finding these stories and healing the wounds the soul suffered during previous incarnations can transform present-life problems.

Not all previous incarnations cross to the Light at death. People seem to be able to reincarnate even though a previous incarnation is still earthbound; however, this situation makes a person feel soul loss—the sense that something important is missing from life. Physical symptoms and emotional disturbances are often arrows pointing to a past life issue that needs attention. Finding these facets of soul energy and helping them heal and move into the Light restores a person's sense of wholeness.

Lotus Symbol

A thousand-petaled lotus flower is the symbol of the energy center (chakra) at the crown of the head, where the physical body connects to the energy of the Divine realm. Each petal of the lotus can represent one lifetime, and no lotus flower consists of only one petal. For the lotus, the muddier the swamp, the more beautiful the flower!

CHAPTER ELEVEN

The Little Prince

A beautiful and gifted healer named Annabel had struggled with chronic anxiety and depression all of her life. Now in her early fifties and highly intuitive, Annabel was guided to do angelic readings for clients wherein she attuned to angels and let them speak through her. Like Chiron, the wounded healer, she could help others, but she herself could not shake the emotional disturbances that plagued her life.

Several years earlier, her mother had died a very slow and cruel death, having various parts of her body amputated as a result of diabetes before death finally came. As a healer, Annabel was a prime caregiver for her mother. The process of attending to her mother's needs had left her traumatized and severely depleted. She had done a lot of work in therapy to resolve this trauma and received an intuitive message from her mother explaining the extent of her mother's suffering. Her mother felt that her suffering was paying for her guilt from a previous lifetime in which she had been one of the soldiers present at the crucifixion of Christ. Her soul realized the divinity of the One they had crucified and carried heavy guilt at doing nothing to avert this injustice, even though she knew the soldier had no power of his own in the situation and would have been killed if he had refused to follow orders.

Shoulder Pain

At one session, during an episode of depression, Annabel had shoulder pain on her right side. She had been doing lots of Emotional Freedom

Techniques (EFT) self-help tapping for this problem, but the pain persisted. We used this physical symptom as a conduit to access the invisible roots of the problem and muscle tested that it stemmed from a past life issue. Annabel had never done any past life work, but we had developed a strong therapeutic alliance over several years of working together, and she trusted the guidance her body gave in detecting root cause through muscle testing and was willing to give past life therapy a try.

Muscle testing indicated that she had been male in that life and had died at five years old. Without hypnosis, without any further prompting, Annabel intuitively and rapidly accessed the Akashic Record (see glossary) of this life and saw swords. Knowing that a person instinctively shuts down when faced with overwhelming trauma, I steered Annabel away from the swords and asked for the happiest memory of that lifetime. I wanted to get a clearer picture of the child before dealing with the trauma that was creating Annabel's shoulder pain.

Annabel saw herself as a little boy named Nicholas. He was three years old and had curly brown hair and a cute little button nose. He was walking in a Middle Eastern marketplace, holding hands with his mother. She was dressed in gauzy cloth with veils across her face. He was the sheltered son of an important man and did not get to go out often, so this trip was a delight. Nicholas saw a dog, got to taste different kinds of food, and loved the voices and busy marketplace sounds. His mother was doing business, smiling at him, and the day was happy.

Next Annabel felt a dark energy and recounted the following:

Nicholas is walking up a hill to a structure that appears to be a house. Other people are there, with the sound of men's voices and a sense of impending doom. Dark clouds and great sadness come over this lifetime.

A group of men raid the home. His father is fighting these men with swords, but the band of men is so large that he is not able to reach his son. His mother is doing the best she can to fight, but someone hits her and knocks her down. The attackers rip Nicholas from his mother's arms and kidnap him. His mother feels intense pain, fear, and agony around what will happen to her son.

Nicholas cries and screams for his parents as the men carry him on horseback to the desert. They draw a sword, and Nicholas knows he will be killed. He dissociates and goes out of body so he does not feel the physical sensations of being murdered. He thinks of his mother and father, realizing how much they will suffer from his death. He wishes he could do something to save them from this pain, but he cannot.

The men cut his throat and leave his dead body in the desert. Their motive is a deeply held grudge against his father, the king. Nicholas [the little prince] is the only child of his parents, and the men want to cause his father pain by killing his son, his heir.

Annabel is surprised that Nicholas does not feel afraid at this point. But angels are present with him and he is all right, though he feels very sad and thinks back to the day at the bazaar with his Mother when life felt so good. He realizes how life can change in a split second.

We went back to the moment when Nicholas was frightened, right before he dissociated, and made a customized meridian tapping sequence on this soul memory to clear the trauma embedded in Annabel's shoulder. We guessed that the enemies might have hurt his shoulder as they ripped Nicholas from his mother's arms. The deepest level of disturbance was his sadness about leaving his parents and the fear that came with being murdered. Over those feelings was a surface layer of anger and rage. The whole issue was held in place by heartache. After clearing each of these components, Nicholas felt better.

Life Lessons

After Nicholas died, he saw himself floating, with the angels. I asked Annabel to inquire what was the lesson from this lifetime—what was her soul to learn? She reported the following:

I see Nicholas as a little baby. He learned about the bright-
ness of God's Light and the fullness of God's love, a reminder once
again that one never dies. He is in a place totally filled with Light,
love, and happiness. He is preparing for his next lifetime, when he
will go down as another man and sees himself in a strong young male
body, about twenty years old, as a warrior, but for peace. A glow is
around him.

The Akashic record next moved to the time when his mother's soul joined
him in heaven. In spite of the pain she felt, his mother lived to a fairly old
age. Their reunion brought tears of joy, though for Nicholas, the time seemed
like just an instant. The same feelings came when he was reunited with his
father, although his father was a little more reserved in his emotions.

Soul Resonance

Annabel asserted, "I feel that my mother in that life is the same soul
essence as my mother in this life." This lifetime could also have been karmic
repayment of the guilt of her mother's soul around the crucifixion of Christ.
Her mother experienced the grief of losing her son just as Mary grieved over
the death of Jesus.

We asked how this soul work could help relieve Annabel's depression.
Annabel reported: "If death is not to be feared, what else is there really to
fear? The process of death can be scary, but the possibility exists to dissociate
and not get frightened."

Annabel's guides told her: "She [Annabel] needs to remember that she is
a true Being of God and that the gifts that have been given to her, especially
working with other people, are her true gifts. Stop second-guessing and wor-
rying—God and the angels are always with her. What more does she need?
This fear is not necessary."

After this session, Annabel felt a pronounced reduction in her depression and anxiety. Although we hoped that this session would bring long-last-
ing healing, Annabel realized later that one can find things other than death
to worry about! Her emotional state continued to fluctuate, but she also

began to get treatment for the hormonal imbalance behind her mood distur-bance. During the time when her hormones were regulated, she felt good. But when her testosterone level slid down, the depression returned. Gradually, her overall functioning improved. The following chapter addresses another of Annabel's treatment goals.

CHAPTER TWELVE

Jamestown Colony

Later in her therapy, Annabel wanted to release her pattern of being overly hungry. She reported, "My blood sugar mechanism doesn't work." She would eat enough food to satisfy her body, yet an hour later, she would be ravenously hungry again. Since going off her low-carbohydrate diet a couple of months earlier, she had gained about six pounds, which all seemed to go to her belly. She was determined to release the fear of not having enough in general and, more specifically, the fear of not having enough food.

We called in our angels to help us find the invisible roots of this phobia. Immediately, Annabel's angels took over and began sending her information. Annabel's eyes were closed as she watched the screen of her inner vision. Without any muscle testing, she reported, "This fear is from a past life."

I said very little as the source of this fear unfolded. Annabel reported that she had been a "big fat person" named Eleanor who lived in a small Jamestown colony during colonial times. Eleanor felt very upset. She was married to Jim, the same soul resonance as Annabel's present husband, and she sensed the presence of her husband being with another woman. She told me, "After I died, he was with her." We did a clockwise heart massage for Eleanor to help her calm down and tapped the crown chakra to open to the possibility of clearing this turmoil.

When I asked for the happiest memory from that lifetime, she saw her wedding day. Jim was tall and thin, and she was "medium plump." They were square-dancing, with arms looped around each other, twirling around. Everyone there looked like Pilgrims. She was twenty-five when she got married and had been considered an "old maid." Jim was a little older, and they loved each other a great deal. They had three children together.

When the children were ages twelve, ten, and six, the land suffered a drought. Getting enough food was difficult for everyone. Eleanor saved most of her portion of food and gave it to her husband and children. Her body got thinner. She became accustomed to a way of life of nourishing everybody else first. Her body was hungry all the time. She fed herself just enough to keep going. But she felt very tired and weak and contracted a terminal illness.

Jim was inconsolable when he realized he would lose her. A dear female friend of hers was present, comforting Jim, and they got involved. The drought eventually lifted, but the timing was too late to matter for Eleanor. After her death, Jim married the other woman, who cared for Eleanor's children.

In her present life, Annabel had always feared that she would die before her children were old enough to take care of themselves. She was so grateful that this situation did not repeat this time.

After she died, Eleanor felt that she had done the right thing—the only thing she could figure out to do. She could not have borne the pain of seeing her children die of starvation while she had food to eat.

Life Lessons

When I inquired what Eleanor's life lesson had been, Annabel exclaimed, "Being a martyr sucks!" She reflected that one does not have to be a martyr to love. She asserted, "You don't have to give away everything you have until you almost die to be a loving person."

She also saw that Jim loved Eleanor with all his heart, as he had loved her down through the ages in other lifetimes together. Loving her friend, who also mourned her death, helped Jim get through his grief.

As for what she, Annabel, had learned from Eleanor's lifetime, she said:

- Be good to myself! The reason for the ravenous hunger in my current life is to make sure that I nourish myself, to be able to give myself the foods I want.

- Stop calling myself fat and accept myself the way I am, a change already in process in my life.

- Release the fear of being fat and the fear of not having enough food, a phobia that has lurked in my shadow all my life.

We closed the session with energy therapy to release Eleanor's starvation trauma. I gave Annabel the homework of going home, attuning to Eleanor, and feeding Eleanor a piece of apple pie with ice cream and chocolate syrup on top. Annabel was happy to comply, and Eleanor enjoyed the feeling of being well fed!

After the session, Annabel sent this e-mail:

Thank you again for yesterday! I never thought I would be exploring past lives, yet here we are. And the experiences and the lessons are quite profound: they explain so many things.

Several years ago, I attended a workshop with Doreen Virtue and had a reading by one of her students. She told me that I would never be rid of my fears until I went into my past lives. At that point, it sounded so scary.

I have come a long way since then, and because I trust you, and God, and the angels, I am not scared. Thank you for helping me move to a better understanding of who I am from who I was.

Many angelic blessings,

Annabel

Follow-up

After our session, when Annabel had a recurrence of ravenous hunger, she used EFT to desensitize this hunger on the spot. One of the principles of meridian tapping is that these therapies can only clear disturbances on the material that is in awareness at the time of the tapping. So catching a negative emotion "red-handed" is an excellent opportunity to clear deeper levels of emotional disturbance.

At a follow-up session a month later, Annabel noted that she had gone a normal twenty-eight days between menses instead of her former irregular pattern. Her hunger was excessive only the week before her menstrual period, and then it returned to normal after her menses. She also noted that the feeling of being satisfied after eating lasted longer, and she was also able to let herself eat more things, instead of denying herself the foods she most wanted, including carbohydrates and dairy.

Historical Note: Jamestown was the first permanent English settlement in America, started in 1607 in Virginia. The settlement suffered many disasters. Of the original one hundred men who settled there, two-thirds died the first year from malnutrition, malaria, pneumonia, and dysentery. Captain John Smith took control in 1608 and held the colony together. The winter of 1609 was called "the starving time," when only sixty of the 214 settlers survived drought, fire, Indian attacks, disease, and starvation. Pocahontas, the daughter of the mighty Algonquin chief Powhatan, saved the life of Captain John Smith twice. The English captured Princess Pocahontas in 1613, and she converted to Christianity. The following year she married the tobacco entrepreneur James Rolfe. This marriage brought peace with the Algonquins for a time.

In 1619, women were sent to the Jamestown colony to encourage young men to make permanent homes there. We speculated that perhaps as a plump "old maid" in England, Eleanor had opted for the courageous choice to go to the new world as a settler. Famine continued to be an issue for the Jamestown settlement, which was at the mercy of the weather and the arrival of supply ships from England.

CHAPTER THIRTEEN
Unbearable Pain

Sarah is another gifted healer who came to therapy because of the pain in her own soul. She was helping others all the time but did not feel that her own emotional needs were being met. She felt that others did not respect her boundaries, did not arrive on time for their appointments, and did not reciprocate help at times when she was in need. The stress of her life situation had gone into her body as knee pain and an overall emotional tone of disappointment in life, compounded by the recent death of a client with whom she had been doing intensive healing work.

Sarah had known for a decade that she was carrying unresolved trauma from many past lives as a healer. Because those lives had not come to completion, their energy remained fragmented from her soul, bringing her a sense of incompleteness—like something was missing from her life. Muscle testing indicated soul fragments of twenty-seven female lifetimes and three male lifetimes as a healer. Clearly, Sarah was very dedicated to her soul's mission of healing, coming back over and over and bearing the occupational hazards of this role.

Lakota Medicine Man

We worked on the most traumatic of these lives, an incarnation as a male healer of the Lakota Indian tribe in the seventeenth century in the area that is now Minnesota. As a child, Sarah had always wanted to live in Minnesota, a feeling that has carried through to this day. Her name in that lifetime was "Bear," and the happiest time in that life was fishing by a stream. Bear's wife was named Zaira.

When Bear was thirty-four years old, his wife became pregnant, a source of great joy to this couple. But tragedy struck when both Zaira and the baby died in childbirth. Bear felt terrible that, even though he was a healer, he could not save the two people he loved the most—his wife and child. In his role as a medicine man, Bear had taken on the sorrows of others in the tribe. When his own grief was added to the emotional load he was already carrying, the sum total was too much for his energetic system to *bear*. He fell into depression. Two years passed, and he no longer had a will to live. He chose to die. He stopped eating, went off into the woods by himself, lay down, and waited for starvation to free his soul from his body.

Bear's soul did not go up to the Light when he died. Instead, his soul went low to the ground because of the heaviness in his heart. Bear would have grieved for his wife's death no matter how she had died, but his bereavement was complicated by the fact that the cause of death was her pregnancy. He felt responsible since he had had an active part in getting her into that situation. How can a man not feel some sense of shame when his wife dies in childbirth, even though the death is not his fault?

Bert Hellinger, the psychotherapist who developed Family Constellation work (see appendix F), states in his book *Love's Own Truths:* "When someone in the (family) system dies, someone else must die as a compensation. This is an ancient, primitive idea of compensation that works deep down in the soul." According to Hellinger, when a woman dies in childbirth, the husband is often treated as a murderer. The dead women do not blame their husbands, because they knowingly risked their lives in the service of life when they became pregnant. Bear's decision to end his life could be seen as unconscious atonement for his wife's death. Acknowledgment of the deceased woman's sacrifice in the service of life restores her dignity and gives her the respect and honor she deserves. Then a compensatory death is no longer needed as atonement.

Occupational Hazard

The anger, rage, and shame that Bear felt at Zaira's death were also emotions that Sarah felt in her current life at the death of the client with whom she had been doing intensive work. Healers walk the razor's edge with people who are tottering on the brink between life and death, and we support the part of our clients that votes for life. Even though we know we are not in charge of everything, healers still often feel devastated when death comes to their clients. The greater the bond to a client, the more sadness we experience. When we have been working with a family member who dies, the sense of failure as a healer is even greater. Bear had so much on his emotional plate that he could not handle the load.

Anger and rage are part of the grief process, and they come from the helplessness of not being able to stop the process of death when it comes. The only way to find peace is to realize that, ultimately, life and death are in God's hands, not ours. Even though we do our best to help our clients heal, sometimes death snatches them out of our hands. We do not have the control to keep death away. Yet Bear could invite death by making the choice to stop nourishing his body. He chose to stop supporting his life and to join his wife and child in death.

We made a customized meridian tapping sequence for Bear to help him release his anger and rage toward himself for not being able to save his wife and child. As Sarah tapped away Bear's shame about the whole situation, his soul came to peace. Bear was finally able to go to the Light and join his family. And as Sarah made a special place in her heart for Bear, her soul experienced much emotional relief.

CHAPTER FOURTEEN

Trail of Tears

The archetype of Chiron, the wounded healer, permeates this book, as many healers come to work on their own deep soul trauma, following the shamanic path of learning by direct experience. Rasha, a beautiful, soulful bodyworker in her midfifties, had already done extensive therapy to heal the wounds of an emotionally and physically violent childhood. She pulled her life together and started a long-distance relationship with a highly spiritual, full-blooded Navajo man named Don. As the gift of the deep love connection between them blossomed, Rasha's past life pain surfaced in a way that was impossible to ignore.

Several days before Don would visit, her eyes became itchy, red, and swollen—as if she had been beaten. At first these symptoms cleared before Don actually arrived, but later the eye redness persisted into his visit, and then got worse after he left. Concurrently, Rasha got flashbacks of walking the Trail of Tears as a Native American woman in a past life, being stripped of her home and land and forced to march a thousand miles to relocate in Oklahoma. She recognized the soul essence of her husband in that life as the same soul essence in her new partner, Don, whose presence triggered this buried memory. Don had been displaced in this lifetime too, being ripped from his home at age six and sent to school far away in an attempt to break his ties with Native American customs.

The Trail of Tears is one of the black marks on the soul of our nation. A chapter of American history left out of most textbooks, this wound affects us all, whether our skin is red, brown, yellow, black, or white. Telling the story is essential to healing the wound.

This terrible event occurred because early settlers wanted land to grow cotton and coveted the land of the prosperous Cherokee nation, which numbered approximately 17,000 in and around the state of Georgia. At that time, nobody thought that the United States would ever extend west of the Mississippi. On May 28, 1830, President Andrew Jackson signed into law a U.S. policy called the Indian Removal Act, which sought to relocate all Native Americans living east of the Mississippi River to land west of the Mississippi. After much political interaction and scandal, the federal government forced the Cherokees to leave their land and march all the way to Oklahoma in groups of around eight hundred on what has become known as the "Trail of Tears," a harsh journey that took the lives of approximately four thousand Native Americans.

Our country was founded on the premise "that all men are created equal, and that they are endowed by their Creator with certain inalienable rights, among these the right to life, liberty and the pursuit of happiness." But these rights were applied only to the European settlers, not to the slaves or the indigenous people.

Rasha's Vision

In her current life, Rasha had a vision of being invited into a tipi. Inside was a circle of white stones, with a fire in the center containing more white stones. A Cherokee chief handed her a stick with a white stone attached and asked, "Will you be a leader now?" Rasha knew she had to take this hammer and break the white stones in the fire. The chief then asked, "Will you now speak for my people?"

She answered, "Yes, I will."

The same sequence was repeated with chiefs from four additional tribes.

Next, the vision broke into a scene of natives with knives, tomahawks, and spears charging from the forest into an open area of land where a row of kneeling bluecoats with long guns fired at them. Then a row of standing bluecoats fired. Natives dropped right and left. Their consciousness was so perplexed at being killed without the test of strength and bravery involved in hand-to-hand combat that they could not move into the Light after death, and their souls remained earthbound.

What follows is Rasha speaking now for the Cherokee nation in that lifetime.

Rasha Telling Her Story

As hearts pour forth their carousel of hurts, one begins to see the Divine threads of meaning. And as we journey through timelessness, the wound that limits this Life unfolds before us as if the Heart sees all…as now. By Grace, I share this with you. This is a Soul Story told by My Heart.

—Rasha

"For the fourth month now, I awaken to swollen, red, and itching eyes. My eyelids are so inflamed that they crack and peel. Wrinkles form from each night's swelling. My physician tells me nothing is really wrong and that the problem may be an allergy. Then, without an injury, my back begins to ache intensely, with pain ripping up my spine with every movement. Kundalini is coming—consciousness of a deep story rising within me. As I look within, my breath and heart are caught in agony as I witness flashbacks of a native woman walking the Trail of Tears in great grief and pain.

"I had experienced awareness of my 'Self' in past lives before this, as an Egyptian, Phoenician, Roman, Jew, Native American, African, and Tibetan. But the heartfelt experience of seeing those lives had no physical or emotional pain attached."

When the Soul demands evolution, one must trust you are up to the task, and that the way will be provided. Awakening is not an invitation to a curiosity, but rather a breaking through of Divine Mind, inspired and invited by Love.

—Rasha

"Don's love is awakening my heart to heal. As I stare into his face, I know that he is deeply important to my soul's history. As I feel life flowing to me through his eyes, my heart hears the echoes from the sound of our love in a different lifetime. Each day I grow stronger until, finally, the love we live together is enough to heal the wounds stored in my soul from other lives."

The hurt that reins in the power and beauty of our present life waits until we have the strength and compassion to heal our wounds through embracing and allowing all that we are.

—Rasha

"My native woman remembers the soldiers coming into our settlement to gather us as if they are herding cattle. We have homes similar to the English—some better, some not. But more beautiful than our homes is the element of belonging—to the land, to the water, to all beings, to each other, and to our God, Great Spirit. We exude the strength and peace that come from satisfaction with our lives and ourselves. We know that our land and our God take care of us. God is present wherever we look. We trust our brothers and the hand of Great Spirit to take care of us. Until you took us from our homes, I did not understand that you settlers did not feel these things about your brothers and your God.

"I am walking along the dirt paths that connect our homes when the soldiers ride in. My long hair is braided to the side, and I am lucky to have my light leathers on my feet, as winter has not yet come. The noisy armed white soldiers on horseback order everyone out of their homes and into the walkways.

"My husband is gone, and I search everywhere for him. The soldiers drive us out of the settlement, with the children crying, the elders very confused, and everyone frightened. I keep praying for my husband to be with me. Did he get away? Did he find out what was going to happen and escape? Does he have a plan to save me later?

"They march us out of sight of our homes and then bark out, 'The government of Andrew Jackson orders you off your land, which is hereby confiscated by federal and state offices for redistribution to citizens of the American government.' Our homes and our belongings will be taken by others or destroyed. Food will be hunted along the way. If we resist, we will be killed.

"Insult and anger flood my being as we are ripped from our homes and the Spirit friends who have supported our lives on our land. You will deny me food, water, and warmth because the God in my body is not a God that warms yours? One day we are a people, prospering and safe in the home next to yours, sharing heart and hand with your very lives. This day, we are treated as animals!

"Getting to the new land takes months. Most of the rations and blankets we were promised were given or sold to whites. We meet other natives that have been allowed to bring some belongings, but my people were taken too quickly to gather anything.

"I watch the heartbreak as hope drains from our eyes. We march in anger, grief, hunger, illness, loss, injury, shame, fear, and pain. Many die along this march, and many lose God along the way.

"I leave my father, weary and worn, sitting against a tree because he can walk no more. I pray he will die in its embrace. We do not stop for sickness, hunger, or death. We only stop when the soldiers order us to. Mothers carry their dying and dead babies and children, sometimes for days. They cannot bear to leave them in unknown land. What would happen to their spirits? How would Great Spirit and their ancestors find them? Finally, exhausted and spent in grief, as rest comes to the walkers, we try to dig a hole for the dead, pray, and cover them.

"When the wailing stops, the silence is deafening. We pass piles of charred remains of natives. Maybe they got a disease. If water is nearby, they lay our sick or dying bodies in the current to be carried away by the rivers and streams. Sometimes we see only bones, from someone who fell behind and was attacked by animals. We are always afraid to be at the end of the line. Food is scarce, and sometimes we have nothing to eat or drink for a long time. Our feet are cut open by the rocks. The big gash on my right foot cannot heal, and my arms and my back are sore from carrying others who are hurt worse than me.

"My eyes have searched through every face of the hundreds in our group for my husband. Oh God, I miss him so much. I need him to care for me and to remind me that I am good, loved, still important, and that I have done nothing to deserve this punishment!

"As Rasha, every morning I awaken to swollen, red eyes as this native woman shows me something more of her brothers and sisters shuffling along this walk, bent in loss. Each time, her heartbreak brings me to tears.

"In a shamanic healing ceremony, tears pour out, and my back screams in pain as I cry for her, for my brothers and sisters on The Walk, and for myself. You see, we couldn't cry then. We couldn't stop to feel or honor each other or our dying. By the time we got to the new land, we had lost the life in our hearts. The back of our culture was broken. Tears pour out as I remember placing my father against that tree. My back screams in pain as I cry for him and for myself.

"As my native woman tells her story, and I feel the feelings we could not express then, the chains that had bound her spirit to the earth are released, and she crosses into the next world.

"But after two days of my eyes and my back beginning to heal, my lower back grabs me in pain that makes every position hurt. The chiropractor says nothing is injured. Desperate to find help, I go to other healers. The native woman comes forward again in one of these sessions, talking about how hard life was in Oklahoma:

'We have no food or shelter when we arrive, and in the chaos, our people are fighting each other to survive. We have lost honor and pride. We do not have the concept of an individual relationship with God that could be different for each of us. Great Spirit is a tribal god who belongs to us all the same. Worse than losing our homes and our power is losing our connection to Great Spirit.'

"I yearn desperately for the presence and protection of my husband, wondering why he does not come get me. I am angry with him for not being in Oklahoma with us, and yet I love him so deeply, I can't let go. I go through the motions of burying my people, body after body, chanting the death chants like a zombie—not feeling, not really present anymore.

"As the tears finally recede, the pain in my back is nearly gone, but my eyes are still feverishly red."

Domestic Violence

Rasha continues:

"My next healing session focuses on traumatic memories from my present lifetime. Before my birth, my mother had been desperately trying to get away from her abusive husband. My inner sense of knowing tells me that she fell in love with another man and was hoping he would help her out of an impossible situation. My mother conceived me by this other man. After my birth, she placed me in an orphanage and fled with my older siblings. But eventually her husband found her and dragged her back. At age two, I went from the loving hands of the Sisters of the Sacred Heart of Jesus into a home filled with violence as my mother was forced back to the abusive man I was told was my father.

"I could not understand why everyone hated me so much. I did not know I was secretly an illegitimate child. I felt like I was a 'hate sponge,' absorbing virulent negativity from the bizarre craziness in my violent home. More than once, I was attacked by family members and injured so badly that I went out of body. I remember dying, going through a tunnel, and wanting to stay in that peace and light. But I kept hearing, 'Dear Rasha, you are not done yet. It is not your time. You have to go back.'

"Since I did not want to return, not all of me came back! Part of me split off. Like the Cherokees being taken from their homeland, the part of me that had been loved and cradled in God and safe community vanished when I was exiled from the orphanage. My personality split, and a two-year-old part of me built a protective wall around herself that I could not get through.

"Once again, my eyes are so red that I have to cancel my clients."

Tunnel

Lying on a massage table in another healing session, Rasha experiences the following:

"I feel a gray, deadening wedge cut through my brain, re-experiencing the process of dissociation. Still lying on the table after the session has ended, I feel my mother sitting down where my bodyworker had been. Mom cups her hands underneath my head, holding me and gently saying, 'You see, Rasha, no one really dies. Death is only the experience of resistance and shutting down to life. Our consciousness does not experience death, but simply leaves this body and moves on.' I feel the love she offers me as she speaks these words. (My mom passed on nearly ten years ago.)"

Soul Detective Session

Rasha reports:

"My eyes are still red, but having taken another step toward healing, I next call Barbara Stone, my dear mentor, friend, colleague, and therapist. Tears well up as every cell in my body screams in rage and horror. As Dr. Stone leads me through energy healing techniques, my native woman reveals that her name is Maria Rosa, and her husband is called John."

Just as Rasha dissociated in this lifetime when her childhood trauma was more than she could bear, Maria Rosa also split into two parts. When pain is greater than the nervous system can handle, a person has two choices: insanity or dissociation. The agony from the loss of her mate and the devastation of her people was so great that Maria Rosa could not bear its load. Of the two options available to her, she chose the healthier one—dissociation. Her personality divided into two parts: Maria and Maria Rosa. A wedge went through her brain, and a wall went up around the pain in her heart. The rest of her just went through the motions of living.

But when the personality has split, only the part of the person conscious at the moment of death has the opportunity to cross into the next world. The other parts are left behind, trapped by the barriers of their suffering. In this native woman's case, both parts of her—Maria and Maria Rosa—remained earthbound when she died. In a previous session, Rasha had found the core personality of that life, Maria Rosa, and had helped her to cross over to the Light. Half the job was done, but the native woman's other part, Maria, was still earthbound, chained by the pain of her people. Deep down was the fear that she would never see her husband again, and over that fear was a layer of rage, held in place by shame and heartbreak.

As we treated these layers of emotional disturbance with customized meridian tapping sequences, Maria calmed down. As we tapped for the fear that she would never see John again, we added the affirmation, "I know he will find me again, even though it will be in our next life. I know I will see him again, because he found me in 2006!"

Once Maria cleared her trauma, I asked whether she was ready to move into the Light. A very blank feeling came up, and I realized I had made the wrong therapeutic move. Maria was deeply bonded to her people, the Cherokee Nation, and many of them were still earthbound—unfinished business. Here, Rasha resumes telling her story.

"When Dr. Stone asks me if Maria's spirit is ready to pass, Maria wants to go, but with all the passion and longing of her spirit, she will not leave without her people! So she summons a grand Medicine Wheel and calls to the spirit guides of all of her people who are still earthbound, locked in the suffering of the Trail of Tears. We call Bear Spirit, Eagle Spirit, Snake Spirit, and all the other animal spirit guides to bring their people into this sacred circle. Maria stands in the center in a beautiful beaded buckskin dress as a shaman, with arms outstretched, calling the spirits of her people to go home together. One by one they come, until thousands are in the circle. In native dress, they dance and chant, drumming and fluting, moving round with each other in the sacred circle.

"But John is not there, as the invitation went only to those who had walked the Trail of Tears. When Dr. Stone inquired whether Maria would like to go find John, the answer was obvious! The longing in her soul for the man she loved immediately connected her with the essence of his spirit."

John's Story

"John had been approached by soldiers outside of our settlement and asked if he belonged there. He lied and told them that he was returning to his people a few miles away. The soldiers ordered him to go back to his home immediately. Sensing that trouble was brewing, John carefully left the area and hid out until the gathering of our tribes for The Walk was done. He had made friends with a white woman, who helped him during that time. In his heart, John knew that he did not have the strength to survive The Walk and would have died. He also knew Maria would not leave her people to stay in Georgia with him.

"As the years passed, John felt deep guilt around his choice, because his wife needed him so very much, and he needed his people. As he aged, this trespass tormented him. When he died in his early fifties, his guilt and remorse held his spirit earthbound.

"John begged Maria's forgiveness for leaving. Seeing his suffering, Maria's heart broke open in compassion, like the shattering of the white rock in the fire in her vision. She released her anger toward him. Maria realized that she would have lost her husband either way, whether he went on The Walk or not. She could not have gone on if John had died along the way. She realized that holding on to her husband's memory had kept her alive, and she forgave him.

"Maria reached for John's hand, and they walked back into the sacred circle together. As John entered, he lowered his head in shame for not choosing to walk with* his people. An elder placed his hand on John's shoulder, comforting him, 'Son, do not let this trouble you. We all lost our way, and we all lost ourselves in different ways. Forgive these things. We are returning and recovering our happiness, our belonging, our honor, and ourselves. We are no longer lost. We are going home!'

"With those words, a large spirit in Medicine Man clothing appeared in the circle. His enormous headdress had a wide cylindrical gray fur roll with

---

*To "walk with" means to journey with/to travel the path together with your loved ones, sharing heart, mind, and experience.

a large bullhorn coming out of each side. Wearing a quilled breast cover and brownish leather pants, he held a spear in his left hand and guided us with his right hand. When I told Dr. Stone that he was the crossing guide, she roared with laughter, knowing this was Archangel Michael in his native attire. Our people would never have trusted white skin with long, flowing white robes and feathery wings.

"Our spirits floated in alignment through some invisible channel until everyone in the circle had crossed, and the space was filled with peace. Welcome home, my people! We are restored."

Correlation with Present Life

As both parts of Maria healed and went into the Light with their beloved John, a template was set for healing dissociation. Then Rasha needed to heal her dissociation from her radiant, loving inner child that had been walled off in this life.

In our second session together, a past life memory held by her dissociated inner child came to light. This little girl inside was pleading in terror, "Please don't make me see this again!" I explained to the inner child part of Rasha that the reason she did not want to see what happened was because bad feelings were attached to the memory. I assured her we could take away those bad feelings with our TFT tapping game so that seeing what happened would not hurt anymore.

We used a distancing technique I learned from Fred Gallo, PhD, of putting whatever she did not want to see again into a box and then tapping on what was in that box. Muscle testing indicated that the root cause of the trauma in the box was a past life when Rasha's soul had incarnated in India in 14 BC and had starved to death at the age of three. Though Rasha had no conscious memory of that life, we made a customized meridian tapping sequence to desensitize the sadness and trauma associated with the horror of starvation for this little girl. Something cleared.

Going Home

Coming back to the present life, Rasha recounted how she had yearned and begged to return home to the orphanage. Since she could not do that, an inner child part of Rasha split off and created an internal "home" with walls for protection from the distress of life on Earth. But she also locked a piece of her heart behind that barrier. Because her heart space could not be fully open, she had difficulty trusting in a deep love relationship with the man in her life.

As we worked to dismantle those inner walls, Rasha realized the depth of her ambivalence about staying alive. Part of her had "spiritual homesickness" and wanted to disincarnate and go back to heaven, to God. We used affirmations to release this ambivalence and to strengthen internal coherence with the statements, "I choose to be fully here now. All parts of me release our resistance to being here in a body." Rasha noticed that even though her eyes were still red, some of the complexity around the issue was gone, and fear dissipated as she integrated the parts of herself.

The day after this session, Rasha called, exuberant. Finally, her eyes were healing. She reported:

"I realize what all of these stories are about: helplessness. And I realize that no matter what happens, I don't have to move into that feeling. Now, if I lost everything tomorrow, I would not move into helplessness, because that feeling locks in the trauma and victimization. Now, if I were ordered to evacuate, I would say to myself, "OK, so let's go to Oklahoma and see what we can do there.

"I can choose what to do with fear. Even if I/others get sick and die, change will happen, but I am not helpless. Life is movement, and it is going to change. I have choice. If I allow myself to move with the flow of life, I will have joy, connection, and power, one way or the other. Hallelujah!"

Follow-up

After our second Soul Detective session, which built upon the insights of many other healing sessions with other practitioners, Rasha's eyes healed completely. She knew she had found the invisible roots of this symptom, because her eyes never got red again. Soon her insight was tested as new challenges entered Don's life. Rasha came to a deeper understanding of his soul essence as she watched him face soul issues similar to the ones he had faced as John. Once again, Don's choices separated him from Rasha. This time, Rasha's personality did not split, and she did not move into helplessness or lose her connection to God. She took time to heal, to choose her power, and to allow herself to move on with the flow of her life. Rather than getting stuck in grief and rage, Rasha chose to focus on gratitude for all that she learned from this experience.

Rasha's Gratitude List

- My soul has recovered its strength and my heart its dignity.

- So much past life healing came to me, to Don, and to my brothers and sisters in the Cherokee nation who walked with me on the Trail of Tears.

- My inner child parts are now integrated.

- I know that whether I walk with or walk alone, either way, I can stay connected to my heart and to Great Spirit.

- I accept and trust life's movement as the ultimate journey of the soul—the great, all-embracing seed of consciousness.

- White men have no secret to a loved and valuable life. It is each man and woman's right and choice, and that choice continues on and on.

- The life truth hidden in my soul is now freed. I fulfilled my vision of speaking for my people. The silence is over!

CHAPTER FIFTEEN

Stonewalled

Rose, a fifty-year-old single mother, called for a telephone session, feeling overwhelmed, unhappy, lonely, and unable to stop her weight gain. Her father was in the process of selling the family farm, an event that brought up anger and resentment from the past and blocked her ability to feel love for her father. She was supposed to go to a family meeting regarding the sale of the farm right after our session. Quite self-aware, Rose recognized that her energy field was out of balance.

Her parents had purchased beautiful farmland fifty years before for $17,000, with $10,000 of the purchase price coming from her mother's inheritance. When Rose was twelve years old, her mother died from leukemia. Her mother intended for each of her children to inherit a piece of land from the farm to build homes on. After her mother's death, Rose's father had full legal ownership of the farm and did not honor those wishes.

New England farmland has a lot of stones, and as a child, Rose had played in the pile of stones pulled out of the field, setting up a play "Stone Store." The year before this session, Rose had asked her father to give her a couple of truckloads of stone from a stone wall on the property. When her father refused to give up his best stone wall, her anger toward her father for not giving her a part of the farm burned hot. She felt "stonewalled."

Past Life Connection

We began by having Rose scan her physical body to find where she carried her disturbing emotions. She felt the anger and resentment in her gut, but more strongly in her throat. Pressure constricted her throat area, as if hands were around her neck. Muscle testing indicated the disturbance originated in a past life. With the help and guidance of our guardian angels, we muscle tested that Rose had an incarnation as a male in sunny southern France in the ninth century. This man was strangled to death at age thirty-three.

I inquired what this man would like us to call him.

Rose replied, "He won't give a name—just says 'I am that I am.'"

I commented that "I Am" is a very powerful name of God, so we called him by that name. Rose attuned to the situation and felt that another man had killed I Am in a fistfight. Bizarrely, they had been arguing over a stone wall, a boundary dispute.

Rose asked, "Am I just making this up?"

I responded that even if she had fabricated the story, her spirit could use the lessons learned from this drama to heal the blockage in her body that was making her life so unhappy in the present moment.

Rose reported that I Am was very entrenched with the thought, "I am right! Why can't you see I am right?" The other man was equally sure of being right. I Am had tried peaceful means to settle the disagreement, without success. I Am did not need this land to ensure the livelihood of his family. The issue was only about the principle involved. As Rose moved forward to the day of the fight, intense feelings came up. She felt tension in every part of her body as I Am felt called to duty, to defend his principle. A brutal outdoor fistfight ensued. He was knocked down by the other man and was lying on the ground in the wet soil when he was "throttled."

I Am still felt, "But I'm right!" He did not realize he was dead, so we told him the bad news. He responded, "No wonder I'm so tired!"

We made a customized treatment to help I Am feel better. The first intervention was rubbing his heart clockwise and repeating, "I fully accept all of my feelings, how right I am, and I love and accept myself even though I got killed trying to be right." Then Rose tapped meridian points for his rage, allowing him first to accept how enraged he felt and then forgive himself for losing his life over this fight to be right—dead right!

Soul Lesson and Resonance

After this tapping, I Am crossed to the other side. We then asked him to talk with his Soul Council to find his soul lesson. He felt this experience was about letting go of being right. I asked specifically how the soul could do that, and Rose replied, "Just give up and put it in God's hands." Then she added, "If that is the lesson, it applies to the issue about this farm too!"

Next I asked Rose to examine intuitively whether the soul energy of the neighbor who had killed I Am resonated with anyone in her present life. No answer came, so I surrogate muscle tested (see glossary) that the person was in her present life and was a member of her family. She felt that the energy of the other man was like her father, so we did forgiveness work with his soul. She easily forgave the other man in that life, because I Am had a big part in causing the fight. They had fought to the death, and the other man had won because he had been a little stronger.

Karmic Debt

I found myself asking Rose, "When someone kills another person, this act incurs a karmic debt. Has your father fulfilled his karmic debt to you?"

Rose responded, "Yes. That time, he took my life; and this time, he gave me my life."

We formulated forgiveness affirmations, including, "I release all anger and resentment toward my father from this life and all past lives. I ask Spirit to balance the energy between us."

Then we came back to current time and did another body scan. Rose did not feel much agitation in her body now. Her throat energy was clear. She had released trying to control what her father did with the farm. Even though her mother's dying wish was for Rose and her siblings to get part of the farmland, her father had no legal obligation to follow that course of action.

Rose realized, "Trying to get my father to do what my mother wanted is not worth dying for and not worth making my life miserable!"

With this clearing and this new perspective, she was able to attend the family farm meeting in peace, putting the whole affair into God's hands. During the meeting, she stayed calm and just observed the proceedings, realizing she had no authority in the matter. Later, her father finally gave her permission to take some of the stones from the wall for her present home. She was no longer stonewalled!

CHAPTER SIXTEEN

Sister Maria's Peace

Resolving a past life trauma also held the key to transformation in the following case. A trusted colleague named Geri referred a client struggling with cancer for a telephone session with me to complement his support team of medical and holistic practitioners. Dana, a sixty-five-year-old teacher, had never been ill before getting colon cancer, which metastasized to his liver. He remained vigorous, swimming and bicycling furiously throughout his chemotherapy. I asked what Dana wanted from our session, as I work from the goals people set. Dana wanted the cancer in his liver to go away.

I asked if part of him wanted to die, a very direct question. As a cancer survivor, I knew my own former ambivalence about staying in my physical body. To assess the strength of his will to live, I asked him to divide one hundred points between how much of him wanted to get well and how much of him wanted to go home to heaven.

Dana choked with emotion at this question and replied that he does not usually tell people these things. He felt inundated by pain from childhood events and severe disappointments around his divorce nine years earlier, which he felt was unjust. He had trouble holding the conviction that anything good was left for him. The deep feeling of not being cared for by the people closest to him made him plunge himself into work and exercise. He felt unappreciated and really did not know what to live for.

"Memory is a tough thing," he observed, as he disclosed his own self-hatred, sense of betrayal, and feelings of worthlessness. Even though he had been in an intense process of therapy, recovery, and compensation, he still felt most people did not understand or appreciate him.

Seeing that Dana did not have a firm commitment to life, I reflected that whether he was going to live or die, the therapeutic work was the same. If he were to live, he would need to clear these negative emotions so he would have more physical strength to heal. If he were to die, he needed to clear them so he would not have to work on the whole lesson again in his next incarnation. We revised our goal from getting the cancer to go away to resolving the deep disquiet in his soul.

Past Life Framework

Surrogate muscle testing indicated the primary cause of the disturbance in his soul that set up the cancer was unresolved trauma from a past life in which he was a woman who had died at age forty-five. She was unmarried, had no children, and was killed by an act of war in Italy in 1600. As many factors can decrease the accuracy of muscle testing, I asked Dana to let me know right away if any of my testing results differed from his perception.

Dana reflected for a moment on the information I had just offered and then asserted, "She was a nun."

I asked him to look into his soul to see if he could find this woman and go to the happiest time in that life. After about fifteen seconds, he reported, "I see her in the garden at the nunnery; she's about twenty-three years old. Another very fulfilling time is when she accepts Christ, which makes peace with her soul. She is very placid and wants us to call her Maria." We did not need to use muscle testing to gather any further information since Dana had now made an intuitive connection with Sister Maria.

Next we moved the memory toward the time right before she realized that the war presented real danger to her. Dana reported that she saw fire outside in the sky but remained inside the convent.

He solemnly stated, "There her placidity was disturbed." With hesitation and emotion, Dana realized a soldier had raped her. She fought at first, then was overpowered and surrendered.

When I asked how Maria felt about the rape, Dana was so choked with emotion that he was unable to respond. I asked Dana to tap under his lips, as if tapping under Maria's lips, to clear the shame of the rape. Soon after this intervention, he resumed the story. After the rape, Sister Maria rearranged herself and closed her eyes—not in denial, but moving to a more profound state.

The rape impregnated her. She did not quite know what to do, as the situation was a lot to bear. She named her little boy Giacomo. She wanted to forgive, but she resented this child, conceived in a state of peace that was disturbed. For the rest of her life, she feared the soldiers might return and disturb her peace again. Sister Maria felt betrayed by God.

We next moved to the days preceding her death. Still at the convent, she was mostly alone, with only one or two people attending her. She had a stomach ailment in the same place where Dana's body had been hurting. The outside circumstances were not war.

My original surrogate testing had indicated that Sister Maria was killed by an act of war, but Dana's soul memory was different. The act of rape during the war set in motion a chain of events that led to a premature death. My surrogate muscle testing also indicated that she had no children. This discrepancy could have come from three factors:

- My testing was inaccurate.

- The rape was so disturbing that the mention of the child temporarily reversed Dana's system, giving me the opposite answer.

- Her rejection of Giacomo because of the rape was so strong that he did not register on her soul imprint as her child.

Whenever my testing differs from what the clients feel, we go with their experience, as they are the experts on their own history.

At the time of Sister Maria's death at age forty-five, Giacomo was in his twenties. Sister Maria accepted the end of her life, but she did not know how to make sense of the middle of it. We turned the clock back to just before she died and made a customized treatment for Sister Maria, opening up her connection to God and then clearing her shame and rage. After tapping, Dana reported that Sister Maria felt peaceful.

I asked him to tune in to what happened when she died. Dana saw the soldier who had violated her come to get her, dressed in his full military regalia. Dana could not tell whether he was still alive and came physically or whether he was deceased and came in spirit form. Either way, he was present, and he reconciled with Giacomo. On her deathbed, Sister Maria had a slight smile on her face. She felt pleased that now this soldier had finally taken some responsibility.

Soul Lesson and Resonance

I next asked Sister Maria to cross through the veil and ask her Soul Council for the soul lesson from that life as it applies to Dana. The answer came through Dana's voice loud and clear: "That anything can be forgiven and must be forgiven!"

Next I asked Dana to investigate whether anyone in his present life resonated to the soul essence of Giacomo. He correlated his current son to Giacomo and his ex-wife to the soldier who had raped Sister Maria. Dana felt raped in his present life by the divorce, which stripped him of his home, community, neighbors, companion, money, and children. He felt that he had lost everything. Though their genders were switched in this lifetime, these feelings of violation revisited the violation Sister Maria felt. Since the lesson was recreated, I asked what his Soul wanted of him from this lifetime.

Rebirth

Dana answered clearly that his soul wanted him to be "born again." He could not stay in this body with this cancer. The purpose of the cancer was to take him out of a life in which rape was possible. He realized, however, that if his soul lesson were not mastered, the stage would be set for another rape in his next life.

He firmly stated, "The only way out of this situation is complete, utter forgiveness, letting go of every trace of resentment, so I am peaceful and no longer bothered by what has happened. No other avenue can heal. My heart's desire is to transform that experience to reach a state of peace—to get to the underlying love that exists, that is beyond comprehension."

I applauded his goal, reflecting that before the rape, Sister Maria had an innocent, untested state of peace. But for the soul to mature, that peace needed to be tested so he could master the wisdom of forgiveness under all circumstances. Then he would not have to recreate the same rape situation in his next incarnation.

We then did a Theta Healing process to delete all programs of "I am angry, I am vulnerable, I am unforgiving, and I am raped." We then replaced these with the program, "Everything can be forgiven and must be forgiven."

As I witnessed the Creator pulling out the old programs, they seemed to be coming out of Dana's torso. In place of the negative programs, the glow of forgiveness created a ball of light in his belly, like a Buddha belly with a glowing inner light. Dana enjoyed that image, but then fear surfaced. He was afraid that he would relapse into his old programs of feeling betrayed and abused.

To ground these newly installed programs of forgiveness with a self-help intervention Dana could use as needed, I presented to him the simple and elegant Lindwall Releasing Process (see glossary).

Lindwall Releasing Process
(from Isa and Yolanda Lindwall)

When you say, "I release _____ (fill in the blank with whatever you want to release)," the subconscious mind deletes that program from your energy field. The subconscious mind is a faithful servant and does whatever you ask it to do.

Then verbalize a positive program to replace the negative one.

We released the following programs:

- I release my rage at feeling raped again in this life.
- I release all anger toward myself for not being able to forgive.
- I release all anger and rage toward my ex-wife for the unfairness of the divorce.
- I release all feelings of victimization.

We replaced these negative programs with the positive affirmation "I claim the power to forgive everything, always."

We closed our session with another Theta Healing prayer for Dana's physical body. As I again witnessed the Creator working on him, I felt joy radiate from his heart—just a trickle at first, then spurting out all over. In my mind's eye, I saw Christ embrace Dana, saying, "I now heal your soul." The golden glow of the Christ presence permeated every cell of his being. After the healing, I shared with Dana that when I had cancer in 1991, Christ came to me in a vision, touched me lightly on the torso, and said the very same words to me: "I now heal your soul." Very moved by this experience, Dana felt he had accepted the healing of his soul.

Transformation

Several months later, Dana decided to surrender to the process of his physical death instead of continuing to fight it. He not only put every detail of his financial life in order, but he also put all of his important personal relationships in order. At the wake, a long line of Dana's family members and ex-girlfriends came to Geri to thank her for the changes that had occurred in Dana through the team of people who had helped him during his illness.

They reported that Dana had formerly been fierce and aggressive in his interactions with them, always intimidating people and carrying an overwhelming threat of physical violence. (He seemed to be responding as if he was Sister Maria and they were trying to rape him.) After his divorce, he directed his rage and violence toward himself and attempted suicide. Although he would do anything for his family, he had also expected them to think like he did and to conform to what he wanted.

With therapy, he softened. For the first time, his ex-wife and children could be near him without being afraid he would hurt them. Dana's fear of victimization had blocked his ability to develop intimacy with others. As he released his fear, an incredibly tender inner part of him emerged, and he was able to relate to people in a new, nonthreatening way. He allowed some true soul connections with significant people in his life.

Noting Dana's transformation, three of his ex-girlfriends came to Geri for therapy. She joked that she should go to more wakes!

Geri reflected that Dana was able to accomplish quite a bit in his soul journey during this lifetime. He created a team of loyal people that nurtured him as a healthy surrogate family. This team was the first time he had ever been connected to people without interpersonal conflict. In addition to his team of physicians and Geri, he also worked with a naturopathic doctor, an acupuncturist, a Reiki master, and me. He strengthened his associations to kindness and decreased his coherence to the energy of anger, putting into practice his life lesson of complete, utter forgiveness. Dana used the ending of his life to make a huge commitment to peace.

CHAPTER SEVENTEEN
The Fallacy of Humans

Abeautiful young woman named Raquel came into therapy after a feng shui specialist pointed out she needed to clean out her basement, a symbol of her unconscious. Raquel noted that whenever she thought about cleaning out her basement, anger and rage surfaced. Muscle testing confirmed she had an issue of rage in her unconscious. As we began, the tension in her body mounted. Anger and rage flooded in from the following past life.

Ninja

Raquel's soul had incarnated as a warrior, born in China in 1315 A.D. and dying at age eighteen from an act of war. This young man named Tiv (pronounced *Teev*) was part of a select group of trained assassins. Their job was thrilling, and Tiv had all the confidence in the world. People in the community respected them—or possibly feared them. Tiv did not have to do manual labor, because his work was playing with swords and "beating up my friends." Food was just given to them. The shadow side of this lifetime was secrets, violence, lies, and betrayals. Raquel felt the façade of respect for Tiv was fake.

Raquel reported, "When it came right down to it, we were lied to. Somebody deceived us. We were on a night mission to assassinate someone who didn't agree with our beliefs and had a stronghold with the populace. We needed to 'take him out' so more people would follow what we wanted. Our teacher betrayed us and sent us to be killed. When we arrived, they had triple our number of warriors."

As she recounted this past life memory, her back began to ache tremendously. She stood up, trying to feel how Tiv had been hurt, and realized that a blow had broken his back. Since he was one of the best warriors, he was one of the last to go down. The enemies saved two or three of the opponents to torture for some "testosterone fun, a warrior's prize, to make somebody else feel pain."

With his back broken, Tiv was stretched out and then pulled apart, killed by being dismembered. During this process, he was not angry with the enemies killing him, because that is just what they did to each other. His group had done the same to them before. But he was in absolute rage and pain toward the person he and his fellow warriors had worked for, their spiritual leader and teacher, who had taught them to honor themselves. This teacher was like God to them. Tiv felt that his teacher had not been sincere and felt totally deceived and betrayed—that everything his life had stood for had been crushed.

Soul Lesson

During the process of dismemberment, Tiv's body reached the threshold of the amount of pain it could bear and then went numb, dissociating from any further pain. After death, his spirit floated and then "went home." We asked the Council of Souls that guides Raquel for the lesson of that lifetime. She replied in a very solemn voice, "Your lesson in that life was to acknowledge the fallacy of humans."

This lesson made me rethink what had happened to Tiv. Could he have had an error in perception? I asked Raquel to inquire of her Council of Souls whether their teacher had actually betrayed them. To her amazement, the answer came back that he had not. Someone within their own group—someone Tiv trusted—had betrayed them instead. Raquel was so surprised to get this new information that she asked me to repeat it and to muscle test its veracity. Slowly, she absorbed the truth that the betrayal by her teacher that she had believed in for almost seven centuries had never happened. That erroneous belief was one of the fallacies of humans.

We revisited the memory with this new knowledge, realizing that the foundation had not been pulled out from under everything she believed in and lived for in that life. She saw their group of about a dozen men going into the main entrance of a circular area made of stones and sand under a dome. Candles lined the inner and outer circles. As they passed through the arch to the center of the circle, where their target and just one or two others were supposed to be, someone from the back of their group stayed in the outer circle and went through the perimeter instead of the front. At the time, his action was not suspicious, as they assumed he was positioning for an advantage later in the fight. But this traitor never rejoined their group. Once they all got inside, down came three times as many enemy warriors and they overwhelmed the assassins. This time, she no longer felt as angry, knowing that their teacher had not betrayed them and that she got a new body and reincarnated as Raquel.

A Very Happy Birthday

Before this realization, Raquel had felt that the soul of the teacher from that lifetime resonated to the soul essence of her eldest son, who was six years old at the time. She had felt a lot of rage toward this child. His birthday was coming up soon, and as with every previous one, she would have been glad for an excuse not to celebrate it.

After the revelations of our Soul Detective work, she talked with the soul of her son, apologizing for blaming him for nearly seven hundred years for something he did not do and asking his forgiveness. In her heart, she felt him responding, "I know, Mom," and giving her a big hug. She noted that even though she had yelled at this son a lot, he was a most compassionate child. We asked why he had incarnated to her in this lifetime. The answer was "to facilitate her awareness."

At the end of this work, Raquel felt absolutely amazed at how correcting her error in perception dissolved her anger and rage toward her teacher and toward her son. Then she was really looking forward to her son's birthday. She had one party for him on the actual birthday and a second party for friends on the weekend, and the celebration was so very sweet!

CHAPTER EIGHTEEN

Everything Serves

A student at one of my workshops was feeling very discouraged because she could not master the art of muscle testing on herself. After trying many different methods of self-testing without success, Hannah mentioned that a psychic had told her she needed to deal with issues from past lives regarding being a healer. The following story emerged as we found the invisible roots of this blockage.

A Life in India

Hannah's soul once incarnated in India as an upper-caste Brahmin male named Anon. The happiest memory in that lifetime was walking through the streets, carefree, feeling strong and powerful in his male body. Anon was happy and jovial and loved people. He was very well dressed, wearing satins.

Next Hannah saw Anon sitting at a heavy table, writing, with several round stone globes before him on pedestals. He heard an altercation outside in the street and ran to see what was going on. People were fighting with whips and injured a man. Anon tried to stop them from hurting this person, and in the fight accidentally fell backward onto a green copper fence spike that impaled him. As he lay dying, with his eyes open, looking up at the people staring at him, Anon thought, "I have failed. It's all over. I can't believe I'm so young and am leaving now. So much is ahead of me. It's not supposed to be this way!" He and the others present were all in shock at what had happened.

Anon lamented, "I blew it! I just wanted to help, and I blew it."

(Hannah still held this residual fear in her current life: If she tried to help, she would stumble onto something and someone would get hurt. She also believed that if she was successful, trouble would come. In reality, she was a highly skilled psychotherapist. We treated these fears with Thought Field Therapy [see appendix E]).

Then Anon closed his eyes and his spirit rose slowly from his body, but stayed nearby. He tore his attention away from his own body to the man the people had injured with whips. Anon felt protective of this man. He wiped the man's brow and put one hand on his forehead and the other hand on his heart, trying to comfort him. The distraction of Anon's death saved this man; the people did not return to beating him.

Anon stayed around while his family prepared his body for burial. He put his arms around those who wept and tried to say good-bye. He went to his mother, father, brother, grandmother, and a good friend who was like a brother. His body was laid on a platform in a room with a lot of green metal. Lots of people came to pay their last respects. Being at his own funeral and witnessing everyone's grief was very hard for him.

Hannah was moved with grief as she recounted his story. At this point, we inserted an intervention for Anon of tapping under the lips while saying the affirmation, "I accept all of my feelings about what happened. I love and accept myself completely and totally."

Anon followed the funeral procession to a tomb. They shut the tomb and closed the door. Now what should he do? Stay or go? Nobody knew he was there, so staying made no sense, but where should he go?

Realizing that the part of Hannah's soul energy that had incarnated as Anon was still bound to Earth, we next asked a Being of Light to come help him.

Hannah reported that Anon then felt a Being of Light, a young man, reach down for him. He realized this action was a sign he could go, took the hand of this Being, and went up.

Anon's crossing may seem too easy, but it reflects the "quantum" aspects of healing which can occur in an instant when the remedy is correct and precise. Remember also that we had just asked a Being of Light to help, and this Being responded with exactly what Anon needed.

Soul Lesson and Resonance

From the other side, we asked Anon to reflect on the lesson he had learned in his lifetime. He answered: "Everything serves its purpose. It is right and good. Anon did the only thing he could, and the man's life was saved. The lesson now in this lifetime is to 'Get it right.' Remember that everything serves."

We also saw that the man Anon saved resonated to the soul essence of Hannah's adopted son in this life. This child had been giving her a lot of trouble and stole all the money she had saved up for this workshop. Spirit advised her, "Hold him with the love you had for him when you gave your life for him. See him as a wounded one, not as an enemy. Hold him with love."

While this message did not solve all the problems with her son, it shifted her attitude to be able to cope with the difficulties from a more loving perspective. She also was able to trust herself enough to master at last the art of self-testing.

CHAPTER NINETEEN

Learning Self-Love

Mariana, a beautiful widow in her sixties, was taking medication for a blood condition in which her white blood cells were normal, but her platelets, red blood cells, and hemoglobin were too high. Although her medication lowered the abnormally high cells, it also lowered her white blood cell level. She wanted to investigate the invisible roots of this disorder as a complement to her medical treatment.

Muscle testing indicated that the root cause was a past life in which Mariana was a young girl named Claire, the only child of parents who loved her and doted on her. Born in the 1700s in the area that is now the state of Michigan, she was very pretty, with blonde hair, and the family was wealthy. Her mother was warm and cultured.

Claire began to get very tired and bruised easily. Physicians did bloodletting to try to cure her, but this treatment did not really help. Claire became frightened. Her parents tried everything, taking her to different doctors and to places they knew she would enjoy, but they could not find a cure.

They propped her up in bed the last few days of her life, when she had hardly any energy. Since Claire loved music, they had special musicians come to play for her. Dear friends read her stories.

At the time of her transition, she was extremely weak, but she was calm because an angel made herself visible and held her hand. The room got very quiet and started to fill with light. Claire had difficulty breathing. She felt as if she had to let go of some pressure, something she had not accomplished yet in her life. Then she took a step and was looking at herself from another dimension. She felt confusion, and then the presence and warmth of the Light as the angel told her everything was all right. She had died of leukemia at age twelve.

Mariana noted the synchronicities of her life as Claire and her present life. Mariana was born on August 12, the Feast of Saint Claire. Both Mariana and her mother almost died when Mariana was born, one of fifteen children. Mariana never had children in this life.

Soul Lessons and Resonance

One of Claire's lessons was "letting go," as she had wanted to hang on to her wonderful family. Another lesson was overcoming fear. Her mother had almost died when giving birth to Claire. Everyone had been clustered around her mother to save her, and the first impression Claire had of this world as a newborn was that this place was not safe. She felt abandoned and was afraid of not having enough love. Then her father came over to her, and she was comforted. Her mother did not dare have any more children. Claire cleared her trauma as a newborn by tapping an energy point under the lips and saying affirmations.

The purpose of the lifetime as Claire was teaching her soul to love herself completely, no matter what. Mariana applied this soul lesson to her current lifetime by realizing that she could have compassion for herself and not identify herself as her illness. She also felt she needed to realize the full extent of her power and not bottle it up inside.

Mariana connected with her guardian angel, named "Feely" (short for Fearless), and reported: "I am not alone. All kinds of love are around me. Feely is a strong, gentle, loving female, but sometimes takes on a male form. She knows just when to step in. I am to trust that everything will be OK."

Mariana felt that the soul essence of Claire's father resonated to the soul essence of her late husband. She felt her husband's presence from the other side and his regret that he was not physically present to help her, but he also let her know that he could be present to her in a more real way by being in spirit. She felt his heart open to her in love and compassion. The next step was learning to have that same love and compassion for herself.

Long-Term Results

After this work, Mariana was able to stabilize her blood condition with the help of medication adjustments. In the years following this session, she poured her newfound energy into studying various forms of healing work and then focused on Healing Touch. Just before her seventieth birthday, she was pinned as a Certified Healing Touch Practitioner by Healing Touch International. Many friends celebrated and honored her. Mariana felt that this soul retrieval work was one of the most significant modalities she experienced in getting ready for her certification. Her heart resonated with the lesson of learning to love and honor herself completely, and she has been able to help others do the same.

CHAPTER TWENTY

Progression of Past Lives

Skye (from chapter 6) moved rapidly toward her goals after releasing the trauma of her friend Pearl's death. The most important treatment goal she had set for herself was staying in recovery from her dependence on alcohol. She not only met this goal, but she also became very active in Alcoholics Anonymous, working the steps and helping others achieve sobriety. In the course of four months of therapy, Skye met all of her treatment goals except establishing a long-term healthy relationship with a man. She did have a fiancé in her life that lived in another state, but their connection was stormy—on and then off again, over and over. This man loved her deeply, and she loved him. He was not firmly established in his own recovery from alcoholism, however, and she refused to let anyone—even her lover—pull her back into the trap of addiction.

We muscle tested that trauma from seven past lifetimes was still affecting her. She wanted to get this entire trauma cleared so she could move forward in the fullness of her strength. We worked on all seven of these lives in the course of three sessions. Here are her stories and the soul lessons she learned.

Lifetime One: Raya

Raya was a happy little three-year-old Native American girl living in the Southwest. She loved being by her mother's side while Mom was baking bread in the stone hearth. Raya caught pneumonia and felt pain in her lungs. She had great difficulty breathing, and her mother was delirious with crying.

Finally, little Raya could no longer breathe. A light came through the wall. She tried to tell her mother how pretty it was, but her mother could not hear her because Raya was not in her body anymore. Her ancestors came for her and took her to a beautiful happy hunting ground.

In Skye's present lifetime, she had almost died at three years old when an ice cube got stuck in her throat. She could not breathe and turned purple. Her father saved her life by jamming the ice cube down her throat.

Soul Lesson

Raya's life lesson was the importance of the bonding of the tribe. A big turnout of ancestors came to greet her when she crossed over. Raya saw animals and noticed they were not hungry, as they had been when she was in her body. Skye reflected, "Family is very important—these people will put their life on the line for you."

Lifetime Two: Damien

Damien was a proud young soldier in ancient Greece. His happiest time was engaging in sports, competing and running. He moved up in the military from being a foot soldier to an archer to a charioteer, as he had a military bearing and the mind of a great strategist. Damien had a younger brother and was from a military family. He felt pride at being in this profession, fulfilling his family obligations. He also had a wife and a son.

Every time he went into battle, he said prayers to his God and thought of his family. He always knew he could be killed. One day in the heat of battle, a spear hit him and knocked him out of his chariot. He rolled on the ground, trying to get out of the way of the chariot wheels. The spear cut his aorta, and he bled to death rapidly. Although he felt some regret and loss for dying at age thirty-three, especially for missing out on the growing-up years of his young son, Damien knew this death was his destiny. He had chosen to be a soldier, and he was well prepared for this transition.

Soul Lesson

His death held great meaning because of the glory, prestige, and honor it brought to his family. The army came and got his body and had an elaborate ceremony to honor the sacrifice of giving his life to defend his country.

Damien did not fear death and went into the Light with calmness. He knew his son would have the legacy of his father and would enter the army at a higher level because of him. Skye also saw that the soul of Damien's son resonated to the soul essence of her firstborn child, a son in this life too. They are very close, and she has always felt proud of the fine young man he has become. She got to see him grow up this time!

Lifetime Three: Thaddeus

Thaddeus was a brilliant scholar, a professor who was also a scribe who wrote an illuminary, a beautiful manuscript. The happiest time in his life was with other students while he was earning his degree.

Thaddeus did not have a strong family backup and had to scramble and fend for himself in the world. A benefactor financed his education, and Thaddeus did well in school and was well respected among the students. But in time, this male benefactor also asked for sexual favors. Though unwilling to participate, he was forced to comply. Thaddeus felt guilty and angry that the person who had promised to take care of him coerced him into sex. The price of his education was very high.

Thaddeus isolated himself from other people and retreated from his wounded feelings into the mental realm. He never had children and had no connection with God or the church during this life. He died at age fifty-three, sad and gray, with nobody to mourn his death.

Soul Resonance and Lesson

We treated Thaddeus to release his shame. Skye saw that the soul of the benefactor in that lifetime resonated to the soul essence of her father in this lifetime. Skye's father loved her, but he also crossed the boundary again by committing incest with her. Skye was able to release, from both lifetimes, the rage and anger that come to the soul when one's protector is also one's abuser.

Skye realized that one can attempt to escape from painful feelings by denying them and trying to dissociate from them by putting up an emotional wall around the heart; however, living with a closed heart conflicts with establishing emotional bonding to a tribe. She reflected, "Retreating into a fantasy mental world, cut off from emotion, is no substitute for a real life."

Lifetime Four: Ven

Ven was a happy little baby who had just completed his first year of life. He was hanging in a little basket outdoors in the verdant jungle in Mexico, enjoying the warmth of the sun on his body, the sounds of birds, the scents of tropical flowers, and all the glory of nature. Suddenly, a jaguar pounced on him. Ven was startled and snatched away from this reverie. Then the Light got bright, and oblivion came.

Several emotional issues from this sudden death carried over into Skye's present life. Skye had trouble sinking into nature and feeling at one with all of God's beautiful creation. Her fiancé was pushing for living in nature in the mountains, but Skye always got a creepy feeling around "too much green" and felt as if she were about to be pounced on again. She needed to be able to see another house close by.

First, we desensitized her phobia of too much green so she could feel at ease in nature. Next, we called upon the spirit of the jaguar to ask why she had done this deed. The jaguar communicated that she just saw an opportunity and took it. Ven asked, "Where was my mother?" Skye saw that the mother had been preoccupied with women's work, as she had many other children. A sibling was supposed to be watching Ven. The jaguar needed only an instant of diverted attention to get her meal. The one in charge of the baby felt guilty, but everyone understood the way of nature. Although sad, they accepted this death as part of the cycle of life feeding on life.

Soul Lesson

The power of the jaguar was so strong that Ven had felt helpless being dragged into the darkness of the jungle. But once Ven's life force went into the jaguar, their souls became intrinsically connected. She realized that the power of the jaguar had been with her all along, though unconsciously. Skye reflected, "There is no way I should have been able to get through all I have come through in my life." Now Skye consciously calls upon the strength and power of the jaguar—it is her right. She also noted that in this life, she loves to sleep in the sunshine, like all cats.

Lifetime Five: Mara

Mara is a Hebrew name that means "bitter," and Mara was born into a family of privilege in the Middle East in the 1300s. The happiest time in her life was her coming-of-age celebration at fifteen. She had been betrothed to her fiancé for a long time. She liked him very much, and he was a friend of the family, possibly a distant cousin.

She was very pretty and enjoyed her status as a young woman, doing makeup and wearing fine clothes. But a dark cloud intruded on Mara's happiness when her face started to get blotchy. Her illness was very disheartening and disruptive to her family, as they had high hopes riding on her. Mara had the plague. Her worst fear was losing her betrothed. Social convention prohibited him from coming near her, since her illness was contagious and fatal.

Mara was frightened and very weak. As she lay dying, her fiancé broke society's rules and came to her side. He told her that he still loved her and would find her again in another life. He stayed present for her death, and she went peacefully, enveloped by his love.

Soul Resonance and Lesson

Mara's fiancé loved her from a very deep place, for who she was, not for her beauty or wealth. He was there because his soul loved hers. Skye felt that her fiancé in this life resonated to the soul essence of Mara's fiancé and that he had found her again. She reflected, "My essence does not change, even with gender changes, cultures, customs, and outfits—something about me is unchangeable and eternal. I had believed in this soul essence from religion, but seeing the proof from these soul stories is really great."

As a child, Skye had loved to play dress-up. Now she could see the soul as just putting on one outfit, then another. With this knowledge, she was able to drop the frantic quality that this is her only life and she has to make it work.

After this session, Skye changed the way she was relating to her fiancé. Formerly, she would distance from him whenever she got afraid, and then her fiancé felt like she was dying on him again and turned to alcohol to drown his sorrow. Skye stopped this pattern of disconnecting when she was upset. She reported, "I feel alive again. I have plans, dreams, and hopes. I have been calling on my powers, and I feel as if I have come out of a coma."

Over time, her fiancé relapsed into drinking, so standing in her power meant she needed to leave that relationship. To have a healthy relationship with a man, the man himself must be healthy. Skye needed to sacrifice this connection, even though they loved each other, to make room in her life for a healthy male partner.

Lifetime Six: Gila

Gila lived in ancient Palestine. Her happiest time was gossiping with the townspeople in the warm weather at the well, which felt like an oasis in the midst of the desert. At age nineteen, Gila got pregnant by a man she did not love—the man her family had forced her to marry, against her will. This man was cruel to her and caused a lot of grief in her life. She was not happy about having a baby by this tyrant.

A teacher named Jesus came to town, and Gila was very drawn to him. When she wanted to become a follower of Jesus, her husband reacted with rage and absolutely refused. He beat her savagely, knocking her down in the sand with his fist, and then breaking a table over her pregnant body. Men could freely do these kinds of things to women back then without consequences. Gila realized she was overpowered and cowed to him in resignation after this beating. She decided that she would have the baby, but she would not stay in the marriage to this ogre.

The beating brought on labor, which came hard and fast with a lot of ripping and tearing. Her mother and other women were there, and they delivered a healthy baby girl. Gila knew she was not going to pull through this ordeal, and she did not want to live under her husband's cruelty. Gila felt a lot of pain after the birth and got steadily weaker as she slowly bled to death. Then there was the Light again! This time the Light was much brighter than the other times, because Jesus was in the world now. She loved Jesus and knew he loved her. His presence was with her as she crossed into the next world.

Soul Resonance and Lesson

The trauma that had persisted from Gila's lifetime was the deep sadness she carried that her daughter grew up without her. When Skye asked the angels what happened to Gila's daughter, she saw that the baby was cared for by the women in the village and had a good life. Then she was astounded to see that the soul of Gila's baby girl was the same soul essence as her beloved friend Pearl! Joy flooded her soul as she made this connection.

In this incarnation, an angry husband murdered Pearl. Gila's death was also a direct result of the wrath of her husband, similar to Pearl's death. We did energy therapy to release Gila's sadness from missing out on seeing her baby grow up. Skye felt overjoyed to realize that this lingering trauma of longing to be with her daughter was fulfilled in this lifetime in the closeness of her friendship with Pearl. Skye noted the everlasting presence of love and life.

In her current lifetime, Skye's ex-husband had been violent and had threatened to kill her. Women's rights were progressed enough by this generation that Skye was able to get a divorce and leave the situation alive. Plus she got to see her children grow up. Skye made a firm resolution with the affirmation, "I reclaim my right to have a joyful connection with a man."

As an afterthought, Skye commented, "After that lifetime, we all learned to be a lot quieter about following Jesus."

After the breakup of her engagement, a childhood sweetheart came back into Skye's life. Not only was he loving, but he was also steady and dependable, a great joy and comfort. The work she had done to heal her soul wounds regarding relationship paved the way to meet her goal of having a long-term, healthy relationship with a man.

Lifetime Seven: Lao

The last of the seven lifetimes we worked on had the longest life-span. Lao, a Chinese man born in the 1400s, lived to the ripe age of seventy-eight.

Lao had a wife and three children. They had financial problems as a young family with too many mouths to feed. They were happy but very poor. Lao wanted to be able to provide so much more for his family.

In Skye's present life, her family of origin also experienced poverty before she was born. Skye faced severe, grinding poverty when she divorced her abusive husband. Twice she had to grovel to get a one-year moratorium on house payments, and she had no money for Christmas presents or new clothes at Easter. Skye realized that, with her brains, she could have put her children into day care, gone into the corporate world, and made lots of money working fourteen hours a day. But instead, she chose to spend more time at home with her children. After Gila's lifetime, she did not want to miss out on the miracle of seeing her children grow up.

Lao was a talented craftsman who produced and marketed his wares throughout his life. With persistence, he prospered. The happiest time in his life was as an old man at a festival, surrounded by his wife, his children, and many grandchildren. The party included lots of food, music, and laughter. In the evening, people put lanterns in boats on a beautiful lake and watched the light of the lanterns reflecting off the water. Like Christmas today, this celebration was definitely about children and making a joyful occasion for the little ones.

Soul Lesson

Skye had always worried that her children did not have a very good child-hood. We did energy work to release her fears of not being able to survive during the time they were so very poor. Afterward, she verbalized, "It all balances out: a little less at the beginning, and a little more at the end." Skye felt her lesson was persistence, realizing that time has to go by to get into the comfort zone financially. She also realized she is still a very talented crafts-person and moved into trusting herself to prosper in this life too.

Reflections

Reflecting on the therapy she did with these seven past lifetimes, Skye was very glad that working with Thaddeus gave her a chance to forgive and release the trauma of her sexual abuse in this lifetime. The lifetime with Mara was when she first found her fiancé, and healing that incarnation put her present ability to establish a loving relationship with a man into a state of grace and ease.

Skye has always loved Jesus, and realizing that she was one of the very first Christian martyrs grounded and gave a deeper level of reality to the personal relationship she has always felt with the Christ energy, the Christ consciousness.

Working on Lao's lifetime released her from the guilt she had felt about the hardships of the early years with her children. She was able to sink into the fullness of this present life and the joy of bouncing grandchildren on her knee. Fear had been preventing her from stepping up to current challenges of making a living and creating a dynamic, healthy partnership with a man. With the release of all these traumatic feelings, she stepped into the fullness of who she really is, complete with her many gifts and strengths.

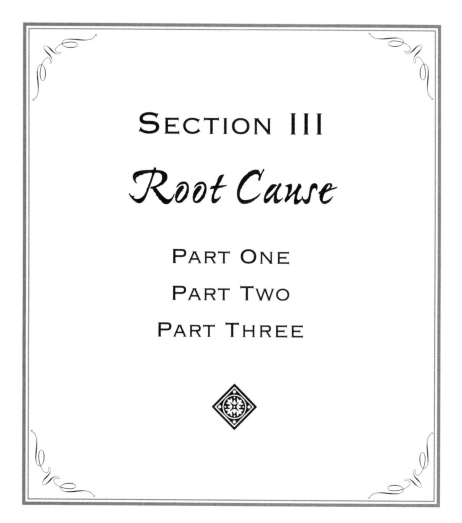

SECTION III

Root Cause

PART ONE
PART TWO
PART THREE

The gravel driveway leading to my shed grows weeds. If I chop off their tops, the weeds think they are being pruned and grow twice as big. To eliminate the weeds, I need to pull them up by their roots. Likewise, for lasting therapeutic results, we need to find and eliminate the root cause of an emotional disturbance.

If the root cause is misdiagnosed, the problem will not get fixed. If a patient goes to the doctor for headaches, the doctor needs to find the root cause of the pain. No physician would want to do brain surgery if the problem was stress, nor prescribe headache medication if the problem was a brain tumor. Likewise, for lasting emotional relief in Soul Detective work, we need to find the root cause of the emotional problem.

In the 1990s, Dr. Jon Kabat-Zinn hired me to teach in the Inner City division of his University of Massachusetts Medical Center's Stress Reduction and Relaxation program. An old hospital gave us classroom space. The first day there, I saw white paint flakes on the carpet in one corner of the room. I called maintenance. They arrived about an hour later and cleaned up. The next week, I noticed more paint flakes in that corner. When I alerted Jon to the problem, he brought me an old sweeper so I could do the job myself without waiting for maintenance. The next week, more paint was on the floor. The old sweeper did not work very well, so Jon bought a new belt that improved its performance. I continued sweeping up the paint each week. After several months, I looked at the ceiling above the paint flake corner and saw a white pipe leaking, causing the paint around it to flake off.

The moral of this story: The emphasis in Western medicine is getting bigger and better sweepers to clean up the paint on the floor. But until the root cause of the leaky pipe is fixed, the problem will continue to regenerate. The holistic approach emphasizes finding and clearing the root cause of a problem.

PART ONE

Levels of Healing

The human energy field is comprised of different interpenetrating bodies—physical, etheric (energetic), emotional, mental, intuitive, and spiritual. Each of these biofields vibrates at a different rate and opens up a potential level of healing.

Different Levels of Healing

5. **Spiritual Body**   Connection with transpersonal energy

4. **Intuitive Body**   The interface between the mental and spiritual

3. **Mental/Emotional Body**   Our thoughts produce our feelings

2. **Energy Body**   The flow of life energy through the physical body

1. **Physical Body**   The flesh-and-blood physical anatomy

Note: These levels come from the holistic work of Dietrich Klinghardt, MD, PhD, a practitioner of neural therapy. He combines the emotional and mental levels. For a free PDF chart of the Five Levels of Healing, see his website at www.neuraltherapy.com.

Working at a higher level has a pronounced trickle-down effect on the levels below it, as the higher levels have a higher vibration. However, the lower levels have little or no trickle-up effect on the higher ones.

1

Physical Body Level

Physicians work primarily at the physical level and have developed miraculous skills in repairing the human body.

Physicians have saved my life three times so far—from pneumonia at eight weeks old, a ruptured appendix at age sixteen, and breast cancer at age forty-two. All three times, I would have died without medical intervention, so I deeply appreciate the advances of modern medicine. Having developed potentially fatal illnesses three times, one could ask why I was in such a hurry to disincarnate! In truth, a part of me could not stand the brutality of this planet and wanted to go back to Source energy. When, at age forty-two, I found the malignant lump in my breast, I knew it could be my "ticket home." I immediately changed my mind about wanting to die: I did not want to go through the suffering that is often involved with death from cancer.

If the root cause of a physical problem stems from a higher level, the problem will recur unless addressed at its level of origin. For example, bypass surgery may temporarily restore circulation to the heart, but if the underlying problem is emotional, another blocked artery is likely to occur. If a patient is treated for heartbreak along with the surgery, the energy of the heart will be able to open, bringing more life energy to the organ, improving circulation, and decreasing the likelihood of another heart problem.

The physical level is the domain of physicians, naturopaths, and dieticians. Some common physical level interventions are surgery, chiropractic, vitamin supplements, herbal medicine, and medications. Often, treatments involving medication, such as high blood pressure medication, need to be continued on an ongoing basis since they cover symptoms but do not eliminate the root cause of the disorder.

Generally, we refer physical problems to physicians who have sophisticated diagnostic tools. If the root cause of an emotional problem muscle tests at the physical level, one can further test to rule out these issues:

1. Allergic reaction to a medication

2. Contamination from toxins

    a) Air pollution

    b) Water pollution

    c) Mercury poisoning from silver-mercury amalgam dental fillings

3. Food sensitivities

    a) Reaction to a specific food

    b) Pesticides or other contaminants in the food

If one of these issues shows up, consult a specialist in these areas, such as Allergy Antidotes, Thought-Energy Synchronization Therapy (TEST), Bioenergetic Emotional Access Method (BEAM), or NeuroModulation Technique (NMT). (See appendix F.)

If none of these issues shows up, seek medical consultation.

2

Energy Body Level

This level looks at the flow of life energy through and around the body and can also be called the etheric biofield. Energy comes in through the central channel, a vertical line of energy running through the center of the body. Energy spins through energy centers called "chakras" and then flows through the meridian system to the organs. Traditional Chinese medicine mapped this system of meridians (energy channels), which consists primarily of twelve basic meridians and two "extraordinary" meridians (the Governing Vessel and the Conception [or Central] Vessel) that regulate the life energy flowing through the body. The twelve basic meridians are named after the primary organ or body part they feed: Lungs, Large Intestine, Stomach, Spleen/Pancreas, Heart, Small Intestine, Bladder, Kidney, Pericardium, Triple Warmer/Thyroid, Gallbladder, and Liver.

Traditionally, the energy body level is the domain of interventions such as acupuncture, acupressure, laying on of hands, massage, and neural therapy. All of these treatments remove blockages in the flow of life energy through the system and restore balance and harmony to the electromagnetic field.

If the root cause of a problem lies at the level of the energy body, muscle test this submenu for more specific detail about the origin of the blockage:

1. Meridian imbalance

    a) Lung

    b) Large Intestine

c) Stomach

d) Spleen/pancreas

e) Heart

f) Small Intestine

g) Bladder

h) Kidney

i) Pericardium

j) Triple Warmer/Thyroid

k) Gallbladder

l) Liver

m) Conception Vessel

n) Governing Vessel

2. Chakra imbalance

a) Root chakra

b) Sacral chakra

c) Solar plexus

d) Heart chakra

e) Throat chakra

f) Brow chakra (Third Eye)

g) Crown chakra

3. Pollution from an electromagnetic field (EMF) that is too high for the body's energetic system to handle.

If the root cause is EMF pollution, you can use a simple device called a Gauss meter to locate the source of the EMF causing the problem. Perhaps your bed is placed near the spot where high power lines enter the house. If so, move the bed to a placement in the room with a lower EMF field. If the EMF pollution comes from sitting under fluorescent lights, change the lighting to incandescent or, better yet, to full-spectrum bulbs. If the EMF source cannot be easily changed, you may want to research products used to modulate its effects, either something worn on the body or placed in a room.

Energy Level Case Example

Marge wanted to release the high level of tension in her body that prevented her from being able to sleep well at night. We muscle tested that the root cause of her insomnia was at the energy body level, more specifically due to an imbalance in the Stomach meridian. With this information, Marge suddenly realized her insomnia had started only after she had children. Her C-section surgery cut right through the bilateral Stomach meridians, which run down the front of the body from head to toe. Usually, a horizontal "bikini-cut" C-section will also cut the Central Vessel, the bilateral Kidney meridians, and the bilateral Liver meridians—seven meridians in all. Energy could not get through properly to Marge's stomach since the lines had been cut and scar tissue blocked the flow.

Fear and anxiety are emotions that surface when the Stomach meridian is out of balance. We did a Directional Eye Movement Therapy protocol from Jaffe-Mellor Technique (JMT; see appendix F) to restore the energy flow through the scar tissue. Subsequently, Marge's tension level went down, and she was able to sleep well again.

If a meridian is out of balance, muscle test whether tapping can restore the proper flow of energy to the meridian or whether acupuncture or another therapeutic modality would be the treatment of choice.

If the imbalance is in a chakra, many energy therapies have protocols to release the imbalance and restore proper flow to the energy center.

3

Mental & Emotional Body Level

The mental and emotional bodies impact and intertwine with each other. Both the emotional body and the mental body are included on the same level since our thoughts precede and determine our feelings. For example, the thought "I am stupid" produces the feeling of shame. The thought, "I'll never have a love relationship that works" produces feelings of hopelessness and loneliness.

This mental-emotional level is the domain of psychotherapy, including the new field of energy psychology, which empowers clients to rapidly achieve their treatment goals. Thought Field Therapy operates in this realm, as does homeopathy (an energy medicine).

The Emotional Body

The emotional body, sometimes also called "the astral body," is magnetic in nature and centered in the heart chakra. When we lose someone we love, our emotional biofield contracts because of this wound to the heart.

Emotional Level Case Example

Joanne, a deeply spiritual person, lost her only child, Ryan, in a hiking accident when he was twenty. Two years later, unrelenting grief drove her into therapy. She still could not talk about Ryan without tears welling up in her eyes, a lump choking her throat, and a huge aching hole penetrating her heart.

Although she went to church every week, she felt as if she were just going through the motions of worship without feeling any connection to God. On Ryan's birthday, she had to take the day off work to stay home and cry.

Joanne and Ryan were very close. Every time Ryan left after a visit, Joanne would say, "I love you," and he would say it right back to her with deep feeling in their parting hug.

Shortly before Ryan's death, one of his friends died in a car crash. When Joanne was discussing the accident with Ryan, tears came to her eyes, and she felt sick inside. She hugged Ryan, choked up, and told him, "I don't know how I would ever handle losing you."

Ryan hugged her and comforted her, "Don't worry Mom—it will never happen!" Those words haunted her.

At the intake appointment, Joanne told the story of Ryan's death. He had gone camping with some friends over Memorial Day weekend. Ryan was a social person and always got people to laugh and have fun. After dark that night, he hiked down the mountain to meet a friend on the other side for a trip the following day. The friend heard his whistle from afar and put on her headlights so he could locate her. The whistle got nearer and nearer, then suddenly stopped. She waited for Ryan, thinking that he could be up to one of his practical jokes, maybe sneaking up behind her to surprise her. But he never appeared.

Joanne and her partner joined the search party, along with the police. She was almost at the top of the mountain when the others called to her that they had found him. The police roped off the area and would not let her go to the scene. They told her that Ryan fell from a cliff at a treacherous spot on the trail, landing in some trees and dying instantly from a blow to his temple. The autopsy showed no drugs or alcohol in his system. Ryan was an experienced and capable hiker, not prone to taking risks. His death was a pure accident.

At the end of the intake session, we created a customized meridian tapping sequence to take the edge off Joanne's grief. First we treated the feeling that the protection around her heart had been ripped away and then her mother-guilt at being unable to help her son.

Joanne's second therapy session was the day before Ryan's birthday, a very emotional time for her. We started with a power therapy called Eye Movement Desensitization and Reprocessing (EMDR; see appendix F) and identified Joanne's negative idea as "I am permanently damaged." She desperately wanted to believe the positive idea "I can let go."

Joanne judged herself as selfish because she was stuck in her own point of view about Ryan's death. She knew Ryan was in a better place, but she could not accept his absence in her life.

As we began the EMDR, Joanne felt a disturbing sensation in her gut move up to her heart, then to her throat—a feeling like something was stuck that she could not swallow. To her surprise, she felt anger and rage toward God for allowing the death of her only child.

We took a short break from EMDR and did some customized meridian tapping to ease this rage. Joanne reflected that she had no grounds to be angry with anyone else over Ryan's death, as nobody, including Ryan, had done anything wrong. The dangerous spot on the cliff was a pure freak of nature. God was the only one she could blame!

After more EMDR, Joanne felt the full force of the myriad feelings in her heart and her body around the loss of her son. We ended with an Integrated Energy Therapy (IET; see appendix F) treatment to remove the imprint of negative emotions that had built up in her body. Joanne could literally feel the IET pulling out anger, rage, guilt, fear, and sorrow from the organs of her body. At the end of the session, Joanne felt exhausted from the letting go of these negative feelings and allowing love and forgiveness to fill her heart.

After this session, Joanne had a vividly clear dream in which Ryan told her, "Mom, it's OK. Let go!" She felt his presence, and the tone of voice he used was the same loving way he would let her know when he could get along without his mother hovering over him. The dream helped her heal and to truly let him go.

At the third and final therapy session, Joanne felt like a new person. She had gotten through Ryan's birthday with no problems. She was able to talk about him without tears streaming down her face and to reconnect with the joy of having this precious child in her life for twenty years. She reflected, "Life is so precious! You go through life thinking there will be a tomorrow, and sometimes there won't be. If I close my eyes, I can still feel Ryan's hug— you can never get too many hugs! Before, I was so angry that he was not here that I could not feel him. Now I can visualize him."

Often, clients want to feel better and get over their problems, but they just don't know how to do it. Energy psychology is a guide to find out how the emotional problem is encoded in the energy field and then to systematically decode the problem so the natural flow of radiant wellness can be restored to the person. In the following case, we traced the invisible roots of the anxiety to an unexpected source.

Mental-Emotional Case Example

Alicia, a lovely Hispanic woman in her forties, came to her therapy session reporting that she did not know why she had started feeling shaky and nervous while cutting up vegetables for supper. In fact, whenever she was using a knife, she began to feel panic. Alicia agreed to try an energy psychology method called Thought Field Therapy (TFT; see appendix E) to desensitize this phobia of knives.

We started by having her massage the area over her heart while saying the affirmation, "I totally accept myself even though I have this problem." One round of tapping the TFT algorithm (sequence of tapping points) for trauma completely desensitized this phobia. Then I gently asked Alicia whether she knew why she had developed this fear.

"It was him," she answered softly. The father of her children had repeatedly chased her with a knife, threatening to kill her. She left him because of his violence toward her. Two years ago, this man killed his new girlfriend with a knife in a fit of rage. He was sentenced to a hundred-year prison term for this murder. From his jail cell, he continued to write letters to Alicia, threatening, "You are next!"

Even though she knew she was safe from him for at least the next one hundred years, her fear of this man had crystallized into a phobia of knives. TFT freed her from this fear.

The Mental Body

Cognition and belief are functions of the mental body, which works much like a computer. Thoughts precede and determine feelings. Psychotherapy can correct cognitive distortions in the mental biofield that produce dysfunctional emotions. People often believe distortions of the truth, feeling guilty when they are innocent and losing their sense of value when abused. For example, if a woman invites a girlfriend over for supper, and the friend is badly injured in a car accident on the way, the hostess may feel guilty. Even though she did not cause the accident, she may claim "false guilt" because her girlfriend got hurt on the way to her house.

The negative beliefs we hold about our lives form an attractor field that draws in more experiences to verify those beliefs. If we believe we are unlovable, we will push away anyone who approaches us with genuine love. If we believe we do not deserve healing, this limiting belief blocks recovery.

Mental Level Case Example

Gabriel, a dynamic Latino male in his late thirties, was just coming out of his second divorce and was establishing his profession in the healing arts in a new country. An outstanding practitioner, he was able to address many layers of the human energy field with his training in massage, acupuncture, counseling, and various forms of energy work. A physician asked what Gabriel's fee would be to travel to a neighboring state to work with the doctor and his family. Gabriel tossed and turned the whole night, trying to set a price.

Muscle testing indicated the problem was the basic negative life belief, "I have no value." Deeply buried feelings about his parents emerged as Gabriel reconnected with the confusion and emotional violence of his childhood that had set in place this limiting belief.

His father had died suddenly in a car accident when Gabriel was twelve, and this loss left a huge wound in his heart. In her loneliness, Gabriel's mother had him sleep with her for two nights while the family was in another country making arrangements. Being in his father's place in bed with his mother felt wrong and confusing for Gabriel, even though no sexual contact occurred. His mother gave Gabriel the house keys and the responsibility of locking the doors. As the oldest child, he was, in effect, the male head of the house. Gabriel felt devastated two months later when a distant relative of his father began staying with them and displaced Gabriel in his role of protecting the women in the house. He never bonded emotionally with this man, who later became his stepfather.

Although his mother never physically transgressed sexual boundaries with Gabriel, he felt her sexual attraction to him, which confused and violated his sense of value, producing overlays of anger, rage, guilt, trauma, and shame.

His mother had also been invasive mentally, reading his thoughts. The first time Gabriel brought a Playboy magazine into the house, she went straight to his room, found it, and lectured him. The first time he ever got drunk, she called up the house where he had been drinking to say that she knew he was drunk and not to come home. His mother accosted him the morning after the first time he had sex. Because he was too young at age sixteen to take responsibility for a child should a pregnancy occur, she advised him to abstain and admonished him at least not to have intercourse without protection, showing him how to use a condom.

As we tapped a customized Thought Field Therapy meridian sequence to treat these emotional disturbances, Gabriel vomited over and over, expelling the anger and rage over the abuse and the sense of guilt and shame he had carried from it. He cried out, "Mom, why did you do it? Why did you do it?"

A new wave of grief and despair surfaced as he tapped on the base of the middle fingernail to treat the pericardium meridian, where sexual abuse is stored. Gabriel got in touch with a deep sense of having been abandoned by God. Through the tears, the convulsions, and the pool of vomit on the floor, he cried out over and over, "God, where are you? Where are you? Please don't leave me here like this."

My heart opened in compassion for Gabriel's suffering. Usually negative feelings just dissolve with Thought Field Therapy, and the client does not move into an emotional catharsis. The model Gabriel used in his own counseling practice, however, helped others connect and release their deepest feelings by expressing them—crying and yelling or whatever was necessary to get the energy of the "e-motion" into motion. He was not afraid to do his own inner work and to give voice to the turbulence within. We added a heart massage to his treatment with the affirmation, "I deeply and profoundly accept myself and all of these feelings."

After a few minutes, he calmed down, smiled, and told me, "I have never before felt how deeply all of these emotions were buried in me. Thank you so much!"

The radiance in his face showed that the hole in his heart had healed. The roots of doubting his own value had been removed from his system by tapping meridians and at the same time allowing full expression of his intense feelings.

He now muscle tested strong to the statement "I have value." He was able to set a price for the work with the physician that reflected his true value. For several days after this therapy session, Gabriel's voice was slightly hoarse. When others asked him if he was getting ill, he replied, "No, I had a powerful emotional release, and I am getting well!"

4

Intuitive Body Level

The intuitive body forms an interface between the mental/emotional body and the spiritual body. Since it contains information we cannot obtain through cognition alone, some ways to access this knowledge are intuition, telepathy, dowsing, and muscle testing. This realm has traditionally been the domain of shamanism and the occult, as it involves the workings of supernatural forces and psychic phenomenon.

Many mental and emotional problems have their roots at this level and are thus missed by traditional psychotherapy. For example, if a client hears voices, a psychiatrist will often prescribe antipsychotic medication to subdue these "auditory hallucinations." Soul Detective work would differentiate whether the problem stemmed from mental illness, a seizure of the auditory nerve, a spirit guide trying to get through, or an earthbound spirit attachment. If the problem is mental illness, then medication could be an appropriate intervention to improve the client's quality of life and prevent psychiatric hospitalization.

Intuitive Level Case Example

Helen was a teenager who came into my office having difficulty in school and bothered by hearing voices. She had a broad range of affect, unlike the presentation of schizophrenia, and her intelligence was obvious. Muscle testing indicated she had a spirit attachment. She easily identified one of the voices she had been hearing as a friend who had died in a freak skateboard accident. She was a highly sensitive young woman, and he could communicate with her. So he just stayed around. Once we explained the situation to him and the benefits of moving on into the next world—both for him and for his friend Helen—he crossed, and that voice stopped. Another earthbound spirit affecting Helen was a former resident of Helen's home. Lights would go on in the kitchen while everyone in the family was in the living room. Sometimes the dog would sit in the doorway of the "empty" computer room and bark nonstop. Once we helped this spirit understand her situation and move on, that voice also stopped.

Psychiatry would have prescribed medication for Helen, but Soul Detective work solved the underlying problems.

If muscle testing indicates a problem originates on the intuitive level, then check the following sub-menu to narrow down the root cause:

1. Earthbound spirit attachments

2. Curses and hexes

3. Ancestral wounds

4. Family constellation issues

5. Archetypes

6. Dreams

7. Soul loss

8. Energetic cords

9. Vows

10. Evil spirits and entities

11. Past life trauma

12. Other—put on your Soul Detective hat!

Part two of this section goes into more detail on ways to work with each of these intuitive level categories.

5
Spiritual Body Level

I f muscle testing indicates that the root cause of a problem lies at the spiritual level, then the problem is in the client's personal relationship with the realm of the Divine, which can be called by many different names: Creator, Almighty God, Lord Jesus Christ, Holy Spirit, Divine Mother, Allah, Source, Great Spirit, and so on. Just as I am called Barb by my family, Mom by my children, and Grandma Stone by my grandchildren, no matter what name they use, it is all me—Aunt Barb, Mother, "Gamma Tone." Sometimes the word "God" carries associations of a judgmental, authoritarian being, so call Divine energy by whatever name you can best access this connection.

As this realm stands at the highest level, if there is a problem at this level, then all other levels of being will be affected, right down to the physical. No healer or spiritual leader can change another person's relationship to the Divine. As Dr. Dietrich Klinghardt, formulator of this model of the Five Levels of Healing, tells the client, "That issue is between you and God, sacred ground." If the client wants spiritual mentoring, however, and both parties feel comfortable with the therapist in this role, the spiritual arena can be explored, but the ultimate relationship with God belongs only to the individual.

People may project onto the Divine punitive qualities experienced in their earthly parents. If the root cause of a problem lies at the spiritual level, one could muscle test the statement, "All parts of me (inner child, adult, wise person) believe that God is one hundred percent loving."

Spiritual Level Case Example

Clara came to therapy with the goal of freeing herself from the sadness and heaviness that sat at her heart center and moved up to her throat. Her life lacked joy. Muscle testing indicated the root cause was at the spiritual level. When I told her that psychotherapy does not usually deal with this sacred relationship with God, she felt even sadder, as she did not even know where to begin to untie this knot in her heart. I inquired whether she was willing for me take on the role of spiritual mentor and to explore together where this sadness came from. She responded, "Yes!"

I questioned, "Did you ever get mad at God?"

Clara wept as she disclosed that since she had been a little girl, she had always felt a deep personal connection with God. She loved God and talked with Him often. Then at age eleven, she got juvenile rheumatoid arthritis. Her mother told her, "No man will ever have you now because you are crippled."

Clara felt betrayed by God, got angry, and exclaimed, "God, I'm not going to pray anymore!" In her anger, she disconnected from God. Ironically, the fear of separation from God was at the heart of her sadness. But God never gave up on Clara, and as an adult, she experienced a Kundalini awakening, which propelled her deep into her own healing journey as she struggled to cope with the strange sensations moving within her.

The sadness in Clara's soul was fed by three past lifetimes in which she had been burned at the stake. Each time, she had felt betrayed and abandoned by God, the same feelings she had in this life when she was crippled by the arthritis. But since she did not die this time, she had a chance to work to heal the illusion of separation from God.

Lifetime One

Many lifetimes ago, Eliza was burned at the stake at age twenty-five for her radical belief that we are perfectly designed to heal ourselves. As Clara remembered this lifetime, her back felt like it was on fire and the back of her head hurt. We made a customized meridian tapping sequence to aid Eliza in releasing the fear at the core of the disturbance and the rage on top of that fear. Eliza came out smiling!

Lifetime Two

Next, a love story unfolded. Betrina, a commoner, fell in love with a man of noble birth, someone she was not allowed to love. The man's mother was furious with this seventeen-year-old girl who was not the right status for her son and devised a plan to get rid of her. She brought false accusations against Betrina, who was convicted and burned at the stake. This time, our customized tapping sequence was more complex. In addition to the trauma and fear at the heart of the issue, Betrina also had great sadness at being separated from the man she loved.

Lifetime Three

In Africa, around 400 A.D., Joseph was a young black man who heard the gospel and embraced the Light of the Christ. Others in his tribe refused to accept Christianity, however, and martyred Joseph. In a state of numbness, shock, and disbelief, Joseph was hung upside down and burned at the stake.

Clara's soul lesson from her life as Joseph was to follow the truth no matter what—to feel the strength of aligning with spiritual truth. Great joy came as Clara remembered Joseph's spirit going into the Light after his death.

Untying these knots in the fabric of her soul helped Clara release her sadness. Months after our session, she e-mailed: "The work we did together was very helpful. I felt noticeably lighter and happier and just more content to be. I feel more peace and less tension in the back and chest since we worked, more openness to the world." She also found a yoga teacher who helped her deal with her Kundalini awakening.

PART TWO

Working with Intuitive Level Issues

Intuitive Level Issues

1. Earthbound Spirits

2. Curses and Hexes

3. Ancestral Wounds

4. Family Constellation Issues

5. Archetypes

6. Dreams

7. Soul Loss

8. Energetic Cords

9. Vows

10. Evil Spirits and Entities

11. Past Life Trauma

12. Other—Put on Your Soul Detective Hat!

Volumes could be written about each of these twelve topics, but then this book would be too heavy to carry! Below is a brief overview of each subject and the guidelines I use in working with each issue. I encourage readers to get more training in the areas of greatest interest.

Multiple factors, called "interference patterns" in several energy psychology therapies, could be impacting a given symptom. To get an overview of the situation, some practitioners test at the outset of therapy for how many of these patterns are present. These initial numbers tend to be large; however, since clearing one issue often resolves other issues—like one domino falling over and knocking down a whole line of dominoes standing behind it—

I usually muscle test for the category of the issue that needs to be addressed first. In other words, I find the most appropriate entry point for treatment. Then I muscle test whether more than one element in this category is involved. For example, if the intuitive level root cause indicated is past life trauma, then I muscle test how many past lives were involved. In one case, I discovered that three past lives were impacting a person with an anxiety disorder. After clearing the male lifetime that needed to be addressed first, only one other past life needed to be treated—a female lifetime.

1

Earthbound Spirits

What Happens After Death?

People have different assumptions about what happens to a soul after death. Western fundamentalist religions teach that good people go to heaven and bad people go to hell. Tibetan Buddhism teaches that the spirit goes from this world to an in-between world called the "bardo" to prepare for reincarnation. Some people believe nothing happens after we die. Others believe that all people who die go back home to God, to heaven.

In *Memories, Dreams, Reflections,* Carl Jung wrote, "Critical rationalism has apparently eliminated, along with so many other mythic conceptions, the idea of life after death" (p. 300). Yet, while the intellect would judge all ideas of an afterlife futile speculation, he adds, "To the emotions, however, it is a healing and valid activity; it gives existence a glamour which we would not like to do without" (pp. 300–301). Jung wrote about the paranormal experiences that came to him and formed his ideas of the afterlife. One prominent example is when, in 1916, Jung and his family experienced poltergeist activity, which culminated in his front doorbell ringing frantically with no one in sight. Jung was sitting near the door and could see the doorbell button moving as well as hear its sound. Jung felt a crowd of spirits present and could scarcely breathe. "Then they cried out in chorus, 'We have come back from Jerusalem where we found not what we sought'" (p. 191). That was the beginning of his book *The Seven Sermons to the Dead,* written under the pseudonym Basilides of Alexandria (1917, currently unavailable).

The experiences that my clients report to me when investigating the root cause of their emotional disturbances do not always fit into traditional frameworks of thought about the afterlife. Many people may be opposed to the concepts I report here, just as the colleagues of Dr. Semmelweiss in the mid 1800s opposed his theory that tiny organisms called bacteria were responsible for puerperal fever, which killed 16 percent of the women who gave birth at his hospital in Vienna. At that time, the theory of bacteria was not part of commonly accepted beliefs. Likewise, the theory presented here of the possibility of earthbound spirits attaching to the energy field of a living person and draining the life force of the host is not a commonly accepted belief in my culture.

The approach of Soul Detective work is to listen with an open mind to what seems to be true for the client and proceed in therapy *as if* it is true. I suspend judgment on whether or not the situation has empirical truth, and I work with the story that comes up as having absolute metaphorical truth— and it just might have inestimable spiritual healing for the earthbound spirits that we help get back home!

Earthbound spirits are people who lived a life as a human on the Earth plane and then at death failed to cross into the next world. They may also be called "waywards" or "spirit-walkers." Sometimes they settle into a physical space, such as the home they used to live in, and at other times they attach to the energy field of a living person. Earthbound spirits are different from evil spirits, sometimes called demons or entities, which are thought of as autonomous negative energy packages that were never in human form.

Earthbound Spirit Case Example

Beth, a healer, noticed a problem with her fourteen-year-old son, Jack. Ever since he was a tiny baby, Jack's immune system had not functioned correctly. Any insect around would find Jack and bite him more than anyone else, and any infectious agent would hit him harder than others. A brilliant child, at age five, Jack had already been planning how to end the war between Israel and Palestine. Jack had been out sick for six months of the past school year, but even with this health challenge, Jack taught himself at home and got straight A's.

Beth's pregnancy with Jack, her firstborn, had been so difficult that she and her husband left their humanitarian work in South America and returned to the United States to get better medical care. When Jack was two months old, they went back to South America to work in a child welfare program in Bolivia.

Beth detected some breaks in Jack's energy field and repaired them, but the damage kept regenerating. She worked to dissipate the black cloud of energy around Jack, but it kept returning. She also sensed a male presence around Jack that she did not know how to handle.

As we called in the guardians and guardian angels for both of us, for Jack, and for the male presence, we felt disturbed emotional energy enter the room. Muscle testing indicated we had spiritual permission to work with this spirit attachment of a six-year-old male, unknown to Jack. This little boy, named Emanuel, did not know he was no longer in his body.

Emanuel had been an orphan living on the streets of Bolivia. As a two-month-old baby, Jack had picked up this spirit attachment when the family moved back to South America. Emanuel was drawn to the spiritual light emanating from Jack. As both Beth and I are bilingual, we did the session in Spanish so Emanuel could understand us better.

The happiest time in Emanuel's life had been with his mother. At age six, he lost both of his parents. As a street orphan, he had to steal food to survive. One day he got caught. He ran away, but some very angry men chased him, captured him, and violently beat him to death. The top layer of the emotional distress we treated was sadness, which we replaced with the readiness to accept joy. Underneath this sorrow was Emanuel's core issue, a layer of pure adrenaline-charged fear. Emanuel felt much calmer after we tapped a customized meridian sequence to release the terror of his fatal beating.

We asked if he would like to go be with his mommy, to have her come get him and take him home with her. Zap! Instantly, Beth felt the presence of Emanuel's mother come from heaven like a beam of light to get her son. Standing outside time, she had been waiting for this moment. We both wept with joy at this ecstatic reunion, and the angels lifted Emanuel to heaven in a cloud of bliss.

We next prayed for forgiveness for those who had killed Emanuel, to let their souls know that his spirit was all right now. We asked that the violence done to them in their lives, the violence done to the ones who did violence to them, and the whole chain of violence in the world be healed. We also asked Spirit to erase the negative karma these people had incurred by their brutality to Emanuel.

Beth saw that Emanuel had been drawn to Jack, a wise, kind soul, because of the outstanding goodness and radiance of his spirit. Not knowing that he was dead, Emanuel was clutching on to Jack "for dear life."

Beth sensed that the soul lesson of this experience for Jack is to work for and to know peace. Jack's openness to the pain of the violence in the world motivates his soul to work for conflict resolution.

Next we prayed for the angels to repair the damage that had been done to the grid work in the layers of Jack's energy field from the attachment of Emanuel's emotional turmoil. The angels repaired the links in Jack's system, sealing up all the energetic holes.

Before closing our session, I sensed the presence of other discarnate children who had been watching our work with Emanuel. We called out to them and summoned their mothers, grandmothers, and great-grandmothers to come get them and help the angels take them back to God. We felt a huge happy flutter of angel wings in the room as all these little ones went home! Indeed, Beth has been a worker for child welfare on many levels.

Jack was interested and intrigued when Beth told him about our Soul Detective session. He reported he had not noticed much difference, but he was feeling good and liked the idea that a little boy had found him to be a safe haven.

In the course of the following year, Jack did very well. His family returned to the United States, and Jack had no major health problems, only a couple of colds. So many variables were present in the situation that ascribing credit for the improvement in his immune system to our work with Emanuel, the move, or any other one factor would be difficult. What really matters is that healing came, and everyone rejoiced.

A Better Offer

As I searched the database on spirit releasement work, I found some therapies that simply expelled an earthbound spirit by commanding it to detach from the host. An analogy would be telling a fan in a row high in the bleachers at a sold-out football game, "Get out of here. You can't stay for the game!" This situation could create hostility. Instead, Soul Detective work addresses the well-being of the discarnate spirit as well as the host. In essence, we ask the fan, "How would you like to move to a front row seat at no extra charge?" We offer the earthbound spirit the therapy needed to be able to cross to the Light—a much better offer—and the host gets free from the attachment.

No matter whether the earthbound spirit I am working with is a nun, a gangster, an innocent child, or a mass murderer, I treat the person with the unconditional love the Creator has for all that is. Since we are all connected in the web of life, giving a person who has made mistakes a chance to repent helps to uplift the consciousness of the entire planet.

Note: This work is not for the fainthearted! Not everyone feels comfortable delving into the underworld, but others like me just have to know what is underneath the symptoms I see. Some therapists will feel comfortable working with past life trauma but not with earthbound spirits. Still, knowing the symptoms of spirit attachment will help these therapists know when to refer a client to a "ghost buster."

Reasons to Stay Earthbound

In the course of my clinical experience, the following theories have emerged as to why spirits stay earthbound:

- When strongly bonded loved ones are unable to "let go" of the deceased, this emotional pull seems to bind the spirit so that it cannot move into the Light. For example, if a wife is unable to release her deceased husband, he may just stay with her in spirit form and attach to her energy field. If a grandchild is unable to release a deceased grandmother, Grandma may stay close and attach to the grandchild, thinking she is helping. Sometimes we need to do therapy for both the living and the deceased to help both parties realize that the spirit attachment is mutually detrimental. Spirit attachments may also be nested, as in a mother who cannot release the soul of her stillborn child, carrying the child as a spirit attachment; then when the mother dies, both the spirits of the mother and the stillborn baby attach to a living daughter.

- When strong negative feelings are present at the moment of death, these dense, heavy emotions seem to chain the spirit to Earth's gravitational field. For example, in a war, if a mother witnesses the murder of her child just before being killed herself, the anger and hatred toward the offender may keep the parent earthbound. War has rules, and soldiers are only supposed to kill other soldiers, not women and children.

- Most people do not know what to expect at the moment of death. Some people think that when we are dead, we cease to exist—"lights out." Those who think that death is the end may not realize their spirit is no longer in their physical body, because consciousness remains, with seeing, hearing, and emotions.

- When people are confused or disoriented at the moment of death, they may not realize they are deceased. Death from brain tumors or an impact to the head may compromise cognitive function. Also, people with dementia sometimes have such compromised mental capacity that they may not recognize what is happening when the spirit leaves the body. According to spiritual teacher Vianna Stibal, as explained in her book *Theta Healing*, at the moment of death, a window of light opens up in the latticework grid system around the human energy field. This doorway back to the Creator stays open about nine days after death and then closes. If a person misses this window of light, they are trapped by Earth's magnetic pull and need help to reconnect to Source.

- When a person fears retribution for misdeeds, the spirit may turn away from the Light. People may think they are going to hell or to purgatory if they leave the Earth plane. The truth seems to be that the Divine does not judge us; we judge ourselves and condemn ourselves to the hell of separation from our creator's love.

- Suicide may chain the spirit to Earth, but not always. The circumstances around the suicide are important. Some spiritual teachers say that if a person takes his or her own life, that person must stay earthbound for the length of time the person would have lived. If a person has a terminal illness with unbearable pain and is already very close to death, suicide as euthanasia does not appear to chain the spirit to Earth or prohibit entry to heaven, according to Bill and Judy Guggenheim in *Hello from Heaven!*

- A curse or a hex may keep a spirit earthbound, as in the case in the following section on curses and hexes in which a man was so angry at losing his property that he put a curse on the land so nobody who died there could cross into the next world.

- Having unfinished business may also keep spirits earthbound. The television show *Ghost Whisperer* and the movie *Ghost* are about people with unresolved issues staying earthbound until they can set a situation right. Once they are at peace, they can cross over.

- Some people become so attached to their material possessions in this world that they are unwilling to leave the Earth plane for the realms of Light. For example, a man was very attached to his beautiful little cabin on a lake. After he died, his son tore down this cabin to build a big house on the same spot. Unbeknown to the son, the father had been staying in the cabin after his death and became very upset about the cabin being torn down. The father then attached to a friend of the family who visited the site. This woman recognized the invasion of her free will by an outside influence, brought the earthbound spirit to therapy, and helped him to cross over into the next world.

Energy Drain

The energy field connected to the human body receives a constant stream of spiritual energy from above through the crown chakra and from Mother Earth below through the root chakra. We also take in life energy through the front and back of the chakras on the torso. We also get energy from the food we eat, the air we breathe, and sunshine. After death, earthbound spirits have no way to generate energy on their own, so they take it in from their surroundings, and their presence depletes the energy in any area they enter. A room that has an earthbound spirit present usually feels chilly—a coldness that penetrates to the bones.

When an earthbound spirit attaches to the human energy field of a living person, this attachment drains the life energy of the host. The situation is like the host riding a bicycle up a hill with another person on the back of the bike, unable to help pedal.

Symptoms of Attachment

Pay attention to these symptoms of earthbound spirit attachments in yourself, a loved one, or a client:

- The person feels unusually tired, exhausted, and drained of energy even when getting adequate sleep and nutrition.

- A cold breeze wafts through the room when the person enters. The chill goes right to the bones. Turning up the heat does not seem to shake off this freezing feeling, and you can't seem to get your hands warm. Having no power source of their own, earthbound spirits drain energy from their surroundings.

- Following the death of a close loved one, a person suddenly has severe emotional problems beyond a normal grief response. The earthbound spirits often feel confusion, emotional turmoil, and depression because they are so cut off from others. These feelings may imprint on the host.

- A person complains, "Something is wrong. I don't feel like myself. I feel as if someone else is inside of me."

- A person's level of functioning takes a sudden, sharp downward turn.

- A person improves significantly after an electroconvulsive therapy (ECT) treatment, and then gradually deteriorates again. The ECT shock may temporarily expel the spirit attachments from the energy field; however, unless the break in the energy body that allowed these attachments to connect is repaired, the person is likely to gradually pick up more spirit attachments after the ECT treatment.

- Following an operation, a patient has a sudden personality change. Being under anesthesia leaves a psychic gate open, and earthbound spirits may attach.

Soul Detective Earthbound Spirit Protocol

When the root cause of an emotional problem muscle tests that it is from an earthbound spirit attachment, Soul Detective work finds these earthbound spirits and does energy therapy to help them realize what has happened, clear their emotional disturbances, and cross into the next world in peace.

Advice to all Soul Detectives

Keep your mind open at all times and expect the unexpected!

Think outside the box!

Getting into Your Center

In Soul Detective work, both the therapist and client need to be centered, or the muscle testing results might not be accurate. Complete details on the way I do centering are in appendix C, including diagnosis and corrections for each of the three vectors of the energy field: up-down, front-back, and left-right. Other modalities use different ways to clear factors that imbalance the biofield, termed "systemic energetic interference" in the certification program of the Association for Comprehensive Energy Psychology (ACEP).

When polarity is reversed on the vertical axis of the energy field, if I hold a pendulum over the heart chakra, I find that it rotates counterclockwise. In this situation, energy flows backward through the meridians (counterflow chi), and answers from muscle testing will be exactly the opposite of the truth. The correction for vertical polarity is easy to do and feels great even if the polarity was already correct. Just to be sure the heart chakra is rotating clockwise, place the right hand over the heart and circle the hand clockwise while saying affirmations appropriate to the situation. For example:

"I deeply and profoundly accept myself with all my problems and limitations. I accept all of my feelings about the spirit attached to my energy field. Even though I have a 'hitchhiker,' I deeply and completely love and accept myself."

Getting Permission

To assess permission, muscle test the statements: "We have spiritual permission to work with this spirit attachment" and "Working with this spirit attachment is safe and appropriate," versus "We do not have spiritual permission to work with this spirit attachment."

I do not work with every client who calls for an appointment. I need to refer some people, because they are outside the scope of my expertise. Likewise, a negative test on spiritual permission to work with an attachment can mean one of several things:

- I do not have the skills necessary to deal with the trauma this earthbound spirit is carrying. When I test this issue, I am really asking Spirit whether or not I have the tools to handle whatever would come up.

- Something else needs to happen first.

- The timing is not right. Perhaps not enough time is left in the session to complete the necessary work.

Always get permission first before starting to work with an earthbound spirit attachment. If permission is denied, do not work with that spirit.

So far in my practice, I have only been refused permission once. I was working with a woman who had both her father and her grandfather's spirits attached to her. We asked for spiritual permission to work with the father and were denied. We asked for permission to work with the grandfather and we got permission. After the grandfather had cleared his issues, then we got permission to work with the father.

When we test that we do have spiritual permission, then we proceed with the confidence of knowing that the end result will be positive for everyone involved.

Getting Spiritual Help

When working with spirits, get spiritual help!

A rescue worker would never jump into a stormy, choppy ocean to save someone without having a lifeline attached to the ship. Likewise, no self-respecting Soul Detective would attempt to work with an earthbound spirit without first calling on a lifeline of help from the realm of the spirit world to make this interdimensional communication possible. We need a connection to a supernatural source of strength and wisdom to work with supernatural phenomena. In *Hands of Light: A Guide to Healing Through the Human Energy Field,* author Barbara Brennan teaches that we access this realm through a layer of the spiritual plane she calls "The Celestial Body," through which we reach the point of "being" where we know our connection with God and the entire universe.

A Native American shaman calls on Great Spirit and the spirits of animal guides when doing soul retrieval. Christians might call on the Holy Spirit, while someone of Islamic faith would feel most comfortable calling on the power of Almighty God. Many religious traditions speak of angels as being messengers from the Divine. Since angels are nondenominational, many clients can connect with their presence.

Angels always stand ready to help, but they cannot interfere with our free will. We simply need to ask for their help and they joyfully spring into action. Sometimes angelic help comes in response to the prayer of another person, such as the account of a mother sensing that her daughter, who was out on a hiking trip, was in mortal danger, as related by Marilynn Carlson Webber and William D. Webber in *A Rustle of Angels.* The mother implored God for help. At the very same time, the daughter fell off a cliff. Miraculously, angelic wings caught the daughter in the middle of the fall and lifted her back to solid ground at the top of the cliff.

One client asked for help from the angelic realm during her therapy session and then did not want to bother them again, because she thought the angels must be busy helping other people. This idea was a misconception. Angels come from another dimension, outside time and space, so they can be everywhere helping everyone all at once. Our asking for help in no way diminishes the help available to others.

Step-Down Transformers

If we saw the full presence of God, the brilliance of God's light would blind us and burn us to a crisp instantly. Angels intermediate between God and humans. Just as a transformer steps down the energy from a high-voltage power line into 110 voltage for our homes, the angelic realm steps down the power of the Creator to the exact amount of energy each individual can handle. The word "archangel" means "chief angel" and designates a higher-ranking angel. Michael is generally considered the archangel of protection. He is most often depicted standing on the head of a vanquished dragon or demon with a sword in his hand. Archangel Michael is thought to be the angel in charge of safe passage from this world into the next one.

The three main trainings I have drawn from to connect with the angelic realm are (see appendix F for details on all):

- **Integrated Energy Therapy (IET).** I am an IET Master-Instructor and have been teaching IET classes since 2001. IET works most specifically with archangel Ariel and also with other angels and archangels.

- **Psychoenergetic Healing.** The work of Martin F. Luthke, PhD, and Linda Stein-Luthke sets therapy inside pyramids of light, anchored into time and space at the four corners and the apex of the pyramid by the archangels Raphael, Gabriel, Uriel, Michael, and Zadkiel. Creating this sacred inner space establishes a safe workplace to connect with the presence and help of the Beings of Light. The Luthkes call these pyramids magnifying glasses of higher vibration, the access points through which we communicate with our omnidimensional nature as Beings of Light.

Pyramid sculpture by Eric Perelman, stained glass and quartz crystal.

- **Theta Healing.** This therapy teaches that each person has several guardians to help with his or her spiritual development. These guardians may be angels, ancestors who have crossed over into the Light and come back in spirit form as guides, or religious figures from the person's spiritual tradition, such as Divine Mother, White Buffalo Woman, Jesus Christ, or the Hindu god Ganesh. Everyone has at least one guardian angel. When I begin spirit releasement work, I call in a treatment team including all of the guardians and guardian angels for my client, for me, and for the earthbound spirit.

Both IET and Theta Healing work with the concept of attuning and reprogramming DNA, which was formerly conceptualized as static. All three of the therapies come together and overlap with the field of microbiology with the discovery that DNA emits biophotons, which are ultra-weak electromagnetic waves in the visible spectrum of light. Although too weak to be seen with the naked eye, they can be measured with special equipment (Bischof, 1998) or accessed in altered states of consciousness or when attuning to the spiritual realm (Narby, 1999). Healing work can access this realm, which lies beyond the limit of normal perception, through linking with the spirit world and then using this connection to move the blueprint of the organism toward healing.

Once we have permission to proceed and have our spiritual team assisting the process, we are ready to find out who has hitchhiked into therapy today.

Gathering Identifying Information

Some very intuitive clients may already know the answers to the following queries without even muscle testing. In this case, muscle testing is not necessary. Most clients need muscle testing to get some identifying information and then transfer to a direct intuitive connection somewhere during this process.

Gender

The first main classification to help establish identity is muscle testing for gender. The safest statement to test is "This person is male," versus "This person is female." Always test both statements to be very sure about gender.

Note: I used to muscle test the statement, "This person was in a female body." The unconscious mind is very literal in giving results of muscle testing, however, and that statement is literally true for everyone since we all grew inside our mothers. We can get "false female" responses with this wording.

Age at Death

The next main clue to a person's identity is finding out how long a person lived. Working with a child spirit attachment is very different from working with a disembodied adult.

Bearing in mind that many attachments may not know they are dead, one tactful way to find out age is muscle testing how old this person turned on the last birthday, the one right before people stopped talking to them and started ignoring them.

Muscle test the statement, "This person lived for at least twenty years." Always preface a number with a qualifier such as "at least," "more than," or "less than," so you will know whether the number you are testing is too large or too small. If the muscle test for at least twenty years is true, keep increasing the number to something like, "This person lived for at least forty years."

Once the larger number tests false, then back up by half the distance between that age and the previous one. For example, if forty years tests false, then test, "This person lived at least thirty years." Continue going forward and backward by half until the age of death is established.

Some spirits have been earthbound for a very long time. For further clarification, one can muscle test the year of birth, as in: "This person was born before 2000 [before 1990, before 1980, and so forth]."

Cause of Death

Usually the trauma that prevents a spirit from crossing into the next world is the manner of death and the emotional turmoil that accompanied dying, so expect some violent scenarios. Rarely, the unresolved material will be around sexual abuse or unresolved guilt. Trauma that results in a death, mortal trauma, is more severe than current-life trauma, which usually does not include dying. The only exception to this guideline is that people who have been clinically dead and then come back to life report they have absolutely no fear of death. They have seen the peace, love, and Light on the other side and often return from their near-death experience feeling great sadness at coming back to the Earth plane, feeling "homesick for heaven" and longing to return to the plane where they were surrounded and saturated with love.

Muscle test these major categories until one tests true:

1. Illness

2. Accident

3. Act of war

4. Murder

5. Execution/martyred

6. Suicide

7. Natural disaster (tsunami, earthquake)

8. Starvation

9. Abortion, miscarriage, or stillbirth

10. Sacrificed in a ritual

11. Other

Known or Unknown?

The next differentiation to make is whether this spirit attachment is someone known to the client or unknown. Test: "This person is someone known to this client," versus "This person is someone unknown to this client."

If known, then test whether the person is family or non-family. (*Note:* Include people related by marriage as family—husband, wife, mother-in-law, and so on.) When doing an intake, if a former mate is deceased, I recommend muscle testing to find out if the former partner is attached to your client as an earthbound spirit. Since spirit attachments often do not know they are dead, they do not realize they are released from their marriage vows of "till death do us part." Furthermore, carrying around a former partner in spirit form can put a serious kink into any future love relationship with a new mate!

• Case Examples of Spousal Attachment

A client awoke in the middle of the night to her three-year-old daughter's cries. Smoke filled the house. A delicious feeling of oblivion within her said, "It will all be OK—just go back to sleep." She had to fight hard against the effects of smoke inhalation, because part of her knew this situation was really not OK. She roused her husband to go get the baby and headed for her daughter's room. Very sadly, her husband was overcome by the smoke and died in the fire along with both of the children. My client certainly had enough grief to cause depression just from this catastrophic loss. Thirty years later, she was still cycling through periods of intense depression.

In the meantime, she remarried and then divorced after having two children by her second husband. When she came for therapy with me, she was highly committed to her third marriage, though the relationship was a challenge, especially with the dynamics of their ex-partners and stepchildren.

During one very intense period of depression, we muscle tested that her first husband's spirit was still attached to her energy field. He did not know that he was no longer in his body. How do you think he felt about his wife sleeping with those other men?

When we explained the situation to him and helped him cross over, a great weight lifted from this woman. She came back to her next session truly happy.

Another client had listed with an Internet dating service for a few months with no real responses. The day after she released her late husband's earthbound spirit attachment to her, she got five different Internet responses from men. One or two could have counted as a synchronicity, but five showed that she had definitely opened up her energy field to become available.

If a spirit attachment tests as known but not a family member, then test a sub-menu of friend, teacher, boss, business partner, enemy soldier, and so forth.

If the spirit tests as unknown, then test whether it is a stranger. If the spirit is a stranger, then proceed with the next step.

An attachment can be unknown but also be family, as in an ancestor who died before the client was born. In this case, muscle test how many generations back and then mother's side/father's side and so forth to identify the individual.

- **Length of Time Attached**

An additional piece of information that will shed light on the situation is finding out how long this earthbound spirit has been attached to the client. Muscle test: "This spirit has been attached for at least a week [month, year, and so on]."

- **Further Identifying Information**

Optional: For unknown attachments, further identifying information can be tested including marital status, children and their ages, and anything else one would like to add to better understand the discarnate person.

Finding a Name

Somewhere in the search to find out more about the spirit attachment, ask what name this person wants to be called. Using a name shows more respect than addressing someone in third person and makes the therapeutic work more personal.

Originally, I asked my clients what this person was named. The client would hear several names and then become confused, unsure of which name was the "right" one. So I changed the wording of my question to avoid this problem. Now I advise clients, "Ask what name this person wants to be called by, and the very first name that comes to your mind will be the right one. It doesn't have to be the person's real name, just what they want us to call them in this session." Then we use whatever name comes, and everyone is happy.

Explaining the Situation: Good News

Once we have the preceding information, gently explain to the spirit attachment what is happening. Rather than bluntly saying, "You are dead," ask your client to attune intuitively to the attachment and let the spirit know we have some very good news. Explain things in terms appropriate to the situation. For someone who died from an illness, you could use the following script:

"We think we have figured out what your problem is. Remember how sick your body was? Your spirit is not in that physical body anymore, and we are going to help you get your new body, your spiritual body. When you go into the Light and get reconnected to the Source energy from which you came, you get a new body made of Light—a spiritual body. And the really good news is that you can make it look like any age you want to be!"

One might ask if the spirit has noticed being ignored much of the time. Inquire how this person has been feeling since people started acting as if he/she is not there. Let the person know we have good news, a way out of his/her trapped situation. By this time, most clients are able to make an intuitive connection with the person attached to their energy field, especially because this person is and has been attached to the client's core energy. The situation is like talking with someone while squeezed into a telephone booth together. The "telepathic" connection comes very easily!

Desensitizing the Trauma

Most people in their bodies have never heard of tapping meridian points, so offering this therapy to people not in their bodies needs to be proffered with great tact and diplomacy. A good place to start is to inquire, "Would you like to try something we could do to help you feel better?" The magic words in this sentence are "feel better." Getting therapy implies someone is defective in some way and needs help. Many self-respecting spirits might refuse the offer to get therapy, but everyone wants to feel better.

Add that what we are offering may seem really silly, but it has helped a lot of other people feel better. Then see if the spirit is willing to give it a try. Informed consent is essential, even with earthbound spirits. If they are hesitant at first, I demonstrate a little tapping sequence so they can see what it looks like.

Note: The client taps on the points as I tap, and the earthbound spirit gets the benefit since he/she is attached to the energy field of the client.

First, I clear limiting beliefs that might block the success of our treatment (see appendix E). Then I almost always treat by making a customized meridian tapping sequence, also called Diagnostic TFT, so that I can detect the exact emotions that have been disrupted in the earthbound spirit by noticing which meridians were involved—Stomach for fear, Large Intestine for guilt, and so forth (see the chart in appendix E for the correspondence of meridians with emotions). Practitioners can use any forms of energy therapy in which they have developed competence. Emotional Freedom Techniques (EFT) work well with earthbound spirits, as do many other techniques in appendix F. A pastor might simply pray with the earthbound spirit, asking to release all guilt, shame, fear, anger, and rage.

Frontal-Occipital Hold

A simple form of trauma release is holding the front and back of the brow chakra in the frontal-occipital hold. For this: Place one hand on the forehead and the other hand on the back of the head over the occipital lobe and hold for a minute or two or until trauma is released from a memory. If desired, the client can imagine a better ending to the traumatic situation to "reprogram" emotional memory.

Preparing to Cross

Once the trauma of the earthbound spirit is desensitized, ask whether the spirit feels ready to cross into the next world. If not, continue therapy until the earthbound spirit has reached a state of peace. Perhaps the person needs to make amends to someone, asking forgiveness. In *Living Your Soul's Purpose,* Mary Hammond calls this dialogue "Soul Talk." This type of interaction heals the heart.

We all have free will, whether in a body or not, and sometimes a spirit is not yet ready to cross over. If the spirit appears unwilling or unable to cross, you can ask your Divine guidance whether crossing is in their highest and best good and whether the timing is right. Usually, however, the spirit has a reason that can be resolved within the session. Possible holdups are:

- **Fear of leaving a loved one.** The earthbound spirit may be afraid to leave the host all alone, such as a deceased husband not wanting to leave his wife because he loves her deeply. In this case, I honor the love he has for his wife and simply explain to him that his presence without a body is actually hurting them both. Once he crosses to the Light and gets a new spirit body, he can come back to visit any time, and then his presence will be beneficial to his wife's energy field.

- **A loved one needs to come too.** Perhaps a relative, friend, or member of the community is also earthbound, and we need to find and help others so everyone can cross together.

- **Self-unforgiveness.** People who firmly believe in the necessity of person-
ally suffering in hell or purgatory to purify their soul for their misdeeds
hold themselves earthbound. Since I always work within the belief system
of my client, even if my client is discarnate, I use a three-step process in
this situation: 1) We focus their awareness on their current suffering as an
earthbound spirit—feeling ignored and cut off, being stuck and immobilized, not having a life of their own, and so forth. 2) We ask what they
have learned from their experience and how they would do things differently if given another chance in a future life. We offer the opportunity to
repent. 3) I inquire whether the suffering they have already done while
earthbound has been enough to "pay" for what they feel they did wrong in
their lives, reminding them that God is pure love and has already forgiven
them. Now they need to make the decision to forgive themselves so they
can be with their loved ones on the other side again.

Getting Helpers

Once ready to cross, ask who the person would like to have on the welcoming committee from the other side. Do they know anyone already on the
other side—a beloved parent, grandparent, mate, child?

If the spirit wants a specific person to help make the crossing, muscle test
to make sure that person has already crossed into the Light. If the desired
person has not yet crossed, ask that earthbound spirit to join the client so
they can go together into the next world, and find someone else to assist on
the welcoming committee.

If no answer comes, muscle test the statement, "A helping spirit from the
other side wants to assist this person to cross." If true, then subtest whether
it is a parent, grandparent, and so on. If the spirit has nobody from the other
side, as with a small child who does not know anyone deceased, ask the angels
to do the job. Angels are totally capable of doing it all by themselves, but the
presence of someone the earthbound spirit knows is very comforting.

Manner of Crossing

Optional: One can ask the spirits how they want to get to the other
side. Does the soul want to walk up a staircase of light? Cross a bridge?

Go by train? Be carried? Fly to heaven on the wings of the angels? Make the visualization of crossing from one place to the next and the nature of the destination culturally appropriate. In Japan, this transition is imaged as crossing a river. Native Americans have animal totems serving as guides in the spirit world, so one could call the animal guides to carry them to the Happy Hunting Ground. Christians might want Jesus to come get them and take them to heaven.

Shamans in Peru go to a sacred place in nature when they die: a mountain peak, called an *apu,* a river, or an altar rock. The photo above, taken with a film camera, is of the opening to a sacred cave near Cusco, Peru. Our pilgrimage group had just finished doing a prayer ceremony around the huge altar rock carved inside the cave. For two years, I did not see the orbs of light in this photo. Then, when orbs of light started appearing on the photos from my new digital camera, I suddenly noticed that the cave was alive with dozens of orbs of light of varying sizes. Could these be the spirits of deceased Peruvian shamans?

One soul wanted to go on horseback, and Pegasus came! Another wanted to go with her grandmother in a stretch limo, with Archangel Michael as the driver. Two sisters, aged six and two, who died in Hurricane Katrina wanted to go by tricycle, so we ordered two tricycles and asked Archangel Michael to make a ramp to heaven. Then we noticed other souls watching who had also died in Katrina and wanted to go too. We needed to ask the angels for ninety-three tricycles!

- **Manner of Crossing Example**

While I do not normally go around doing random acts of soul rescue, when I walked past a stack of my partner's books, *Left for Dead: A Young Man's Search for Justice for the USS Indianapolis,* by Peter Nelson, caught my attention—as if my spirit guides were exclaiming, "Read this!"

In July 1945, after the battleship USS Indianapolis had sailed from San Francisco and delivered the atomic bomb to a U.S. base near Japan, an enemy torpedo sank the ship. Of 1,197 men on board, only 317 survived the sinking and the shark attacks during the five nights and four days they were adrift before being rescued. Captain Charles Butler McVay III was unjustly court-martialed and blamed for the deaths of 880 of his men. In 1968, he committed suicide.

An eleven-year-old named Hunter Scott chose the USS Indianapolis for his history fair project, brought national attention to the injustice, unearthed new evidence, and started a campaign that cleared Captain McVay's name.

On the hunch that Captain McVay might still be earthbound due to the turmoil preceding his suicide, I asked Spirit whether I had permission to investigate this matter. Permission was granted, so I did a Soul Detective session with Captain McVay. My muscle testing indicated that he was still earthbound and did not know his name had been cleared. After bringing him up to date and tapping to release the false guilt he had been carrying, he was ready to cross.

Can you guess how he wanted to go? He wanted his ship restored! So I asked the angels to put the USS Indianapolis back together and throw the nets over the side. Then Captain McVay climbed aboard and ordered the spirits of all of his men who were still earthbound (or waterbound) and floundering around in the ocean—more than eight hundred souls—to climb aboard as well. They all followed their captain's orders without any further energy psychology treatment, and they sailed off to heaven. Whether this work was real or a figment of my imagination, it brought pure joy to my heart.

If an earthbound spirit has no religious belief system, I use the following elevator analogy. "When you were in your body, you were on the first floor of the elevator. The other side is the second floor of the elevator. At the moment, your elevator is stuck between these two floors. We're going to ask the angels to get your elevator up to the second floor, where your loved ones are waiting." Then we watch the elevator door open and the person step through it into the next world.

Once the person is ready and can visualize a manner of crossing, we call the crossing guides and angels or Archangel Michael to take the person to the other side. We also call the loved ones from the other side to reach a hand through the veil or come to the portal between the worlds with open arms. Then we ask the angels to take them to the other world, back home to their Creator, to the Heart of God.

The Numinous Moment of Crossing

Such joy is present at the moment a person crosses! My soul is so moved, I almost always cry. Think of how it would feel to be lost and alone, trapped between worlds, in a place with no human contact, unable to communicate with anyone and not knowing what is wrong. In the magical moment of crossing, these individuals feel the angels and see the Light and the crowd of kindred spirits waiting to greet them and welcome them back home. The unconditional love that flows from the heart of the Creator begins to seep into the very essence of their soul once more. What a delight to be able to facilitate this transformation!

I am often left speechless by the numinosity of this sacred work. When we can talk again, I ask my client whether they feel the person has crossed. Often my client has a visual image of the crossing.

Verifying and Celebrating

After the spirit has crossed, I muscle test the statements: "This earthbound spirit is still attached to my client," versus "This earthbound spirit is on his/her way to the Light."

When we get confirmation that the spirit has crossed, we shout a verbal affirmation to anchor the transformation, like "Hallelujah!" This technique from Seemorg Matrix Work (see appendix F) is like putting the exclamation point on the end of a sentence.

Multiplying the Benefits

Gary Craig, the developer of Emotional Freedom Techniques (EFT), noticed that people watching someone else getting an EFT treatment were able to "borrow the benefits" and reduce their own emotional disturbance just by witnessing the process. Likewise, when a Soul Detective session sets up a pyramid of light and addresses a specific issue, other earthbound spirits resonating to this topic may be drawn to the Light.

I found out about this phenomenon the hard way. After doing a Soul Detective session, sometimes a light switch around my office would turn on or off of its own accord. Twice I found the hot water faucet running in my bathroom when I had not turned it on and nobody else was around (at least, nobody with a body!). At first, these paranormal experiences scared me and I had to do a tapping sequence on myself to desensitize my own fear. But then I realized that someone was trying to tell me by turning on my hot water faucet that he was in hot water, and other earthbound spirits were letting me know by flipping my light switch that they wanted to get to the Light.

For my own protection, I started inviting any other earthbound spirits who had similar issues to borrow the benefits of our session and use this opportunity to move into the Light as well. One can invite any ancestors or other family members of the one who just crossed to join the big family reunion on the other side! If appropriate to the situation, I also extend the pyramid of Light to encompass the whole planet Earth and send out a cosmic invitation for any other earthbound spirits who have been chained by fetters similar to the ones we just broke to take this chance to cross to the Light.

This step is optional. If a client has any objection to shifting the focus off them and onto humanitarian work to lighten the disturbance level of the whole planet, then skip this step. If a client agrees to the process, then let the healing of the earthbound spirit who just crossed resonate out and gather in any other earthbound spirits who are ready to cross with no further energy work. Clients accrue positive karma for this soul rescue! Then ask how many "extras" the client felt crossed, and muscle test the number just for fun. After a moment or two, bring the focus right back to the client.

Sealing the Energy Field

How was the former attachment able to invade the host? An earthbound spirit cannot attach to someone without the host having a break in the energy body. Use muscle testing to find and seal this portal. Usually it will be in a biofield, a chakra, or an organ. Sealing the energy field so no other earthbound spirits will attach can be as simple as asking the angels to correct the problem and waiting until the client muscle tests that the repair work is complete. Therapists with more differentiated skills in repairing damage to the human energy field can use their tools.

Giving Gratitude to the Angels

We always end with a prayer of deep gratitude to the angelic realm for their help, giving credit where credit is due and releasing the pyramids of Light.

Spirit Attachment Checklist

1. Getting centered
2. Getting permission
3. Asking for spiritual help
4. Gathering identifying information
   a. Gender
   b. Age at death
   c. Cause of death

   Illness

   Accident

   Act of war

   Murder

   Execution/martyred

   Suicide

   Natural disaster (tsunami, earthquake)

   Starvation

   Abortion, miscarriage, or stillbirth

   Sacrificed in a ritual

   Other
   d. Known or unknown? If known, then family or non-family?
   e. Length of time attached
5. Finding a name
6. Explaining the situation
7. Desensitizing the trauma
8. Preparing to cross
9. Getting helpers
10. Manner of crossing
11. The numinous moment of crossing
12. Verifying and celebrating
13. Multiplying the benefits
14. Sealing the energy field
15. Giving gratitude to the angels

2

Curses and Hexes

Thoughts are things. They have energy, and they can affect others at the subconscious level. Curses and hexes bind energy in a person or a place, but finding and erasing the energetic imprint can undo this binding.

Sometimes a person curses out of anger and frustration. An example is that a man once owned a resort area that did very well in the days before the automobile was invented. The area was near a train stop, and people from a nearby city frequently came to vacation. After the car came into popular use, people could drive anywhere and seldom came to this resort. Since the man could no longer make his payments, the bank foreclosed the property. He was so angry about losing his resort that he put a curse on the land that all who died there would not be able to cross over into the next world—their souls would stay earthbound forever.

Years later, a religious order bought the land and built a convent and retirement center on the property. Many Catholic sisters spent their last years there and then could not cross through the veil. Energy workers became aware of this situation and called in a Native American healer to break this curse. One witness reported King Neptune himself rose out of the lake on this property to break the chain of this curse. Hundreds of souls made the crossing, which produced a tremendous clearing of the energetic space at the convent and retirement center.

The following protocol for clearing a curse or a hex draws elements from Focusing, Guided Self Healing, Psychoenergetic Healing, and the Tao of Presence protocol developed by Mayer Kirkpatrick, LAc. Once we access the energy pattern, we can interact with this embodied knowledge for healing.

Protocol for Clearing a Curse or a Hex

1. Ask spiritual permission.

    a. If you get permission, call in spiritual help and proceed.

    b. If permission is not granted, then this problem is beyond the scope of what you are equipped to handle. Refer the client to someone else, perhaps a priest, a rabbi, or a minister.

2. Muscle test where the curse is connected to the energy field. I find that a curse or hex will usually attach to several chakras, so test this possibility first.

    a. One or more chakras

    b. An organ

    c. A body part

    d. A meridian

    e. A biofield

3. If more than one chakra or other site is involved, muscle test which of these to clear first and start there. Later, keep finding out which one needs to be treated next until all links to the energy field are severed.

4. Ask the client to visualize or sense her/his perception of the energy of the curse with visual or kinesthetic language, for example, a black cloud around the forehead or a metal band around the heart. If the client has difficulty formulating a perception, then ask for additional information, such as a color, a temperature, a density, or a texture to describe the negative pattern. This sustained focus on the energy helps the client

distinguish the negative pattern from self and shifts its energy. Focusing on body sensations is an entry point for access to embodied knowledge. I first learned this technique from the work of Mayer Kirkpatrick, LAc, in his protocol Tao of Presence. Psychoenergetic Healing and many other energy psychology methods also use focusing techniques. Visualization involves the frontal right quadrant of the cerebral cortex in finding a solution. Having an image of the problem tells us what needs to change for healing.

5. Optional: Have the client inquire of his/her Higher Self why the client has been carrying this energy, when it was received, and what lessons or understanding are needed to relinquish this dark energy.

6. Call in spiritual help to release each aspect of the negativity. If the client is attuned to a religious figure such as Divine Mother or Great Spirit, ask that figure to clear the negative energy and watch what happens. If a client needs more help to change the energetic configuration, then ask the person's guardian angels to eliminate the problem using whatever terms have defined it. For example, if the curse energy is a black cloud in the forehead, ask the guardian angels to remove the black cloud and bring sunshine into that area. If the curse was a metal band around the heart, then ask the angels to break off the band and set the heart free.

7. Repeat for the next chakra, organ, or biofield until all aspects of the curse energy have been eliminated.

8. Give thanks for the clearing and thank all of the spiritual helpers!

Case Example of a Hex

An elderly woman named Naomi was having an allergic reaction to her steroid eye drops. Her friend Jennie confided to her that Randy, a roommate who had died a year earlier from severe asthma, was haunting the house in which they had both lived. Because Naomi's energy was down from the allergic reaction, Randy's spirit attached to Naomi just from hearing Jennie's story. Naomi began to have labored breathing and shortness of breath, Randy's symptoms right before he died.

Randy was attached to Naomi, and he was carrying a hex. So Naomi had two intuitive level issues: an earthbound spirit attachment and a hex. We did a treatment for Randy, using Naomi as a surrogate to clear the hex energy and to free him to cross into the Light. He was attached to Naomi at four chakras, which needed to be treated in the following order:

1. **Solar plexus.** Naomi sensed the presence of a substance that felt like regurgitated vomit in her belly. Archangel Michael swept out the mess with a broom, clearing it from left to right.

2. **Throat chakra.** Something felt like it was trying to be ejected from the throat, like an engine sputtering. We asked the angels to clear this pattern, and the engine took off.

3. **Sacral chakra.** The hex was also connected to the anus and urethra, giving a lack of control of bowel and urinary function. While Randy was still living, he could not hold an erection nor hold sexual feelings. As we worked, Randy felt so very sorry for what he had done in a past life. He had been a man and had left the woman he was with. In anger, this rejected woman put a hex on him so that he could not function sexually with any other woman. Her revenge found its mark, because that curse extended into his next lifetime! Through feeling true remorse for what he had done, Randy was able to clear the hex energy from his sacral chakra.

4. **Crown chakra.** The last place where Randy had been blocked was the crown chakra, one's access to the Divine. Once the other chakras were cleared, Naomi sensed that the crown chakra was like a teakettle with a lid that was on too tight. We asked Archangel Michael to take off the lid and whoosh! Randy's soul went to the Light with no further instructions necessary.

We gave thanks for this healing, with gratitude that we could help Randy. We also prayed for forgiveness and healing for the woman who had hexed him. Immediately after this work, Naomi was able to breathe better. She still had other health issues of her own, but she did not feel the drain of life energy she had experienced while Randy's spirit was attached.

Threefold Return

If a curse or hex is consciously sent out to someone and the intended target does not receive the curse, the negative energy will bounce back to the sender, triple in strength—a law of energy dynamics. When clearing curse or hex energy, let the client know that unless otherwise directed, the negative energy released will return to the sender. For this reason, we prayed for forgiveness for the woman who had hexed Randy so that she would not be further harmed by what she had done. The client can request an angel of protection to bind the energy, wrap it in a ball of light, and take it straight to heaven to be reprocessed and recycled into Light.

Case Example of a Curse

Another woman I worked with, named Julia, suffered a setback in health just as she was about to step into a leadership role in her profession. The invisible roots of this physical disorder stemmed from a past life in which she died from a curse. Named Gloria in that lifetime, she had been betrothed to a man named Pablo.

As their engagement progressed, Gloria realized that Pablo was attracted to her because of her power, not because he loved her. Gloria broke off the engagement and instead married a man who loved her deeply. The men in the village frequently went off to sea for long periods of time, and the women turned to Gloria for emotional and spiritual guidance. Even after their husbands returned, the women came to Gloria for guidance. She was running the whole town!

Pablo became enraged with her power in the community and threw a curse on her. When this dark energy came her way, Gloria lost her stamina. She had no strength and shriveled up and died. We did energy tapping to release the rage behind this traumatic death.

Julia felt that the lesson for her soul in that lifetime was about freedom, independence, and love. She could follow her heart and make strong decisions. Her only mistake was not resisting the curse. She came into that life with the ability to change the outcome, but she did not believe in her own power. She could have resisted the curse. She just forgot how.

In this life, Julia was on a similar path of leadership and found herself embroiled in a huge power struggle. Multiple health problems could have taken her down, but this time, she reversed the process. Now she has no need to fear dark energies. Gloria doubted herself and succumbed to the curse. But in this life, the soul made the choice to believe in her power and strength. This time she took the right turn at every decision point. Julia regained her health and is functioning highly in her occupation.

3

Ancestral Wounds

Sometimes the root cause of a problem traces to an unresolved trauma that happened to an ancestor. This energetic disturbance gets passed down through the DNA imprint for emotional functioning and needs attention.

Find out which ancestor is carrying the disturbance with the following protocol:

1. Muscle test how many generations back.

2. Find out whether the ancestor is male or female.

3. Find out the relationship. Usually it will be a parent, grandparent, great-grandparent, etc., but it could be the sibling of an ancestor.

4. Starting with the client, trace back each generation to find whether it came through the paternal or maternal line until finding the wound.

5. Do surrogate work for this ancestor to clear the trauma.

For example, suppose an Irish client comes to therapy with the goal of losing weight and tests that the root cause of being overweight is an ancestral wound. Perhaps her ancestors were involved in the Great Irish Famine in which a million people, 12 percent of the population, died between the years of 1846 and 1849 due to failure of the potato crop. A million more people fled from Ireland to other countries because of the famine. Having this memory of watching people starve to death imprinted in the client's DNA could make weight loss very frightening. The client could be carrying extra weight as protection against food shortages. Identify which ancestors carried this wound and then do a surrogate treatment for them to release the fear of starvation. Then the client would be free to pursue her goal, perhaps redefined as "gaining her optimal weight."

Ann Nunley, MFA, PhD, developed a subtle energy generational healing process that is part of the Inner Counselor generational process taught at Holos University in Fair Grove, Missouri. Dr. Nunley and Bob Matusiak, PhD, presented this very moving intergenerational healing process in a breakout session titled "Clearing Generational Trauma: A Transformational Process Based on Five Levels of Consciousness" at the November 2004 Energy Psychology Conference in Toronto (CD available online through www.softconference.com/041111).

Ancestral Wound Case Example

Adrienne came into therapy feeling unloved and uncared for, despite much evidence to the contrary in her life. Her ancestral wound traced back four generations to her great-great-grandmother Ruth, who had lost a two-year-old child while she was pregnant with another. Devastated by this loss, Ruth was unable to eat properly during the rest of her pregnancy, so her fetus did not receive adequate nutrition in the womb. Once the new baby was born, Ruth's postpartum depression was exacerbated by the grief of her other child's death. Ruth fell into a severe depression, and she was unable to give her new baby girl the love and care the child needed. The older siblings helped, so the child survived. Ruth's daughter carried the emotional scar of feeling unloved and uncared for her whole life, and that feeling had passed down the generations to Adrienne through the DNA governing emotional makeup. Through surrogate energy healing work with her ancestors, Adrienne was able to peel off these emotional scars and open her own heart to give and receive love.

4

Family Constellation Issues

An ancestral wound can affect other family members not only through imprinting into the DNA of everyone down the line, but also through wounding the family soul. Just as each person has a soul, each family also has a soul. Bert Hellinger is a radical psychotherapist who developed his own theories of how family dynamics work from astute observation of how things are. In his book *Love's Own Truths: Bonding and Balancing in Close Relationships,* he writes of the natural laws governing love and the intricacies of relationship and resolution. He developed a system of principles required for healthy relationships to flourish, which he calls "the orders of love."

For example, when any member of a family gets left out and then is lost to the family system, the soul of the family suffers. Some examples of ways people get excluded from the family are miscarriage, abortion, adoption, early death, or being cut off from the family because of religious differences or sexual preference. In future generations, an innocent family member will then get entangled subconsciously in the feelings of the one who has been excluded and try to put things back into balance. For example, a family member entangled with the feelings of a child who has been aborted may try to atone for this death by committing suicide.

Hellinger works by having a client place representatives for significant family members into a "constellation" in the center of the room in the positions and relationships to each other in physical space that reflect the positions and relationships of the actual members. For example, a mother and child who were very close might be placed side by side. Someone excluded from the family could be placed outside the circle. Being in the position of a family member enables the surrogate to enter the family field of information, connect with the feelings of the person represented, and speak for that person. Hellinger feels that whether or not the words spoken have historical truth, they will point the way toward resolution for the client. In this novel method I like to call "feng shui for the family soul," Hellinger then moves people into different positions in the constellation to put them into harmony with the natural orders of love. For example, the harmonious order for the family is placing the mother on the left side of the father, followed by the oldest child on her left, down to the youngest in birth order.

If a client muscle tests that the root cause of an emotional disturbance is a Family Constellation issue, then test whether the issue is within the scope of your practice to treat. If it is, do a careful interview to find out who has been left out of the family and work to have that person honored and respected. If the issue is not within the scope of your practice and your treatment skills, then refer your client to someone who does Family Constellation work.

Family Constellation Case Example

Liz was a counselor who carried a pristine beauty and sense of self-worth that did not match the long-standing case of psoriasis that had plagued her life. Several years earlier, she had asked in meditation to see the root cause of her skin problem. To her shock and surprise, she saw a vision of her paternal grandfather, Vito, committing a murder on a train outside a small town.

Shaken by the image and curious, she queried her father for more information. Her father revealed that Vito was not a very nice person, although he was a brilliant inventor and mechanic. No one ever wanted to give him a job because he was so difficult. Upon further questioning, he disclosed that

Vito was involved in bootlegging and had once been accused of murder. He remembered eavesdropping on people talking about the death. The charges were eventually dropped, and the murder was considered an accidental death. Both Vito and his father were in the Mafia.

Shortly after Liz shared this story with her sister, the two women went to a psychic. When Liz searched for the photo of Vito the psychic requested, she could not find it anywhere. When she got home, she found it right where she had already looked several times. She was certain her grandfather had not wanted her to take it along!

The psychic confirmed that an angry Grandfather Vito was present and had been involved in the murder. The psychic warned Liz that Vito did not want her poking around in this business. Determined to find and heal whatever happened, Liz pursued the topic. The psychic told her of a newspaper article about the murder concealed behind a photo in an old, large, leatherbound family album. Liz found this album at her aunt's house, but the article had been removed. Several years later, the article appeared in a collection of her grandfather's papers.

Grandfather Vito had been left out of his parents' will because he married outside their religious faith. When his parents died, a distant relative we will call Mario inherited $11 million, a great deal of money in those times. Shortly after receiving this inheritance, Mario died in a motel fire.

After getting spiritual permission to investigate, we muscle tested that Grandfather was still earthbound; however, he was stubbornly unwilling to communicate with us.

When someone takes another person's life, that murder puts the soul of the whole family into the debt of the one killed. The effects of this family constellation issue showed in problems throughout Vito's descendants: Liz's father had recently gone into hospice for kidney problems; Liz had psoriasis, controlled with medication; her cousin Vito, who carried the same complete name as their grandfather, had gotten deeply involved in drug addiction and was in psychiatric hospitalization.

Since Grandfather refused to work with us, we focused on Mario, who was still earthbound, scared, and confused about what had happened in the fire in which he watched his body burning. He had not figured out that he was no longer in that body. Once we explained the situation, he was willing to let us help him.

Mario remembered getting the $11 million. He had really wanted to enjoy all this money but, instead, found himself anxious and fearful, always "watching his back." Mario admitted that he had broken the rules of the Brotherhood (the Mafia) and had cheated others out of money. He was very afraid of "the men in suits." He kept his money in a metal box he carried with him at all times, even sleeping with it. He deeply regretted his actions, which had led to his early death. He lamented that he had looked so handsome in his suit!

Vito and several other Mafia members wearing suits cornered him on the train and killed him with a blow to the head. They stole his metal box, then took his body to the motel room and set it on fire so the death would look like an accident.

We made a customized meridian treatment for Mario first to accept and admit his guilt and then to release it. Mario asked forgiveness of all the people he had wronged and forgave Vito for spearheading his murder. Mario wanted his father and his sister to be his greeting committee; however, we muscle tested that they were both still earthbound. So we called for Mario's father and sister, and they all crossed into the Light together—a joyful moment! If Mario had not become entangled with Liz's family, he would not likely have gotten into Soul Detective therapy to help his father, sister, and himself cross into the Light. Assisting Mario and his immediate relatives helped pay back the family debt incurred when Vito took Mario's life.

Grandfather Vito had been hiding the whole time we worked with Mario. We told him everything we learned and let him know that Mario asked his forgiveness for wronging him and had forgiven Vito for his murder. Then Vito was willing to do energy therapy to release his own rage and anger over what happened. Once he was ready to cross, we asked whether any other earthbound members of the Brotherhood and their families had been watching. To our amazement, we muscle tested that more than four hundred other earthbound souls were ready to go together to the Light. They decided to form a "Brotherhood of Light" on the other side to work for planetary healing. We also asked the angels to place a golden stairway of Light in Chicago for other earthbound souls to find its light and cross into the next world. Liz wanted to put it at the busy intersection of State and Randolph, so it would get lots of traffic!

Liz put the family history pieces together. The Mafia was a brotherhood formed for protection; fear was its basis. Fear is encoded on the kidney meridian, and her father had kidney disease. While in Liz the fear and anxiety were only "skin deep," these unresolved negative emotions had driven her cousin Vito to addiction and then to mental illness. Uncovering the family secret, helping the earthbound souls forgive and cross over, and righting the wrong by helping Mario healed this wound in the family soul.

5

Archetypes

Carl Jung developed the concept of archetypes—patterns in the collective unconscious that shape personality, behavior, and relationships. Jungian analyst Jean Shinoda Bolen introduced the gods and goddesses of the Greek pantheon as archetypal patterns in *Goddesses in Everywoman: Powerful Archetypes for Women* and *Gods in Everyman: Archetypes that Shape Men's Lives.*

In addition to deities from all religious traditions, some other archetypal patterns are:

Trickster

Magician

Wise Woman

Fool

Warrior

Judge

King

Queen

Devil

Savior

Archetype Case Example

Oppression hit Rose in multiple areas of her life, and despite doing battle on all fronts, she felt like she could not move forward in:

- **Work.** Unemployed, she felt resentful that she had to compete for jobs for which she was overqualified.

- **Parenting.** Her former husband was in bed with a bad back and unable to take their son, so Rose never got downtime to regenerate.

- **Social life.** Her listing on eHarmony brought her some pen pals, but no suitable partner.

The origin of this oppression muscle tested as the archetypal pattern of Athena, the Greek warrior goddess of wisdom. Athena's mother was not present at her birth, as Athena sprang from the forehead of her father, Zeus, fully grown and clad in battle armor. Rose lamented, "But I don't want to do battle with everything!"

We started treatment by setting sacred space with pyramids of light from Psychoenergetic Healing. To free her from the negative aspects of the Athena archetype and connect with Athena's positive aspects, we next used the Seemorg Matrix "Archetypal Presence Protocol," which sets up a dialogue between the archetype (unconscious material) and the conscious mind. The dialogue is based on Carl Jung's soul work technique called "active imagination," in which one attends to the stirrings from deep within to bring life into greater balance and harmony.

In dialogue with Athena, Rose was able to feel united with the positive qualities of Athena's strength and power. Rose realized that she had been carrying a wound in her solar plexus, the seat of her personal power, from grief over her mother's death from cancer when she was twelve. Even before she died, her mother's protracted illness had rendered her emotionally unavailable to Rose. Like Athena, Rose felt her mother's absence from her life.

Next we treated the traumatic pattern "I was filled with grief" with the Seemorg protocol of holding chakras, which entails one hand placed over the solar plexus while the other hand moves through the chakras, placed over each one in turn, moving from top to bottom, until the negativity clears from each energy center. Then we called for help from the spiritual presence of her mother, who is now a spirit guide for Rose. In meditation, Rose sensed the wise telepathic message from her mother, "Bring light into the grief." Together we formulated the affirmation, "I accept my sadness, and I choose to move forward in my life." Rose then installed this affirmation in each energy center and reinforced this new pattern for the next thirty days.

Within several months, Rose found a job and felt she was out of the battle zone.

The Wounded Healer: Chiron

An archetype that affects many healers is that of Chiron, a centaur who was accidentally pierced by a poisoned arrow. This wound would have been fatal, but because he was immortal, he could not die. Chiron's unrelenting, excruciating pain drove him to search for healing far and wide. In this process, he discovered medicine, which he taught to Asclepius, the Greek god of healing.

The Martyr

Another archetype that frequently appears in healers is the martyr. Throughout history, from the dawn of civilization through the crucifixion of Jesus to the Spanish Inquisition to the Salem witch trials, many healers have been persecuted and killed. Then, in this life, when they start practicing a powerful, cutting-edge therapy like energy psychology, they shut down because of the fear of being martyred again. Whether this phobia of stepping into their power as healers comes from a past life or from humanity's history of executing healers, the fear needs to be cleared to actualize healing skills in the present.

6

Dreams

ometimes dreams hold the key to understanding problems and their
solutions. If a client muscle tests that dreamwork is needed, ask what
has held a strong emotional charge in the dream world lately. An
example is a repeated dream of danger or the death of a close loved one.

Some resources for working with dreams, in addition to those cited in
the case that follows, are:

- The work of Swiss psychiatrist Carl Jung.

- The "Seemorg Dream Work" seminar from Seemorg Matrix Work.

- The process of Association for Comprehensive Energy Psychology
  (ACEP) members Robert and Lynne Hoss integrating dreamwork with
  energy psychology, presented at the May 2006 International Energy
  Psychology conference. A complete free download of this process is
  available through their website at www.dreamlanguage.org under the tab
  "Energy Psychology." The recording of their presentation, titled "Energy
  Psychology Meets the Dream World," is available through the ACEP
  website at www.energypsych.org.

Dream Case Example

Jo's primary care physician referred her to me, sensing something outside
the scope of her practice. Jo had a life-threatening autoimmune illness that

continuously relapsed after treatment. The exact nature of the malady was elusive. A primary complaint was feeling as though she had been poisoned. Compassionate and caring, her physician had asked to hear Jo's dreams, knowing the power of dreams to diagnose and heal material hidden beneath the conscious mind. Jo reported the following dream:

> I am with a baby and need to change the baby's diaper. I don't have one, so I leave the baby to go find one. (I don't know why I'd just *leave* a baby like that.) Then I couldn't get back into the bathroom [where the baby was]. My dreams are always a mess. But in the end, the baby was OK.

Her physician felt encouraged that the baby in the dream might symbolize the birth of some new potential in Jo.

Working on the dream led us to discover through muscle testing that Jo's relapse problem came from a spirit attachment, a thirteen-year-old female who had died from an illness and attached when Jo had had surgery twenty years earlier. Being under anesthesia leaves the psychic gate open, and earthbound spirits sometimes enter and attach. After Jo's operation, she had a serious mental breakdown and was in and out of mental institutions. The thirteen-year-old spirit had suffered from mental illness and also a serious autoimmune disease.

When I asked Jo what this girl wanted us to call her, Jo heard the names Ann, Pat, Irene, and Belinda. We then tested whether this spirit had multiple personalities, and she did! The four names were four parts of her, with Belinda the core personality.

Jo's presenting dream had indicated a baby needing diapering, but Jo did not have a diaper; she did not have the means to get this baby dry and clean. Perhaps parts of Belinda were infants, having dissociated due to early trauma. Usually, a person will not develop dissociative identity disorder, formerly called multiple personality disorder, unless experiencing severe trauma before the age of five. The dream picture of Jo not being able to get back into the bathroom after she went to get a diaper is an apt metaphor for not being able to reach a dissociated part of the personality, especially a dissociated part of a spirit attachment's personality. In the dream, Jo reflected, "I don't know why I'd just *leave* a baby like that." Yet, when feelings become overwhelming, the needy, traumatized part of a person does get left behind. The ending of the dream showed that the baby came out all right, however, so we hoped our unusual intervention might work.

Jo had not been able to clear her autoimmune disorder with multiple physical interventions, so she was willing to give Soul Detective therapy a try.

First, we did a NeuroModulation Technique protocol to integrate Belinda's four personality parts. Otherwise, we would have had to treat each part separately, and we did not have that much time in our therapy hour. Then we restored balance to Belinda's system using a customized meridian tapping sequence. The root of Belinda's disturbance was traumatic sexual abuse, with an overlay of anger and rage. On top of that rage was a "psychological reversal" pattern that closed the crown chakra, her access to the flow of Divine energy. After correcting all of these problems with Thought Field Therapy, Jo noticed a profoundly peaceful shift inside.

We explained to Belinda that she no longer had a physical body of her own, and her attachment to Jo's physical body was draining Jo's life energy. We let Belinda know that a brand new spiritual body was waiting for her on the other side, in heaven, and her guardian angel would take her there. We asked Archangel Michael to wrap his wings around Belinda to protect her on the journey.

Jo spoke lovingly to Belinda, assuring her, "Don't be afraid. It's OK to go. It will be all right."

But Belinda was afraid to go. Jo felt Belinda's arms and legs wrapped around her, clinging to her belly like a baby monkey. We both sent Belinda love and compassion and asked the angels to release her fear and help her transition. Then Jo's golden-colored sweatshirt started to glow, and she felt Belinda's presence lift.

After Belinda's release, Jo trembled and felt anxious and lonesome. She had not known about Belinda's presence until just this past hour, but her exit left Jo feeling alone and desolate. We did more customized meridian tapping for Jo to release this anxiety and to put her heart at rest.

Jo then inquired, "Can I send her love?"

We made a special loving place in Jo's heart for Belinda. I asked her to pray for Belinda over the next month, as Belinda was completing her transition. This assignment gave Jo a concrete action to fill the empty space left by her Ann-Pat-Irene-Belinda companion leaving.

Jo calmed down, then reported, "I know that when Belinda gets up to heaven and gets all settled in, she will be watching over me and taking care of me. We are tight. I helped her get to heaven, and she will help me. I know she will!"

7

Soul Loss

Our spiritual essence, the soul, can become fragmented by trauma of many kinds: loss of a love relationship, war, an accident, and physical or sexual abuse. Under these circumstances, some of a person's soul energy may flee the body, leaving the feeling that a part of oneself is missing. In *Soul Retrieval: Mending the Fragmented Self*, Sandra Ingerman writes about the pervasive sense of incompleteness and alienation in our culture: "For most, the sense of not being fully alive is a continual, low-grade pain often masked with drugs, entertainment, compulsive sex, and addictions of many other kinds."

Many cultures have traditional healers called shamans who journey to other worlds to bring back these soul pieces. Anthropologist Michael Harner, author of *The Way of the Shaman*, researched the storehouse of ancestral wisdom in shamanic traditions and brought the principles of shamanic healing into contemporary life through his Foundation for Shamanic Studies. Becoming a shaman requires a long, arduous training and work in the dualistic realm of good and evil.

When a partner breaks off a love relationship, the jilted person may be unable to release the connection and might cling to a soul fragment of the beloved, causing soul loss in the partner. Or a person may purposefully steal part of someone's soul energy to gain power over that person or to cause sickness, as in black magic and the case example that follows.

Several energy therapies have protocols to retrieve lost soul parts. If you do not have a method of soul retrieval with which you are comfortable, start by muscle testing how many soul fragments are missing from the present life and at what age they left. Then treat with energy therapy the trauma that caused each fragmentation.

Unresolved past life trauma is another form of soul loss. When the soul energy of a past incarnation remains earthbound, a person feels deep inside that something is missing. Clearing the past life trauma and helping that incarnation cross into the Light retrieves that soul fragment.

For an all-encompassing affirmation to reintegrate lost soul parts, shout the following (adapted from Vianna Stibal's *Theta Healing*, p. 176):

> "I call back to myself all parts of my soul that ever were. I ask Spirit to release them from their current locations, scrub them clean, and return them to me! And I release any soul fragments I might have that belong to others and ask Spirit to scrub them clean and return them to their rightful owners!"

Soul Loss Case Example

In her forties, Trish threw herself wholeheartedly into the new field of energy coaching. Immediately after making this commitment, she developed multiple severe physical problems. Soul Detective work located the invisible roots of this block in a former incarnation named Maura, born in 44 B.C. in Palestine.

Maura's happiest memory was having many children around her, though she had none of her own. A midwife with dark hair and dark skin, she was highly regarded and surrounded by friends. Her mother and grandmother had passed down their herbal healing knowledge to her.

In her early thirties, a highly contagious illness hit their village—something like diphtheria, which affects children more severely than adults. Many children got sick, and this bacterial upper respiratory disease was more than Maura's herbs could treat. Lots of children died, and the village lost faith in her ability to work healing miracles. Maura suffered temporary soul loss from feeling so helpless to cure these children she loved. She began to doubt herself and turn away people who asked for help.

After the epidemic passed, she recovered emotionally and picked up her work again. When she was around the age thirty-nine, government soldiers harassed her, demanding a report of all the babies she delivered. She did not want to be involved and reported only if the families wanted the births recorded. Most did not, so she withheld the information.

In her forties, Maura was midwife at a very difficult birth for a young mother bearing twins. The woman was very small and not very strong, so the birth was complicated by a number of factors. Unknown to Maura, the father of the babies had abused the pregnant mother and she did not want to live. She had soul loss too. The twins got stuck, and the woman bled to death. All three of them died. Maura wept profusely. This young woman was very special, as Maura had delivered her into this world.

The father of the babies blamed Maura for the deaths. He vowed to "take her down" and attacked her with the fury of his wrath. He set the intention to steal her soul energy. He was bearing extra guilt because he had conceived these children out of wedlock and was married to someone else. Even though Maura had delivered twins before and had done nothing wrong in the situation, she shut down under this attack. She stopped doing her work and fell into a depression at age forty-four.

Alone, bitter, and sad, she discontinued everything. She shut out the people around her, even though they really loved her and brought her food and cared for her. She never showed her appreciation for them, but after her death, they buried her and remembered her kindly. The cause of her death at age fifty-two was soul loss—giving up and feeling broken.

Trish reflected on the soul lesson in her lifetime as Maura, "The attack and my depression closed my opening to God, which is the power. It's always there. When I left my physical form, my soul went straight up, and I got back my full connection to the Divine. I need to honor that this Divine connection is present for me all the time and to let it flow even more. Self-doubt just shuts it down."

As Trish cleared all of her past life issues related to being a healer, her physical body healed simultaneously, and she then launched her new energy coaching career with great success.

8

Energetic Cords

Some energetic cords are beneficial. When we pray for help, an angelic cord is created from the heart of God to our heart to guide our way. A mother frequently has an energetic cord from her heart to the hearts of her children so that she knows instantly when danger is near or when the children need her assistance. None of these energetic cords are problems. If muscle testing shows that an energetic cord is the root of the problem, then it will be a detrimental cord.

Sometimes a person deliberately creates a harmful energetic cord, as in a curse or a hex consciously creating a cord that binds the flow of life energy. An energetic cord can also happen unconsciously. For example, a mother whose life is devoid of meaning outside her role as a parent might become overcontrolling of her children and not "cut the apron strings" for them to grow into independent people. While children need the energetic connection to the parent for nurture and support, a baby bird eventually needs to leave the nest to learn to fly. If the parent binds the child to the nest with guilt and manipulation, how can the child get the flight lessons needed to learn to soar?

Another example of an unconscious energetic cord is the soul loss that happens when someone ends a love relationship and the partner is unable to release the cords connecting them. Sexual partners share soul essence at the moment of orgasm, the inner meaning of the biblical description "And the two shall become one." They entrust their souls to each other. To break up, they each need to give back the other's soul space they have shared. If either partner cannot let go and instead hangs on to the hope of getting back together, that person binds his/her own heart from being able to move on and love again. This energetic cord also has a negative impact on the heart of the other partner.

Powerful negative emotions like rage, revenge, and hate diminish heart energy and create internal cords that bind a spirit to Earth.

The protocol for clearing a curse or a hex can also be used for clearing an energetic cord:

1. Find out whether the cord is from another person or is generated internally.
2. Find where the cord attaches to the client's energy field (a body part, an organ, a chakra, or biofield). Note the cord may attach at more than one place. With multiple connections, muscle test for the treatment order.
3. Have the client visualize the nature of the cord.
4. Release the attachment.

You can also call in an angel of protection to cut a cord placed in the energy field by someone else. One Soul Detective student shared the following:

> "I had an experience with an earthbound spirit who had a cord/ attachment binding him to Earth as the result of a curse. I just had the sense that there was a connection to the ground that shouldn't be there. The angels were there, the Light was there, his loved one was there, and he just couldn't cross. So I asked Archangel Michael to cut the cord—and zoom, he was over."

Drawing on the Earth Release work of Diana Burney, this student asks the following of the angels, visualizing each step along the way:

1. Cut any cords not for the highest and best good and remove their source, circuitry, and receptor sites.

2. Seal the ends of the cords for all time and return the energy to where it belongs.

3. Heal any damage to any of the bodies.

A self-generated negative cord, however, can only be cut by the person who put it there. Since we all have free will, no other person or angelic being can make the choice to release the negative cords we have put around our own hearts.

Energetic Cord Case Example

Rose called reporting a high state of anxiety. This feeling was different from the depression she had felt in the past. The invisible root of her anxiety muscle tested as an energetic cord from her sixteen-year-old son, who had a learning disorder.

A female healer Rose had worked with felt the umbilical cord between Rose and her son needed to be severed—by a man. Rose planned a week at a camp with a male healer to perform this "spiritual surgery." But as the date approached, anxiety welled up within Rose. With his neurological disorder, how could her son ever survive in the world without her assistance?

After praying for help from the angels and asking for the highest good of everyone involved, we found energetic cords to her son in three chakras:

Root chakra. Rose feared that her son would not be able to survive or even breathe without her. Knowing that the Law of Attraction draws to us whatever we are thinking about, we desensitized this fear with Thought Field Therapy, adding the affirmations, "I release this fear. Fear doesn't help!" Rose felt calmer after this intervention. We noted that Rose still had the job of cooking for her son and continuing to provide emotional and mental nourishment by getting him an educational plan suited to his special needs and planning activities to develop his social skills. Rose sensed that she was to continue in the role of guidance to connect her precious child with resources for sustenance his whole life, whenever he asked her for help. This cord of nourishing and helping to keep him rooted in the world did not need to be severed.

Heart chakra. From her heart to his was a beautiful, golden braided cord that radiated love. This cord also did not need to be severed, as mothers have the right to love their children forever.

Solar plexus. But in the solar plexus was a dark, small skinny cord from her belly to his. The solar plexus can be compared to a solar panel that converts energy from the sun into life energy to run our bodies. Her son was attached to her solar panel. When he was in the uterus, he grew from her energy through the umbilical cord, and as a breast-fed baby, he was directly nourished by her life energy. But the time had come to let go of this energetic cord. This connection was depleting Rose's life energy. Without severing that cord, her son would be like a bird with a broken wing, unable to fly, forever staying in the nest. He needed to find his own power and strength as a young man. Knowing that she could keep the heart connection to her son forever, Rose was willing to let go of the dark energetic cord from her solar plexus. She called in the angels. Standing between them, the angels broke the cord in the middle. They brought one end of the cord back into her belly, relocated it, and placed a beautiful shield of golden energy over her solar plexus. Her son had an archangel who took the other end of the cord and did the same for him. Rose felt such a big shift of energy with this process that she sensed the bed she was lying on moved to the side and then back again. To her surprise, she felt joyful security both for herself and for her son.

9

Vows

A vow is a specialized kind of energetic cord that binds the heart. Vows are always made consciously. The vow can be to God, as in religious orders; to another person, as in marriage; or to a group, as in secret societies. The vow can come in a negative form, like the man who vowed to "take out" Trish in the earlier example in the section on Soul Loss. One can also make a vow to oneself, as in vowing to stop abusing a harmful substance. In this case, the part of the person that wants to be healthy vows to stop the part of the person that is self-destructive.

Past Life Vows

Many clients focused on spirituality have been in a religious order in a past life. The vows of poverty, chastity, and obedience taken by Catholic priests and nuns are written on the soul, so they perpetuate into future incarnations.

If the root cause of an issue muscle tests as a vow, then muscle test to see which vow is causing the problem and whether the vow is from this life or a past life. Treat whatever emotional disturbance comes up around the issue. Then, to release the vow, have the client place the right hand over the heart and rescind the vow. Make the wording appropriate to the situation, and energize the statement with strong feeling. An example is to exclaim: "I, _____

[name], of my own free will do hereby rescind from my soul all vows of poverty [chastity, obedience] that I have taken in any and all past lives." Adding an affirmation that reflects the complementary value empowers the release, for example: "And I claim the abundance of the universe as a path to God!"

Marriage Vows

The vow of marriage is made "till death do us part." Sometimes, deceased partners are unaware of their death and cause trouble in future relationships. Divorce is a legal rescinding of marriage vows, but this legal action does not always release the heart from the vows. Making emotional peace with the ex-partner helps release a person from the emotional aspect of the vow, which was made in the heart, as the following case demonstrates.

Vow Case Example

Ellen wanted to change her pattern of reacting to men by getting confused, afraid, and feeling as if she were five years old. We traced the root cause of this reaction to a vow from this life—her marriage vow. Although she had been divorced for many years, she had two inner children, eight years old and five years old, who felt as if they were still bound by the marriage vow. We interviewed these parts.

Ellen was adopted, and her five-year-old part, Ellie, wanted her adoptive father to love her the way she had loved him—with total devotion and adoration. Under the circumstances, he could not do that. After her father's death, Ellen discovered a well-kept family secret: Her adoptive father was also her biological father! Her adoptive mother could not have children, and Ellen had been conceived from her father's affair with a distant cousin. Her adoptive mother forgave her father for breaking his marriage vows. She chose to love and adopt Ellen, knowing what a great gift she was giving the man she loved for him to be able to raise his biological child. Her father could not show how much he adored Ellie because he had vowed to keep silent about the family scandal.

In her marriage, Ellie had wanted her husband to really love her; however, he did not come forth with the love he had vowed to give her when they got married. Ellie did not want to get hurt again, so she froze up and got confused whenever she met a man who had sexual interest in her. We tapped with Ellie to release her sadness about not being loved and to help her realize that even though her husband had vowed to love her, he did not have the emotional capacity to give her the depth of love she needed. The situation was like trying to shake hands with someone who does not have an arm. Ellie was then able to release her husband from this marriage vow.

The eight-year-old part, Ellen Rae, suffered sexual abuse from her older brother, also adopted. She felt like she let him do what he wanted with her, and then he still did not love her. In her marriage, her husband was not emotionally available to her, and the sexual relationship was poor. Like the connection to her brother, the relationship had no foundation in real love. Ellen Rae had given up all hope and trust in men. Now, when an interested male came along, Ellen Rae brought up a hard edge and gave him the cold shoulder.

We made a customized meridian tapping sequence for Ellen Rae to release the embarrassment, shame, rage, and trauma of the sexual abuse. While tapping on the outer eyes, the rage release point, Ellen Rae added, "I forgive myself for being so desperate for love."

Once we had cleared this emotional disturbance, we called in her father's spiritual presence. Ellen reported, "He is very proud of all three of us (Ellen, Ellie, and Ellen Rae). We've been strong. He loves all of us, and has always loved all of us, and his love is gigantic!"

I asked her father to instruct Ellen how to determine whether or not a man is trustworthy. Her father gave her an image of two men and the following criteria:

If the man would be emotionally dangerous to her, she would feel muscles tightening at the back of her neck and her shoulders.

If a man held the possibility of real friendship, her whole body would feel relaxed.

The connection of her inner child parts Ellie and Ellen Rae with their father's love was deeply healing and fulfilling, and Ellen was able to release her ex-husband from his vows to her. Ellen felt the soul lesson behind the multiple ways she had been wounded was developing understanding, love, and compassion.

10

Evil Spirits & Entities

In biblical times, people conceptualized mental illness as possession by evil spirits or demons. Jesus cured mental illness by casting out demons. Many people in the world today still refer to mental illness in these terms. My Hispanic clients often attribute bad behavior by a family member to being possessed by an evil spirit.

Treatment interventions will be more effective if they are framed in the language the client uses for the problem, whether you believe in the concept presented or not.

When testing for the root cause on the intuitive level submenu, check all the other possibilities on the list first. Do this test last, only if none of the other categories hold the key to healing.

If you muscle test that the root cause of an emotional disorder is an evil spirit or entity and you do not feel comfortable dealing with this terminology, then refer the client to another helping professional such as a minister, priest, or rabbi. If you feel confident to address this description of the problem, if you are comfortable working with the extreme end of the scale of mental disturbance, and if you muscle test that you have spiritual permission to address the issue, then use the language of the client to invoke whatever higher power the client believes will release the problem. Then repair the damage to the client's energy field, as we did in the following case.

Demonic Spirit Case Example

Morgan, a competent and empathic psychologist, hired me for energy psychology consultation. As all other family members had crossed over, she was legal guardian for her older brother Edward, diagnosed with mental retardation. Morgan was emphatic that Edward was misdiagnosed, as he had been a precociously bright child until he began having seizures around age two.

Edward became aggressive and hurtful in his teenage years, so the family was forced to place him in the state hospital. Edward was physically abused and raped before his parents could secure a better institutional setting for him. Currently in his fifties, Edward functioned at a two-year-old level.

A hospital worker used a laborious process called "facilitated communication" to enable Edward, who was mute, to communicate with the family members who were still living at that time. He told them, "I try to talk, but I can't because my tongue is too thick. I feel like demons have me."

After a time, Edward refused to continue with the clumsiness of the facilitated communication. Following recent surgery for his bowels being twisted in a knot, Morgan felt he was beginning to check out of this incarnation. Contributing to his health problem was pica, a condition in which a person eats indigestible objects. Edward had a passion for eating cigarette butts and was addicted to nicotine even though he did not smoke.

The priority goal of our telephone session was healing the root cause of Edward's seizure disorder. Morgan's intuition was highly developed and she had a strong telepathic connection with Edward. We began by calling in spiritual help, asking for the highest good of everyone involved.

As Morgan was adept at surrogate testing, I asked her to muscle test along with me. We both tested that the root cause was a spirit attachment, but a spirit that had never been in a human body. Since Edward had claimed he was filled with demons, we next tested the statement, "This spirit is demonic." Morgan got a strong yes on that test, and I got a no. Since our answers were opposite, one of us had to be reversed—and sure enough, I was. This session was my first encounter with a "demonic" force, and my initial fear reversed my polarity so that my testing results yielded the opposite of the truth.

After correcting my reversal with a heart massage, adding an affirmation of deeply and completely accepting all my feelings about this issue, we both tested that the invisible root of Edward's problem was one demonic force. Since we muscle tested that we did not have spiritual permission to address this demonic force ourselves, we called in Archangel Michael to remove this energy from Edward's system, to contain it, and to send its energy for recycling.

As Edward was mute, Morgan's telepathic connection with him was our only way to communicate. She focused on listening to Edward and being his voice during our work. Edward consented to our goal of clearing as many of his difficulties as possible before his time came to cross. When we told him we would be tapping on some energy points on the body, Edward was worried that his hands shook too much to tap. He was relieved to learn that he could use the "Touch and Breathe" method, invented by Dr. John Diepold Jr., instead of tapping.

We got Edward centered by asking his guardian angels to set proper polarity on all vectors of his energy field. He was amazed how good being in his center felt, so we taught him an anchor technique to get centered again any time he wanted to. All he had to do was ask his angels to center him, take a deep breath, and think the word "Center!"

Next, Edward told us that getting better was not possible. We identified this limiting belief in energy psychology terms as a psychoenergetic reversal regarding possibility. To clear this barrier to success, we asked Edward to massage his heart clockwise while saying, "Even though I don't think getting better is possible, I deeply and completely love and accept myself. I accept all of my feelings about everything that has happened in my life. Even though I was abused, I love and accept myself."

Shortly after he started the heart massage, Morgan heard Edward screaming. He had a lot to scream about, so Morgan and I encouraged him to express his feelings and joined him in scream therapy for awhile. When he got to his deep sadness, we wept with him. Then Edward shouted, "I live! I live! I live!" We asked him to thump over his chest like Tarzan, and we shouted with him, "I live!"

When we asked Edward to check with the angels whether he was ready to proceed, Edward wanted to know if the angels were the Beings of Light that he often saw around him. He did not realize that not everyone saw them and had an "aha!" moment as he identified them as angels.

We next used the Soul Detective protocol for clearing energetic cords, curses, and hexes to heal the energetic damage the "evil spirit" had done to Edward's chakra system.

Root chakra. The root chakra healed by calling Edward's mother in spirit form to join the Beings of Light surrounding him. Morgan wept as she felt the presence of their mother filling Edward's root chakra with energy. Edward had been closer to their mother than anyone else and was named after her younger brother killed in World War II several years before Edward's birth. Their mother's presence also evoked deep emotion for Edward and was a turning point in this process. Their mother had a strong Christian faith, and this faith helped Edward put everything together in a context of great meaning for him.

Heart chakra. Edward was afraid to open his heart chakra. He communicated, "In this environment, having my heart open would be very difficult. People don't exchange much heart energy here, and I would not survive."

As the angels channeled red and purple energy into his heart, Edward declared, "Love to me is a larger phenomenon than we as humans can understand. We can approach it at seven different levels. Now you are hearing my voice as stronger, bolder, and more connected. I am speaking from a higher level. I can accept love on the mental level, the only level I am comfortable with and the easiest for my chosen life circumstances. I am not ready to accept love on the emotional level. It just doesn't feel safe. I see the pearls around you."

My mentor, Gloria Karpinski,* had talked about my past lives being like pearls on a string, each one contributing to the growth of my soul. My heart was so moved by Edward's seeing this image that I wept. I thanked him for noticing my past life pearls, and he was very pleased. This image was also

---

*Gloria is a holistic counselor, spiritual director, teacher, and author. Website: www. gloriakarpinski.com.

confirmation that the work with Edward was coming from a very high level of awareness.

Next we cleared Edward's limiting belief that loving was not safe, using tapping on an energy point under the lips with the affirmation, "Even though opening up my heart to love does not feel safe, I love and accept myself. Whether or not opening up my heart is safe here, I love and accept myself. It's safe to love and honor myself at all seven levels."

Sacral chakra. Edward's sacral chakra held a lot of disturbance and was a muddy red color. We had Edward tap his middle fingernail while saying, "I call back all of my energy that I lost from being abused. I renounce the past! I call back my life energy from the past!" Sexual abuse robs power from a person, and this affirmation called back that power.

Brow chakra. Edward reported a rainstorm and lightning in his head. Since he had gone to Sunday School and was familiar with Christian imagery, we suggested he ask Jesus to command the storm inside of his head to be still. Just like the Bible story, the sea inside Edward calmed down.

Solar plexus. Edward reported his belly had a Dementor, a soul-sucking fiend from the Harry Potter book series—great telepathic shorthand to explain what was happening in his solar plexus, the body's power center. I compared the Dementor stealing his energy to the milkman delivering two bottles of milk and the neighbor drinking it all before he could get to it. Edward remembered getting milk in a silver box on the back doorstep when he was a child.

We then called Jesus and Archangel Michael to remove this Dementor from Edward's solar plexus and put the Dementor into quarantine so he could never harm anyone else.

Edward quizzed, "Is Archangel Michael the one with the sword?"

Edward then opened up the silver box. He felt that getting this milk was almost too good to be true. He saw a "ghostly image" of Jesus sitting next to him and could not make that image jive with someone bringing him milk. Then he saw a jolly 1950s TV commercial kind of milkman in a white suit, and Edward knew that this man was Jesus too—an image easier for him to accept. Edward laughed, "You couldn't ask just anyone for milk, and it would be hard to ask a ghost. But it's easy to ask the milkman!"

Edward was amazed when we told him he could ask for milk any time he wanted. He queried, "Could I also have some Oreo cookies to go with my milk?"

Morgan reported that when Edward was little, he would say his name and then the thing he wanted. He loved Oreo cookies and would often insist, "Edward Oreo! Edward Oreo!" Edward asked Jesus for Oreo cookies and got them. Morgan saw Edward with his face full of cookies being totally amazed that he could be a bit of universal light manifesting in such a way as to eat cookies!

Then we asked Archangel Michael to put a shield around Edward so that no other Dementor could ever get into his energy field.

Edward reflected, "It's kind of like saran wrap around me."

Soul Lesson

We asked Edward, "Why did your soul choose this experience? What did the soul want to learn?"

From his Higher Self, Edward responded, "This question needs to be addressed at the causal level. There was no lesson for the soul, because the soul had nothing to learn. The reason for the experience was because of what we are doing now. The pairing of siblings moved the desire for greater understanding of mental health and the spiritual world."

Having Edward as a brother helped Morgan understand that we are greater than we realize, and we can communicate through telepathy from the depth of our essence.

Edward ended with these words of deep wisdom: "Thank you for coming to a place so dark. But was this not your purpose? And are we all not loved? While there is a beginning and an end, there is no beginning and end. Dark and light are the shadows only, and without those shadows, the light would fade—except where there is none but Light. We will meet again, but due to your kindness, my personality can live and be and cross over with far more peace than was originally intended."

When I asked Edward's permission to write about our work together, Morgan reported, "It's hard for him to talk, because his mouth is so full of Oreo cookies! He says, 'Of course!'"

Edward let us know that many of his companions could also communicate telepathically and were all trying to make others aware of this—quite a revelation! Meg Blackburn Losey's book *The Children of Now* reinforces this concept that many children who appear disabled or dysfunctional can communicate telepathically and are actually spiritually advanced beings, forerunners of "the new evolution of humanity."

A few days later, Morgan reported, "I heard a lot more from Edward the following day, and the quality of our relationship has changed. Gone is the feeling that he has had an awful life. I do still wish he could have avoided some of the hurt and pain, but I know now that he is more than that personality experience."

We are both deeply grateful to all the Beings of Light for the healing that came to Edward during this session. As Edward's mind healed, my heart also opened. We could call this opening countertransference, or we could just call it compassion!

Note: In Oriental medicine, a virus is called an "evil spirit"; it invades the body and causes destruction. Since Edward said he had demons, I wondered whether a virus might have been the root cause of Edward's seizures that began at age two. Could a viral infection have caused the nerve damage that impaired his mental and emotional capacity, especially damaging his impulse control? If so, then perhaps the only way Edward could conceptualize healing for himself was to cast out this demon.

Reversal

People who are so dissociated from their own negative emotions that they conceptualize them as being autonomous, malevolent forces (external locus of control) that invade them are at the far end of the wellness to illness spectrum. Saying "The Devil made me do it" could be a way of avoiding personal responsibility for our actions. In energy psychology terms, people with this problem also likely have a condition called "massive psychological reversal," described in appendix C.

Evil is a reversal of the life force. Spell the word evil backward, and what do you get? Live! Also note that the word devil is evil with the letter "d" in front.

Expanding Consciousness

In his book *Power Versus Force,* David Hawkins presents a Map of Consciousness with a logarithmic scale of consciousness from zero to a thousand. This map correlates God-view, Life-view, Emotion, and Process. Our view of God, the spiritual aspect, determines our view of life, and the emotions follow.

Thoughts precede emotions, and we can choose which thoughts to focus our minds on. If we give more "air time" to thoughts of destruction, injustice, and enslavement, these thoughts create feelings that pull us down on the map of consciousness. If we focus our minds on thoughts of acceptance, forgiveness, and love, these thoughts raise our level of consciousness. Researcher Gail Ironson, MD, PhD, found that HIV patients who believed in a loving God fared better with their disease than those who believed that God is judgmental.[†]

Notes in the musical scale sound different because higher notes vibrate faster than lower notes. When a note moves up an octave, its frequency doubles. An analogy in the realm of emotions is that love, peace, and joy are the high notes on the musical scale, and hatred, anger, and shame are the low notes. We can choose which notes to sing.

In *The Genie in Your Genes,* the groundbreaking book published in 2007, author Dawson Church dispels the myth that DNA is destiny. He explains how we are learning to see our cells and our bodies as malleable, influenced

---

[†]Rick Del Vecchio. (2006, April 6) "Berkeley: Conference at Cal about spirituality as research topic/First public talks on scientific study of the inner life." *San Francisco Chronicle.*

by every thought and feeling that flows through us. Knowing this, we can choose to take responsibility for the quality of thought and feeling we host, and choose those that radiate benevolence, goodwill, vibrancy, and wellness. Doing this, we positively affect not just our own well-being, but also that of the entire world of which we are a part—and the great ocean of consciousness in which our individual minds swim.

The genocide in the tiny African country of Rwanda in 1994 is an example of choices in consciousness. Two tribes had a long history of conflict: the lower-class Hutus and the elite group of Tutsis. An extremist militant Hutu group fanned the flames of hate and resentment that the Hutus felt from their history of abuse by the Tutsis and set a goal of "exterminating" all Tutsis from Rwanda. They broadcast a hate radio station that dehumanized the Tutsis by calling them cockroaches, held rallies, and organized a militia. After the death of the Rwandan president in a plane crash on April 6, 1994, and the assassination of Rwanda's prime minister the next day, this group seized power.[‡] From April through July, in a period of a hundred days, nearly a million Rwandans were killed. Most of these were Tutsis and moderate Hutus who refused to take sides against their Tutsi neighbors and family members.

People who witnessed this atrocity said that the militia lost their humanity and were overtaken by evil spirits or the devil. Another viewpoint is that some people chose to feed their racial hatred, which pulled their level of consciousness down to the lower vibrations of fear and separation from the Divine. These emotions close off access to the limbic brain, which allows for complexity and choice, and put the reptilian brain in control—fight-or-flight survival mode. The Rwandan government demanded that Hutus "exterminate Tutsis" or be killed themselves as Tutsi sympathizers. A collective hysteria resulted, and people did things they would not normally do, acting on long-repressed impulses of hatred and rage. Once the blood started flowing, dark collective archetypal forces seemed to take over and make the soldiers even more bloodthirsty.

[‡]PBS Home Video documentary "Ghosts of Rwanda" (2004), coproduced by the BBC and Silverbridge Productions Limited.

The mind is a dynamo that generates energy. According to Divaldo P. Franco, author of *The Dynamics of Our Sixth Sense,* we tune in to certain levels according to the way we are thinking. The bad spirits are in the lower bands. When we think negatively, we open a gap for this tuning to happen. When we mentally and morally elevate ourselves, they cannot reach us.

But not all Hutus chose to lower their consciousness through nursing hatred, resentment, and greed. Some Hutus protected and hid their Tutsi neighbors, risking their own lives in the process. They kept themselves at a high level of consciousness through these brave acts of heroism and altruism and focused on love and forgiveness.

11

Past Life Trauma

Some believe in the theory of reincarnation, some do not, and some are undecided. I never try to talk a client into belief in this theory. Whenever muscle testing indicates that past life trauma is the root cause of a current emotional disturbance, I first inquire whether the client believes in reincarnation. So far, everyone has either believed or been open to the possibility of using reincarnation as a metaphor to resolve an emotional problem that has been unresponsive to other treatment. Seemorg Matrix Work and Theta Healing (see appendix F) refer to past life content as simply "historical" material.

The most important reason for resolving past life trauma is that time is really an illusion, and all of our past lives are actually happening right now, all at once. When we resolve trauma from any one of our lives, that improvement affects all of our lives simultaneously, including the present one.

Past Life Case Example

Rita's elevated anxiety began as a teenager, with no apparent cause. Her first full-blown panic attack happened in her thirties on a highway when she was driving home from visiting her mother in the hospital. Over the next ten years, the panic disorder got worse, becoming so severe that it interrupted her life and limited her mobility. Unable to drive on major highways, she had to take back roads.

During our therapy session, Rita completely desensitized her fear of highway driving. She remained free of this phobia for a whole week, but it returned while driving to her next session. Rita's case came several years before I had developed my Soul Detective protocols. At that time, I just treated the presenting problems and looked deeper only if the issue did not resolve quickly. Since Rita's phobia recurred, we suspected some deeper-level disturbance was triggering this anxiety.

Years before, I had read Brian Weiss's *Many Lives, Many Masters*, which started with the case history of a client named Catherine who presented with lifelong phobias, depression, nightmares, and panic attacks. At the time of treating Catherine, Dr. Weiss chaired the department of psychiatry at Mount Sinai Medical Center in Miami Beach, Florida. He was completely skeptical of parapsychology, past lives, and reincarnation. He inadvertently put a root cause statement into his hypnotic induction for Catherine, however, suggesting, "Go back to the time from which your symptoms arise."

Catherine flipped back into an ancient near-Eastern lifetime in which she drowned in a tidal wave, with the force of the water tearing her baby from her arms. To his surprise, Catherine improved dramatically the following week and was completely cured within a few months, without the use of any medication. I wondered whether Rita's driving phobia might stem from a similar root, and muscle testing confirmed this hunch.

Rita connected with a lifetime around 1900. At age eighteen, she was in love, impetuous, and reckless. She saw herself coming down a grand flight of stairs in a big house, with petticoats flying. She got into her buggy and was driving fast in the rain. As she came around a curve, a buggy coming toward her was in her lane. Trying to avoid a head-on collision, she swerved and her carriage flipped over, flinging her out of the buggy to land facedown in the mud. Next she saw herself in bed, wounded, feeling angry that she was unable to get up. She died of respiratory failure three days after the accident.

For Rita, watching her mother dying of a respiratory illness had touched her soul's memory of her suffering in this past life and triggered her first full-blown panic attack. Her phobia of driving on the highway was a defense mechanism to try to protect her from having another accident and repeating the suffering. Dying as a teenager in the past life also correlated to the sudden onset of her panic disorder at the same age in this life, with no other apparent cause.

Rita released the trauma of having her past life cut short with a customized meridian tapping sequence and forgave the driver of the other buggy involved, because he was at fault in the accident. At the end of the session, Rita disclosed that, in this life, she had a horse and buggy, but she had been afraid to drive it on the road.

This release brought some relief but did not completely resolve the phobia. Since the anxiety only came when she was in the actual situation, we planned a driving session with me along to coach. We began by sitting in her car before the trip and tapping her customized TFT algorithm to desensitize anxiety.

We agreed that if Rita felt any panic at any time during the trip, she would pull over to the side of the road, and we would repeat the tapping sequence. On the way to the interstate highway, Rita tapped again with one finger. She repeated the treatment right before getting on the interstate and several times during the trip. Although the muscles in her legs were tensed and her breathing shallow, she was able to bring her anxiety down to a reasonable level. After that session, the phobia of driving on the highway was completely released and had not returned when she checked in fifteen months later.

Automobile Analogy

One analogy of reincarnation is getting a new car. I'm glad that in my fifties I'm not still driving the same automobile that I was driving when I first got behind the wheel at age sixteen. I love my cars, but they wear out after awhile, and eventually I get a better, newer model. The soul is like the driver of the car, and the physical body is like the automobile itself. Just as I have needed more than one auto to get all the places I want to go, the soul likewise needs more than one body to learn all of its lessons. The body's view of death is very different from the soul's view. The body gets frightened that it will cease to exist. But to the soul, death is just discarding the old worn-out or crashed-up vehicle and getting ready for a brand new car.

Soul Detective Past Life Protocol

Many parameters are similar to working with an earthbound spirit attachment and are repeated here in shortened form.

Getting Centered

Once a client's problem has been identified as unresolved trauma from a past life, the next step is being sure both the therapist and the client are centered (see appendix C). Since access to the information about the past life comes from muscle testing rather than from hypnosis, we need to be sure our muscle testing is accurate. If either the client or the therapist is not centered, the treasure hunt to find the emotional impasse will lead to a dead-end street. Accurate muscle testing quickly leads to a gold mine of emotional information and a dynamic emotional catharsis as the past life trauma is discovered and resolved.

A beautiful way to start the work is for the client to massage his or her heart clockwise while saying positive affirmations similar to the following:

"I deeply and profoundly accept myself with all my problems and limitations. I accept all of my feelings about this past life. I know I got through it because here I am, reincarnated. Even though I was not able to get through the trauma then, I love and accept myself. Now we know how to clear trauma!"

Getting Permission

To assess permission, muscle test these statements: "Working with this past life in therapy today is in my highest good" and "Working with this past life today is safe and appropriate," versus "Working with this past life is not in my highest good right now."

Denial of permission could mean one of two issues:

1. Perhaps the therapist does not have the skills necessary to deal with the trauma this past life is carrying. When I test this issue, I am really asking

Spirit whether I have the skills to deal with the issues that will come up in this past life.

2. The timing is not right. Perhaps not enough time is left in the session to complete the work it will take. While clearing a past life trauma with customized meridian algorithms usually takes me less than half an hour, upon occasion the issue requires a full hour. Only once have I had an extremely traumatic past life that needed two hours to process all of its aspects. Note that past life sessions using hypnosis regularly need around two hours to process the material and are hard to fit into the one-hour session allotted by most health insurance benefits.

Always get permission first before starting to work with a past life. If permission is denied, find out whether you need to schedule the past life work at another time or whether you need to refer the issue to another therapist.

Getting Spiritual Help

Next, call for spiritual help to assist the process of healing. We know that the person ultimately survived this trauma, because the client is right here in therapy. Emphasize this point! But we also know that whatever problem remained unresolved in this past life is still unresolved for the client today.

In your prayer of invocation, call the guardians and guardian angels for you, your client, and the previous incarnation.

Establishing Identity

Gender

The first main classification in establishing identity is muscle testing for gender: "This lifetime was male," versus "This lifetime was female."

Age at Death

The next main clue to a past life identity is finding out how long the person lived. Working with a lifetime that ended at one year old is very different from working with one that ended at age fifty-four. Most of the past life deaths I have worked with came at a young age, in the twenties or under. Rarely did a person survive past fifty.

Muscle test the statement "I lived for at least twenty years in this life-time." If true, keep increasing the number to forty, sixty, and so forth. Once the larger number tests false, then back up by half the distance between that age and the previous one until the age of death is established.

Cause of Death

Natural deaths are not usually traumatic, and spirits cross over. Most often, the unresolved trauma of the past life is the manner of death. On rare occasions, an issue of guilt, sexual abuse, or unfinished business keeps a past incarnation earthbound.

Muscle test these major categories of cause of death until one tests true:

1. Illness
2. Accident
3. Act of war
4. Murder
5. Execution/martyred
6. Suicide
7. Natural disaster (tsunami, earthquake)
8. Starvation
9. Abortion, miscarriage, or still birth
10. Sacrificed in a ritual
11. Other

Further Identifying Information

1. Country lived in
   a. Test whether this life happened on planet Earth or some other loca-tion in the universe. Some souls may have had lives on other planets or in other realms.
   b. If on Earth, then test whether it was in the eastern or western hemisphere.

c. Test above the equator, below the equator.

d. Check for continents in that quadrant of Earth.

e. Test countries in the continent. For ancient lifetimes, use the wording "in the area that is now part of China [current name of country]."

2. Date of birth

a. Born after 1 A.D.

b. Born after 1000 A.D., after 1500 A.D., and so forth. Again, keep going forward and then backward by half until locating the year of birth.

Optional further identifying information can be tested, including marital status, children and their ages, and occupation.

Happiest Time in That Life

We really want to find the most traumatic moment in this past life. If we head straight for this unresolved agitation, however, our client may become emotionally immobilized. So instead, take a detour to the happiest moment in that lifetime as a wonderful way to connect with the essence of this incarnation. The client visibly relaxes with this entry point, and some beautiful descriptions emerge of the happiest times.

Amplify whatever image of the happiest time comes up by asking for further detail, for example: How was the person dressed? Were others in the scene? If so, what did they look like? What kind of landscape was around? What kinesthetic sensations were present?

Almost always, the client makes an intuitive connection with the past life by this time and knows what that person was thinking and feeling. Images and experiences start to flow freely. Each person has all the information about all past lives held in the spiritual layer of the biofield. In his book *Journey of Souls*, Michael Newton writes that his subjects call these records "Life Books" rather than using the Eastern term "Akashic Records." One can also visualize past life memories like cards in a deck, one card representing each life. When we focus on a past life, we are asking the soul to pull out one card from this deck to examine and heal unresolved issues.

An eighth chakra, called the "Soul Star," the book of our soul, holds the complete plan for the soul's mission in the current lifetime and karmic memory of past lifetimes that need to heal. Stevan J. Thayer, developer of Integrated Energy Therapy, explains that though the soul star is generally thought of as being located about four feet above the head, it is nonlocalized, so it is also four feet behind, in front, and to the sides of the top of the head. When a client accesses this information bank, the memories flow.

Finding a Name

Somewhere in the search to find out more about this lifetime, inquire what name this past life self wants to be called. Having a name makes a more personal connection and allows us to address the past incarnation directly. If the name has not already come, ask just after finding the happiest moment.

Naming is powerful. In ancient times, the name conveyed the meaning of the person's life. The Hebrew name for Moses, "Moshe," means savior and "drawn out of the water." The Hebrew name for Jesus was "Yeshua," which means "the messiah, the savior."

Ask the client what name this former life self wants us to call him or her by, and be sure to add that the very first name that comes to mind will be the right one.

Moving Toward the Trauma

Next, to move gradually toward the traumatic material, I ask my client to go to the time just *before* the traumatic event happened, when the first inkling came that trouble was coming. What was going on? Then I instruct the client to move forward very carefully, imagining that we are watching a movie of this life and the client has the remote control.

Desensitizing the Trauma

I ask the client to stop whenever strong feelings come up so we can desensitize the trauma. My clients need less preparation for energy tapping with past lives, as they are usually already familiar with energy psychology. Still, I ask if the past life self would like to try something that might seem really silly but might help the person feel better—a "spiritual informed consent."

I use diagnostic Thought Field Therapy, also called making customized algorithms, with almost all of these cases, not only because this method is rapid and very precise, but also because the meridian tapping sequence indicates the nature of the emotional disturbance. But any form of energy therapy the practitioner has mastered can be used to help a past life self come to resolution: Emotional Freedom Techniques (EFT), Tapas Acupressure Technique (TAT), Healing from the Body Level Up (HBLU), REMAP, Seemorg Matrix Work, Therapeutic Touch, Whole Healing–Easily and Effectively (WHEE), or other method. If the client already has a cue word to desensitize trauma from Be Set Free Fast (BSFF), you can use that.

Since the unresolved trauma is almost always related to the death experience, move forward, desensitizing trauma as you go, to the ending point of that lifetime. Ask what the past life self was feeling at the moment of death, and then treat any unresolved issues.

What Happened Next After Death

After desensitizing all of the trauma and moving through the death experience, inquire what happened to the spirit after death. Which direction did it go? Up and away from the gravitational force of Earth into the Light? Lateral movement? Did the soul wander?

Sometimes the energy of the past incarnation does not cross into the Light at death and instead stays earthbound. The soul can still reincarnate, but without having time on the other side to study and review the life, learn from the mistakes, and integrate the lessons, the soul just starts over at the very same place where it left off. The situation is similar to failing an online exam, not knowing which questions were wrong, and having to take the same exam again without any corrective feedback.

Having a past life fragment earthbound, "frozen in time," is a form of soul loss and leaves a person feeling as if something is missing in life. Crossing to the Light and reintegrating this energy into the core soul energy brings a sense of wholeness and completion.

Crossing If Still Earthbound

If this past incarnation is still earthbound, call the angels or other departed loved ones to help make the crossing into the Light, back into the arms of the Creator. Once the client feels this part of the soul energy has crossed, we celebrate and give thanks to the angels.

Multiplying the Benefits

A research study done by Gary Craig demonstrated that people who simply watched an EFT treatment reduced their own emotional disturbances. Likewise, other earthbound spirits who resonate to the issue a past life has addressed seem to be able to "borrow the benefits" and cross to the Light without any further treatment.

One can send a crossing invitation to ancestors, family members, and community members of the one who just crossed. One might also extend the pyramid of Light to encompass the whole planet Earth and send out a cosmic invitation for any other earthbound spirits who have been chained by the fetters we just broke to take this chance to cross to the Light.

Multiplying the Benefits Case Example

A client felt compelled to eat before going to bed and wanted to break this bad habit. The invisible root of this compulsion to eat came from a lifetime when she was born in northern Africa in the year 228 AD, a precious little girl named Sulee. At age three, war broke out, and Sulee and her mother had to run away to the hills to escape a brutal death. But they did not have enough food in their hiding place. They were both lying on the ground, close to death from starvation. Sulee's mother died first, terrifying Sulee, who died shortly thereafter. Her fright kept her earthbound. Once my client did a heart massage for Sulee and then tapped the TFT algorithm for fear (eye, arm, collarbone), Sulee ran across the bridge from this world into the arms of her mother, who had been waiting for her in the Light.

When we sent out a crossing invitation for any other earthbound souls in the area who had died in the war, my client felt a huge rush of souls crossing the bridge—1,843 people! This group included many different tribes all sitting together on the other side. They decided to form a new group called "Champions of Humanity" to work for the realization that whatever we do in war to our brothers and sisters, we do to ourselves. Once their souls go through the healing process in the Light, this group will become spirit guides for people here on Earth for the betterment of humanity.

As wars like the one Sulee and her mother died from are still going on in Africa today, we also set a bridge of Light from the heart of Africa into the next world with the invitation for any earthbound spirits to go home to their loved ones.

Soul Lesson

Inquire what lesson the soul wanted to learn by incarnating into this life situation. In both *Journey of Souls* and *Destiny of Souls,* author Michael Newton talks about the Soul Council on the other side helping a person design a life to hold the specific challenges the soul wants to master—to "build spiritual muscle." You can ask the client to consult his or her Soul Council to find out what the plans were. Very deep wisdom comes out of clients at this step.

Ask what lesson the soul intended to master. Did it happen? If not, go back and work with the past life self, desensitizing further soul trauma that comes up around the story and the sense of failing the soul test. One simple energy psychology technique to use after desensitizing the trauma is doing a frontal-occipital hold (see the Soul Detective Protocol in "Earthbound Spirits") while imagining a better ending to the story. Similar to Carl Jung's technique of "active imagination," visualizing a different ending to the story with a better outcome also rewrites emotions in the current life, reprogramming the system for increased emotional health.

Once the client comes to a place of peace regarding the events of the former lifetime and finds the lesson the soul intended to master, anchor this wisdom back into the current life by correlating this soul lesson to present life challenges. While in this sacred space, you can also ask the Soul Council or the person's Higher Self for direct guidance on issues in the current incarnation.

Soul Resonance

An optional final step is asking whether the soul essence of anyone in the past life resonates to the soul essence of important people in the present life. Usually characters will be in a similar role. If any of the souls the client had conflict with in the past lifetime have reincarnated as challenging people in the client's current life, find out whether the client needs to do further work on the present-life relationship.

If a past life had a love relationship that felt incomplete, such as a parent leaving behind young children or a mate dying prematurely, examine the present life to see whether the essence of that soul is present in this life. Sometimes the bond between souls is so strong that they find each other in a future incarnation. Making this connection fulfills the intentions the souls set but were unable to fulfill during the previous lifetime.

Giving Thanks

The energy of gratitude has a very high vibration and is an excellent way to close a session. If you called in transpersonal help, give thanks for this Divine assistance. Thank the past life self for coming forward for healing, and thank the client for being willing to do this soul work to lighten the load of trauma on this planet.

Past Life Checklist

1. Getting centered
2. Getting permission
3. Asking for spiritual help
4. Gathering identifying information
   a. Gender
   b. Age at death
   c. Cause of death

   Illness

   Accident

   Act of war

   Murder

   Execution/martyred

   Suicide

   Natural disaster (tsunami, earthquake)

   Starvation

   Abortion, miscarriage, or stillbirth

   Sacrificed in a ritual

   Other (usually natural deaths are not traumatic and spirits cross over)
5. Further identifying information
6. Happiest time in that life
7. Finding a name
8. Moving toward the trauma
9. Desensitizing the trauma
10. What happened next after death
11. Crossing if still earthbound
12. Multiplying the benefits
13. Soul lesson
14. Soul resonance
15. Giving thanks

12

Other—Put on Your Soul Detective Hat!

If the root cause lies at the intuitive level, and none of the other eleven categories fit, then you have the challenge of listening very carefully and together with your client trying to solve the mystery of where the problem has originated. For example, if a client is functioning well in almost all areas of life but says he was abducted by extraterrestrials as a child and implanted with a device to monitor his physiology, then treat the client as if these events truly happened whether or not you believe they really did.

PART THREE

Protocol for Working with Couples on Their Past Lives Together

L ooking at past lives couples have shared can bring light to current issues and add another dimension to healing. Sometimes couples find themselves in emotional gridlock, unable to move forward in their connection, knowing they are working on something important, yet unable to find their way through their issues. If this situation arises in therapy, you could muscle test whether past life interpersonal issues are contributing to the current difficulty.

Couple's Past Lives Case Example

Reynard and Michelle, a couple in their fifties who had recently announced their engagement, knew they had been together before in other lives. They also knew that between lives, when planning their current incarnation, Reynard had asked Michelle if she would marry him in this lifetime. Michelle's soul had responded, "Let me think about that." Both of them had grown children from previous marriages, and both had used the ordeal of divorce to develop a great deal of personal growth and spiritual strength. Michelle knew that Reynard was the right man for her, so she was puzzled at finding herself pushing him away lately.

Muscle testing indicated that Reynard and Michelle had been together in three previous lives. The most recent one was during the Revolutionary War. Reynard had been a furniture maker, and they had no children. In their second lifetime together, they had been brother and sister, with Reynard being the brother and Michelle the sister.

The lifetime that needed treatment was their very first time together, a century before the birth of Christ, set in the country of Gaul, which is now France. During that time, the various Celtic tribes in the area were always

Protocol for Working with a Couple's Past Lives

1. Identify the issues the couple is facing in the current life.

2. Test how many lives the couple has shared.

3. Find their relationship to each other in each life.

   a. Family or non-family

   b. If family, marriage, parent-child, sibling, etc.

   c. If non-family, teacher-student, friends, lovers, enemy soldiers, business partners, etc.

4. Test how many of these lives hold unresolved issues that need to be addressed to resolve current interpersonal conflict.

5. Identify the life that needs to be addressed first, and which partner needs to work first.

6. Follow the past life protocol for the first partner, with both the therapist and the other partner doing the energy psychology treatment along with the person who is working.

7. Offer the opportunity for the partner who is working to ask forgiveness of the other for past mistakes. Make space for healing and reconciliation.

8. If the other partner also carries trauma from the lifetime, then repeat the past life protocol on that lifetime for the second partner, again having everyone tapping and offering space for forgiveness, healing, and reconciliation.

9. Ask each partner to find the soul lessons from then that apply to the current life together.

10. Repeat the whole protocol for any additional lives that need treatment.

fighting with each other and had little unity. Reynard's soul was the older brother, Eyore, and Michelle had been his younger brother, Cig. We all sensed that a lot of trouble had happened in that life.

Michelle wept and burst out, "I think I killed him."

Reynard vehemently insisted, "No, she didn't! Muscle test me for the statement, 'She thinks she killed me, but she really didn't.'" Reynard's statement tested as true.

Cig's Lifetime (129–42 B.C.)

To divert Michelle from the overwhelming trauma that was surfacing, I asked her to remember the happiest moment in that lifetime. Cig's birth in 129 B.C. was the happiest moment. He came in feeling loved and wanted, surrounded by Light.

Historical note: The Romans began their conquest of the southern part of Gaul in 125 B.C.. Later, Julius Caesar penetrated further into the region in the Gallic wars from 58 to 51 B.C., in Cig's lifetime.

Eyore's Lifetime (131–109 B.C.)

The Celts were ironworkers—hot, sweaty labor. Eyore, two years older than Cig, could not remember any happiness from that life. He joined the military at age eighteen to get away from the drudgery of the hard work at home. Cig felt devastated by his brother's leaving. (At this point, we treated Cig to release the sadness and trauma of his brother's departure.) Cig joined the army two years later, as soon as he was old enough to enlist and be with Eyore.

The memory that held the imprint of trauma for Cig was the moment of Eyore's death at age twenty-two:

> We are in the same tent, sleeping on cots, getting up in the morning and putting on our uniforms. Before we can get on our metal caps, suddenly the enemies thunder into camp on horseback. Chaos prevails as they swoop down in a surprise attack. Eyore is standing up in the tent, and Cig is cowering in the shadows, shaking with fear. Eyore calls to Cig to come fight, but he can barely get

the words out of his mouth before an enemy soldier rides into the tent brandishing a sword and decapitates Eyore. Cig feels he killed his brother because Eyore had been defending him, like he always did, and Cig was hiding. The horseman rides out of the tent without even noticing Cig, who survives the battle and lives until the age of eighty-seven, missing his brother and blaming himself for Eyore's death the whole time.

First, we treated Cig while he was in the tent, hiding and shaking. The customized meridian sequence we made for Cig indicated that he had been having a panic attack and was physically unable to get up and fight. Had he been standing, he would have been decapitated along with his brother. A man on foot is no match for a man on horseback.

Once we treated Michelle for Cig's anxiety and the psychological reversal in the brow chakra that held the traumatic emotions in place, she could remain peaceful while remembering Eyore's death.

Next, I asked her to move to her soul's memory of the time when she left her body and went to the Light. Eyore was there to greet her, and the reunion was filled with joy. He had never held any animosity toward her for what happened. At this point in the therapy, Reynard leaned over to Michelle and gave her a huge hug, with the words, "You are forgiven!"

Soul Lesson

Cig's life lesson had been self-forgiveness. From the love his soul had for Michelle, Reynard's soul had volunteered to be her brother and to go through this scenario of dying young so Michelle's soul could learn the meaning of pure love and how to release the grudge she had held against herself that entire lifetime, fabricating the lie that her inaction had killed her brother.

Before this trauma was healed, Michelle had unconsciously felt that if she got close to Reynard, she might "kill him" again. Then she realized that this misperception at the soul level had been instrumental in her pushing Reynard away. Tears flowed as they embraced, feeling the deep love they have for each other. Michelle took home an affirmation of self-forgiveness to reinforce the healing of her soul and reprogram her mind for truth in the connection with Reynard.

Six months later, they had each completed their inner work to be ready for marriage. When I opened the invitation to their wedding, my soul filled with joy.

Appendices

APPENDIX A

Therapist Tips

1. Get solid training for the energy psychology methods you want to learn. The Association for Comprehensive Energy Psychology (ACEP) has a certification program that provides an understanding of the foundational practices of energy psychology. See the ACEP website at www.energypsych.org for complete details and membership and certification applications. ACEP is an umbrella organization unifying a broad array

In the ACEP Workshop photograph note the orbs of light around the group. Though skeptics call them refractions from specks of dust, great minds from around the world gathered in Sedona, Arizona, on May 4–6, 2007, to talk about this phenomenon at the Prophets Conference entitled "Orbs: What Is Going On?" (www.greatmystery.org/events/sedona07). I consider orbs visible signs of the help from other dimensions that guides our work.

of different energy therapies, many of which provide more focused training and certification in their own specialized methods. The ACEP certification program has two tracks: Diplomate, Comprehensive Energy Psychology (DCEP) for licensed mental health professionals; and Certified Energy Health Practitioner (CEHP) for a broad range of allied health and human potential fields and/or those whose academic degrees are in mental health but who are not licensed mental health practitioners. This training includes learning how to make customized meridian algorithms, also called Diagnostic TFT.

 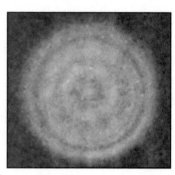

Left: An orb above the head of Doug Parks at an ACEP dance with Her Holiness Sai Maa. Note the smaller orbs inside the larger one.

Right: Close-up of an orb.

2. When doing energy psychology, pay attention to ethical standards and stay within the scope of your practice. If a client's issues are outside the realm of your expertise, refer the client to someone who has the necessary skills. This important guideline is part of the Code of Ethics established by ACEP (see the ACEP website for the complete Code of Ethics).

3. Be sure both you and your client are centered before beginning a treatment method. If the energy field of either the client or the therapist is imbalanced, the treatment will either not work or not last. Details on centering are in appendix C.

4. Clarify the client's treatment goals and priority method. Remember that goals need to come from the client's agenda rather than from what the therapist might think should change. Once the goals are set, muscle test for the priority goal to begin therapy. Then muscle test a menu of the

treatment modalities you have mastered to find the priority treatment method to best help the client reach this goal.

5. In most cases, do the energy treatment along with your client. Tap along as the client taps. If they are massaging the heart, massage yours too. Reasons for this are:

   a) The client initially may not know just where to tap or how to hold a point. Doing the treatment along with the client demonstrates the proper technique when the session is in person and proper timing during phone sessions.

   b) Most of these treatments look quite silly from the outside, and you would not want to sit at the sidelines laughing at your client. Be ridiculous too so you can both laugh at yourselves!

   c) The most important reason, however, is that feelings are contagious, just like the measles. When connecting with a client in deep emotional trauma, the emotional body of the therapist registers the traumatic imprint. Doing the treatment along with the client releases any vicarious traumatization the therapist may experience.

APPENDIX B

Dowsing

owsing is an ancient craft used throughout history to get information that lies beyond three-dimensional limitations. Dowsing is also called "divining," a way of asking the Divine for information. One might call it "communicating with God."

Finding water has been the most universal application of dowsing. After my Amish grandfather's new neighbors drilled down one hundred feet at several places on their new property without finding water, they asked Grandpa to dowse for a place to drill. Grandpa cut a forked branch from a cherry tree and held the prongs of the branch in his hands with the point of the stick facing forward, level with the ground. He then walked the land, focusing on finding a good spot to drill the well. When the point of the branch pulled down toward the earth, he told them to drill the well there—and they found a great source of water only fifty feet down!

The human body is mostly water, and dowsing applications have expanded to gathering information about the human energy field.

Devices and Method

Dowsing can be done with a number of devices, including metal L-rods, pendulums, bobbers, and forked branches. The dowser holds an intention firmly and clearly in mind and then asks the device to respond when approaching the target.

Muscle testing can be considered a form of dowsing—setting an intention and then using a muscle such as the arm or the finger as a dowsing rod. When working over the telephone, I muscle test the strength of my index finger. For example, I focus on the statement, "The root cause of this problem is on the physical level." Then I push down on my index finger with the middle finger of the same hand. If the index finger holds strong, I consider the statement true. If the index finger goes weak, I consider it false.

How Dowsing Works

An instrument that measures electromagnetic fields in units of milligauss, called a Gauss meter, involves a set of complicated circuitry and batteries connected to a moving metal needle that indicates the strength of the electromagnetic field (EMF). Dowsing uses the human brain as the circuitry of the meter, the dowser's energy field as the battery, and the L-rods, pendulum, bobber, or forked stick as the metal readout needle. Clear focus and concentration are essential in the art of dowsing.

Intention

Dowsing attunes to a higher level of consciousness to access information. Whether we call this level Universal Mind or the Holy Spirit, it comes from the spiritual layer of the energy field. Inherent in dowsing is the obligation to use it only for the highest good of the planet and everyone involved. Dowsing will not work if used for personal gain, like identifying the winning numbers in the lottery or showing off one's psychic powers. Intention must be pure to develop skill and accuracy in dowsing.

For more information on dowsing, books, workshops, and conventions, contact the American Society of Dowsers at P.O. Box 24, Danville, VT 05828; (802) 684-3417; www.dowsers.org.

APPENDIX C

Centering

I f a client's energy field is not centered, either the treatment will not get into the system or it will not hold. The biofields around the body need to be balanced and centered to have access to all parts of our brain. When the biofield is distorted, the effect is like being out of range of cell phone reception. When we get centered and balanced, then all the bars appear on our inner cell phone screen, and we get great reception from our own mental fields.

Centering—both for the client and for the therapist—is an essential prerequisite to doing any form of energy work.

I learned to dowse the human energy field to get a visual image of whether it was centered from a prominent dowser named Tom Milliren, whose numerous books on dowsing are available through the American Society of Dowsers. Following Tom's protocol, I ask my L-rods to open at the perimeter of the biofield that I want to measure. The interpenetrating concentric layers of the biofield are as follows:

- The etheric body

- The astral body, sometimes called the emotional body

- The mental body

- The causal body, sometimes called the spiritual body

Each body is made of finer and finer particles of light. These inter-penetrating bodies of light are like cocoons of energy surrounding the physical body.

Systemic Energetic Interference

All of the imbalances that interfere with proper energy flow through the entire system and distort the biofields can be called "systemic energetic interference." Like infectious agents, these systemic imbalances are also contagious. As a therapist, have you ever gone into a session feeling centered and then ten minutes later, felt totally confused? Correcting systemic energetic interference is foundational to doing any form of energy work.

Educational Kinesiology

Paul and Gail Dennison created a system now known as Edu-K or Brain Gym to assess which brain pathways are running counter to the proper flow of energy. Simple exercises that integrate mind and body through movement then correct these systemic energetic interferences, enhancing concentration and cognitive and learning abilities. Clients love watching these simple exercises bring their energy field to center and boost their sense of well-being.

The Process

To dowse the human energy field, I hold in my mind which biofield I want to measure and make my six-inch L-rods line up so they point straight ahead. Then I slowly walk toward the subject, repeating the person's name and the biofield I am measuring. The rods will then swing open, pointing in opposite directions, at the perimeter of the biofield.

Etheric Biofield

The human energy field has three vectors: up-down, front-back, and left-right. First I dowse the front and then the back of the etheric body to see whether a person is centered on this axis. Then I dowse the sides, one at a time, to assess the left-right axis. I also note each measurement for later reference after doing the centering exercises.

The size of the etheric body also indicates the client's overall energy level. A person with an etheric biofield that extends only one foot around the physical body will have very low energy; a person with an etheric biofield extending six to eight feet around the body will have plenty of energy. I can also check for centering on the up-down vector by having the client lie down, then dowsing the etheric biofield above and then below the body. Whenever dowsing indicates an imbalance, I always follow up with a muscle test for the same imbalance so the client can feel the difference in muscle strength before and after the correction for this systemic energetic interference.

Proper Polarity

Our bodies run on minute electromagnetic currents flowing from one point to another as direct current rather than alternating back and forth over the same pathway like the wiring in our homes. In other words, all the energy pathways in our bodies are like one-way streets.

Energy flows from a north pole (receiving) to a south pole (giving), and the proper direction of energy flow in the body is set by having our north and south poles at the right places. When we get too tired or stressed, too hot or cold, or when toxins contaminate us, our poles may reverse. Then energy runs backward through our system. Sometimes this reversal is called "switching." When we are running "counterflow chi," our life does not flow very smoothly. The situation is like trying to drive the wrong way on a one-way street in heavy traffic. Everyone seems to be against us! When reversed on any of the three vectors of the human energy field, a person will be off-center.

Up-Down Polarity Reversal

The up-down axis is the most important vector that needs to be centered. I find that my up-down polarity immediately reverses whenever I get afraid that energy therapy may not work or when I think that I am not doing a new protocol the right way. Then, because I am reversed, the answers I get from muscle testing make no sense or lead me nowhere—and of course, then energy therapy does not work! The therapist needs to be centered to help the client come to center.

When polarity is reversed on the up-down axis, the client will be running a subconscious program of self-destruction. Doing harmful things will feel good, and doing beneficial things will feel bad. We call this situation "massive psychological reversal." These people usually come to therapy only if ordered by a judge to get psychological help after arrest for substance abuse, if the alternative to therapy is prison, or if a spouse delivers the ultimatum: therapy or divorce!

Automobile analogy: Reversal on the up-down axis is like getting the gearshift stuck in reverse. When you step on the gas, you get further away from your goal.

Up-Down Diagnosis

The test to determine proper polarity on the up-down axis checks polarity at the top of the head:

1. First we test the strength of a muscle while the client places a hand palm down over the top of the head. This test should be strong.

2. Then the test is repeated with the client's hand palm up over the top of the head. This test should be weak.

Why the Palm-Down, Palm-Up Test Works

The palm of the hand gives out energy, so its polarity is south pole. On a battery, south is the positive or + side. The back of the hand receives energy, so its polarity is north pole. On a battery, north is the negative or − side.

The top of the head should be north pole, receptive. So when the hand is placed palm down over the top of the head, energy should flow from the palm of the hand (giving) into the crown of the head (receiving). If a person is properly polarized, this muscle test should be strong. When the back of the hand (receiving) is placed over the top of the head (receiving), placing a north pole against another north pole should repel, like putting the minus sides of two magnets together. This juxtaposition of like energy fields should make the muscle test weak.

If a client tests weak instead of strong with the palm down, this situation tells us that the person's polarity is reversed on the up-down axis, because the top of the head is south pole, giving out energy instead of receiving it. When the top of the head is south pole (giving), then when the palm of the hand (giving) lies on top of the head, the two south pole energy fields repel each other, and the muscle tests weak. Likewise, a strong test on palm up shows that energy is flowing from the south pole (giving) at the top of the head into the top of the hand (receiving), which is north pole, and the person is reversed.

Up-Down Correction

Some forms of energy work begin with prayer, which is a centering activity in itself. Prayer sets a Divine figure as a giver, which would be south pole, and the client's brain as a receiver, north pole, ready to take in energy and information from the spiritual realm.

When the up-down axis is reversed, I have also found that if I hold a pendulum over the heart chakra, it will rotate counterclockwise, moving against the natural flow of time. One powerful correction for up-down polarity reversal is putting a hand over the heart and massaging clockwise (as if a clock were printed on the client's shirt) to restore clockwise rotation of the heart chakra while repeating the affirmation: "I deeply and profoundly accept myself with all my problems and limitations. I also accept all of my strengths and gifts."

Always muscle test again after a correction to be sure the imbalance is corrected.

Nonpolarization

Sometimes the north and south poles wander around and get lost. In this case, the system loses its polarization, and the client tests equally strong (or weak) on both palm down and palm up. The common term for this condition is called "brain fog," and the technical term is "nonpolarization."

> **Automobile analogy:** Nonpolarization is like the gearshift slipping into neutral. You're not going backward, but you're not going forward either. The situation is also like typing on an external keyboard without having it plugged into the USB port of your computer: Nothing happens!

The cause of nonpolarization could be dehydration, lack of oxygen, or a temporary imbalance in the flow of energy through the system. Interventions that can restore polarization are drinking water, breathing deeply, the Thymus Thump (see appendix D), and the Over-Energy Correction (see later in this appendix).

Front-Back Polarity Reversal

Have you ever heard the expression, "He kept getting ahead of himself?" When a client fails the test for front-back polarity, my dowsing indicates that the biofield is shifted either forward or backward. When shifted forward, a person will likely feel hyperactive and anxious, racing to get fifty million things done all at once, unable to complete one task before jumping forward to the next, not knowing when to stop.

When the etheric biofield is shifted backward, the person will likely feel fatigue, depression, and weariness. One client described this situation as "the magnet in the couch."

Front-Back Diagnosis

The muscle test for front-back polarity reversal tests the strength of the collarbone points at K 27, the twenty-seventh point on the bilateral Kidney meridian. Muscle test both K 27 points with the palm side of the fingers (south pole) and with the knuckles (north pole) to assess polarity in each of the four quadrants of the cerebral cortex:

1. Two fingers (south pole) on K 27 left side tests *basal left*.
2. Two fingers on K 27 right side tests *basal right*.

3. Hide thumb in the fingers and touch just the knuckles on K 27, right side, to test *frontal right*.

4. Same knuckles on K 27 left side to test *frontal left*.

All four of these quadrants should test strong. If any quadrant tests weak, it is not properly polarized.

> **Automobile analogy:** A weak quadrant is like trying to drive a car with a flat tire. And sometimes more than one tire can go flat!

Front-Back Corrections

Brain Buttons

Stimulate the umbilicus (press, rub, or hook the middle finger into the navel and pull up gently) and at the same time tap or rub K 27 on both sides. Then repeat the process with the other hand at the navel.

Photos in this section by DeeAnne Butler

Brain Buttons

Over-Energy Correction

1. Cross the left ankle over the right one.

2. Place the left hand on the right knee, then the right hand on the left knee.

    (Alternative position: stretch the arms out in front of the body, thumbs down. Cross the right hand over the left, clasp, and twist inward to bring the elbows to the chest and the hands to the heart.)

3. Put the tip of the tongue on the roof of the mouth on the inhalation.

4. Rest the tongue on the floor of the mouth on the exhalation.

    Continue for one to two minutes. Eyes can be open or closed.

    Note: The Over-Energy Correction is excellent for insomnia. When the body wants to rest and the mind races on, this intervention brings the mind to stillness so the body can get the rest it needs.

Over-Energy Correction

Collarbone Breathing Exercise

1. Place two fingers of the right hand under the collarbone where it meets the sternum (K 27; Photo 1).

2. With the fingers of the left hand, tap the gamut spot (in the web between the outer two fingers close to the knuckles; see Gamut Spot and Photo 1) on the right hand at least five times in each position:

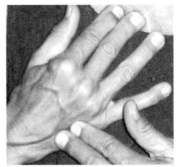

Gamut Spot

Breathe halfway in.

Breathe all the way in.

Breathe in even more.

Breathe halfway out.

Breathe the all the way out.

Breathe out even more.

Breathe halfway in.

3. Move the right hand to K27 on the other side of the collarbone and repeat.

Photo 1

Photo 2

4. Hide the thumb inside the fist and repeat the sequence in step 2 with the knuckles on the same spot (Photo 2).

5. Repeat with the knuckles on the other side at K 27.

6. Then repeat the whole sequence of the four positions with the right hand tapping the gamut spot on the left hand (Photos 3–4).

Photo 3   Photo 4

Left–Right Polarity Reversal

Have you ever heard the expression, "I was beside myself with worry?" When polarity on the left-right axis reverses, the axis slides off center, either to the right or to the left. Because perception is distorted, a person whose energy field is shifted to the right may bump into the left edge of a doorway. The center of the energy field was aligned with the opening—ouch!

Perception may also be reversed, as in dyslexia. Children who have dyslexia write numbers and letters backward because that is how they see them. If the biofield slides to the right, the person will likely be strong on visualization, connecting with feelings, carrying a tune, and feeling connected to Spirit. If it slides to the left, the person may have trouble with everything just mentioned but will likely be strong in math, logic, keeping things in order, and strategic planning—areas that are difficult for the right-brained folks. Corrections for left-right imbalances involve cross-crawl activities.

> **Automobile analogy:** Left-right imbalance is like having the axle of a car tilted to the right or left so one side of the car rides higher than the other side.

Left-Right Diagnosis

Muscle test while the subject is looking at the letter X drawn on a standard-size sheet of paper held two to three feet in front of the subject. This test should be strong. If it is weak, have the client continue to look at the X and test again while the person is counting (a left-hemisphere activity) and then while he or she is humming (a right-hemisphere activity) to identify the hemisphere that needs strengthening.

Muscle test the client while looking at parallel lines drawn on a sheet of paper, again held two to three feet in front of the subject. This test should be weak.

If either test is incorrect, do the following:

Left-Right Correction

Cross Crawl Exercise

Touch right hand to left knee, then left hand to right knee:

While counting to 30, one number for each knee tap.

While humming for 30 seconds.

While circling eyes one way for 15 seconds and then the other way for 15 seconds.

While circling eyes and counting (if possible).

While circling eyes and humming (if possible).

Brain-Heart Integration

To see whether the heart center is integrated with the brain center, muscle test while the client is looking at an X and holding a hand over the heart. This test should be strong. If it is weak, do the following exercise.

Cross Crawl—right hand to
left knee

Cross Crawl—left hand to
right knee

Since my clients had trouble with the original Brain Gym correction from
the Dennisons, called the "Scarecrow Cross Crawl," which involved the elbow
and the shoulder, I simplified the exercise to the following.

Brain-Heart Integration Exercise

1. Hold the hand palm down in front of the body, just below the navel.

2. At the midline, bring the hand up to the horizontal at heart level while
   lifting the opposite knee as if raising the leg like a puppet on a string.

3. Let them both return to their normal position. Repeat with the other arm
   and leg.

4. Then continue the motions of steps 1, 2, and 3 while also counting to 30, one number with each upward motion of the hand.

5. Do the same while humming for 30 seconds.

6. Do the same while circling the eyes one way for 15 seconds and then the other way for 15 seconds.

7. Do the same, if possible, while circling the eyes and counting.

8. Do the same, if possible, while circling the eyes and humming.

Brain-Heart Integration—right arm and left knee

Brain-Heart Integration—left arm and right knee

APPENDIX D

Clinical Kinesiology/ Muscle Testing

Kinesiology is the study of the principles and mechanics of anatomy related to human movement. George Goodheart, DC, developed a diagnostic system he named applied kinesiology (AK), in which he correlated muscle strength to proper organ function. Dr. Goodheart developed a system of diagnosing the function of each organ by testing the strength of a corresponding muscle. If the muscle tested strong, the organ was fine. If the muscle tested weak, the organ's function was impaired. Dr. Goodheart then used muscle testing to determine which supplements would best treat that organ. He further tested for quantity and frequency of the supplements for a treatment plan that was tailored exactly to the individual's need.

The clinical use of kinesiology in energy therapies is known as "clinical kinesiology," used as a true-false diagnostic indicator to determine the locus of the problem and the best solution. The basic premise of muscle testing is simple: A muscle will test strong following a true statement, and it will test weaker following a false statement. An experiment using a computerized dynamometer to measure strength of muscle responses following congruent (true) and incongruent (false) statements found approximately 17 percent more total force over a 59 percent longer time on congruent statements.[*]

---

[*]Monti, D., Sinnott, J., Marchese, M., et al. (1999). Muscle test comparisons of congruent and incongruent self-referential statements. *Perceptual and Motor Skills* 88, 1019–1028.

Much of the skill in muscle testing lies in figuring out what statements to test!

Practice Self-test

If you want to try a simple muscle test, follow this procedure:

1. Sit on a chair and raise one leg a few inches off the floor.
2. Test the strength of that thigh muscle by trying to push down on this knee with the hand on the same side.
3. State your full name and test this muscle again.
4. Then state a different name and repeat the muscle test.

Did the true statement and the false statement test differently for your name and another name? If both tests were the same, see the section in appendix C for correcting for nonpolarization.

Getting Accurate Results

The art of muscle testing is a delicate skill that uses a subtle level of energy. Results can be thrown off by the following factors:

- Both the practitioner and the client need to be properly hydrated. Just as the battery in your car engine needs to have water in it to conduct electricity, your body also needs water to properly conduct electrical signals.

- If the practitioner's mind wanders, results will not be accurate. The therapist needs to focus on the topic being tested and let the mind go blank to everything else.

- The results can also be thrown off by making eye contact during testing, as an eye gaze directs magnetic energy to the recipient.

- If either the client or practitioner tries to influence the result, the test will not be accurate. For example, if a client is testing the statement, "Chocolate is good for my health," some bias might be present!

Muscle testing has been "debunked" by those trying to prove that it does not work. Since intention is so very important, the intention of the debunkers to prove that muscle testing does not work is likely to influence the results, and then sure enough—it does not work while they are watching. But used in a neutral manner to gather information, muscle testing guides the practitioner first to find out what is happening and then to find the best way to resolve the problem.

In Soul Detective work, we are in unknown territory working with other dimensions of reality—past lives and earthbound spirits. Often, we are working with invisible strangers, so we cannot even read clues from body language. We need information that we cannot access in any other way, so we use true-false muscle testing as a guide, asking the Divine to show us correctly what is going on and how to proceed.

Emotions and Behavioral Kinesiology

Psychiatrist John Diamond, MD, was a student at Dr. Goodheart's International College of Applied Kinesiology. He used muscle testing to find the core emotional problems of patients much more quickly than with traditional psychiatry. Dr. Diamond's 1979 book *Your Body Doesn't Lie: How to Increase Your Life Energy Through Behavioral Kinesiology* explains the mechanics of applied kinesiology and explores the role of the thymus gland in health. (The thymus gland is located beneath the sternum in the chest.) Dr. Diamond called his system behavioral kinesiology to distinguish it from Dr. Goodheart's applied kinesiology. At that time, Dr. Diamond had only begun to discover a subtle phenomenon of muscle testing: Your body does not lie unless it is reversed. When polarity on the up-down axis is reversed, muscle tests will give the exact opposite of the truth. Diamond called this phenomenon "a reversal of the body's morality."

Dr. Diamond's *Life Energy: Using the Meridians to Unlock the Hidden Power of Your Emotions* further investigated the role of the thymus gland and its positive attributes of love, faith, gratitude, trust, and courage. Dr. Diamond also developed an energy-boosting exercise on the following page called the Thymus Thump. The thymus gland boosts immunity, and he says everyone should thump the thymus at least a hundred times a day.

Dr. Diamond also mapped the emotional aspects associated with each meridian, including images that strengthen or weaken meridians. He strengthened weak meridians primarily with affirmations.

Thymus Thump

1. Smile,

2. Think of someone you love, and

3. With closed fist, thump on the sternum and say,

   Ha ha ha, Ha ha ha, Ha ha ha!

   Alternatively, bring the fingertips of one hand together and tap with the joined fingertips on the sternum.

Thymus Thump with the fist

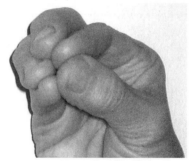

Fingertips together

Photos on this page by Bert Fellows

APPENDIX E

Thought Field Therapy
(TFT)

Roger Callahan, PhD, studied applied kinesiology with Dr. Goodheart and was a colleague of Dr. John Diamond (see appendix D). Dr. Callahan discovered that tapping on the beginning or ending of a meridian would dislodge the negative effect stored in that particular pathway.

Clearing Limiting Beliefs That Block Treatment Success

Dr. Callahan noticed that while tapping meridians worked for many clients, a sizeable percentage either did not get better or actually seemed to get worse after tapping. One of the most important contributions he made to the field was developing the concept of psychological reversal and finding ways to correct this problem. An example of a psychological reversal, also called a psychoenergetic reversal or a limiting belief, is a client wanting to get over a trauma but at the same time carrying guilt and feeling undeserving of getting better.

Clearing these internal conflicts that are obstacles to reaching goals is termed "Willingness to Succeed" in the ACEP certification training. Following are a few psychoenergetic reversals in addition to *deservingness* that block treatment success:

- *Safety:* Getting over this problem is not safe for me or for someone else.

- *Possibility:* Getting over this problem is not possible.

- *True intention:* I want to keep this problem.

- *Willingness:* I am not willing to be over this problem.

- *Motivation:* I will not do what is necessary to be over this problem.

- *Permission:* I do not give myself permission to get over this problem.

- *Vengeance:* If I get over this problem, someone else will have gotten away with hurting me.

- *Benefit:* Getting over this problem will not benefit me or will not benefit someone else.

- *Identity:* I would not know who I am if I get over this problem.

- *Deep level:* I will never be over this problem.

- *Mini-reversal:* I want to keep some of this problem.

Dr. Callahan named his discovery Thought Field Therapy (TFT) because with TFT one only has to think about the problem and does not have to feel the emotions connected with the issue. Frequently, survivors of severe trauma are retraumatized just by talking about the event. TFT avoids this retraumatization and thus is the gold standard for releasing the painful feelings attached to trauma.

Dr. Callahan's most advanced level of training is Voice Technology, done over the phone using computer technology that determines the treatment sequence, currently available for $120,000.

Subjective Units of Disturbance Scale (SUDS)

To measure the effectiveness of TFT, Dr. Callahan utilized a scale originally developed by psychologist Joseph Wolpe, in which a person reports the subjective level of disturbance on a scale of one to ten, with one being a complete absence of disturbance and ten representing the worst disturbance possible. (Since then, other practitioners have started using a scale of zero to ten.) A SUDS rating is taken at the beginning and ending of each treatment to measure progress. In this sense, TFT practitioners are gathering data each time they do an intervention.

Algorithms

Dr. Callahan developed algorithms, specific sets of points in sequence, to treat common emotional problems. The phobia algorithm in his first book, *Five Minute Phobia Cure: Dr. Callahan's Treatment for Fears, Phobias, and Self-Sabotage,* tapped eye, arm, and collarbone for most phobias. He also developed a diagnostic form of TFT, a way to use muscle testing to diagnose a customized sequence of points needed to clear the disturbance around a more complex problem. Also called point-therapy localization in addition to diagnostic TFT, in ACEP's certification workshop, this process is called making a "customized algorithm."

In each TFT algorithm, the sequence is repeated twice, with the 9 Gamut treatment (on the following page) inserted between the two repetitions, forming a "treatment sandwich." For example, the algorithm for treating trauma adds the Bladder meridian treatment point, the eyebrow, in front of the phobia algorithm mentioned, so the trauma sequence is eyebrow (eb), eye (e), arm (a), collarbone (c). Then the algorithm does the 9 Gamut treatment and finishes with tapping the same sequence (SQ) of eyebrow, eye, arm, and collarbone. A floor to ceiling eye roll (er) at the end of the treatment locks in the healing.

TFT Trauma Algorithm
eb, e, a, c → 9 G → SQ → er

Trade Secrets

Trainees with Dr. Callahan must sign a nondisclosure confidentiality agreement that they will not divulge the secret of diagnostic TFT. As a result, many of his students adapted what they learned into other forms of energy work, and then they broke off from him to market their own techniques. Greg Nicosia, PhD, DCEP, calls his work Thought Energy Synchronization Therapies (TEST), and he was the teacher who introduced me to energy psychology. Fred Gallo, PhD, developed Energy Diagnostic and Treatment

Methods (EDxTM). Larry Nims, PhD, developed an energy psychology technique he named Be Set Free Fast (BSFF). Dr. Callahan's attempt to enforce his agreements in federal court led to the removal of the trademark from TFT and the evolution of several forms of Thought Field Therapy. Thus, TFT became the generic description or term for meridian-based energy psychology therapies that subsequently evolved.

The 9 Gamut Treatment

The 9 Gamut treatment (9G) is a brain-activation sequence that involves tapping the spot in the web between the outer two fingers while doing nine different actions:

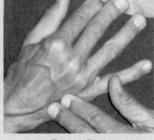

Gamut Spot

1. Close eyes.

2. Open eyes.

3. Move open eyes down to one side.

4. Move open eyes down to the other side.

5. Circle eyes in one direction.

6. Circle eyes in the opposite direction.

7. Hum a few notes.

8. Count to 5.

9. Hum a few more notes.

Explanation: Eyes closed accesses the nonvisual parts of the brain. Eyes open accesses the visual parts. Trauma is stored in the brain by where the eyes were positioned when the trauma occurred, so moving the eyes into different positions may bring up more information for treatment. Humming is an activity of the right hemisphere of the brain, and counting is a left-hemisphere activity.

Emotional Freedom Techniques (EFT)

Gary Craig, another early student of Dr. Callahan, disagreed with him that tapping the meridians in a specific order was necessary. Craig simplified TFT by eliminating specialized algorithms. Instead, EFT begins with a standard treatment for psychological reversal. Originally, the next step was to tap all fourteen meridian points head to toe, several times if necessary. With the progression of EFT development, practitioners now often tap points only on the head and torso, eliminating the points on the hands.

EFT is thus much easier to learn than TFT and is a great technique to send home with clients for self-care. Craig also increased EFT's effectiveness by honing in on the most relevant affirmations to say while tapping. The EFT website at www.emofree.com offers a free download of a basic EFT manual.

Effectiveness

None of the TFT practitioners doubt that meridian tapping sequences work, but people disagree on just why they work. Thousands of case studies have shown rapid, effective, lasting relief from emotional disturbances with TFT and its cousin EFT. As a young science, energy psychology does not yet have a sufficient number of double-blind studies to enable it to be accepted by the American Psychological Association (APA) as an efficacious therapy. Such research is a high priority for the Association for Comprehensive Energy Psychology (ACEP), however, and hard research data are now amassing and are available on the ACEP website at www.energypsych.org.

In my practice, I have witnessed the power of TFT to release trauma, anxiety, and phobias simply, quickly, and permanently. I find it effective upward of 95 percent of the time. The only contraindication for this non-invasive therapy would be a client who is plaintiff in a lawsuit and suing for pain and suffering. Since a TFT treatment would likely significantly reduce the amount of that suffering, getting TFT before the trial might not be in the client's best financial interest, because testimony could be less compelling. Treatment could still be in the client's best overall interest, however.

Diagnostic TFT and Soul Detective Work

When my clients started bringing earthbound spirits to their therapy sessions, I had to figure out how to handle these invisible people. Dr. Edith Fiore's book *The Unquiet Dead* helped me to understand how spirit attachments worked. Then Spirit guided me to this way of using energy psychology tools to help these earthbound spirits heal from their traumas so they could cross into the Light.

Often we are working with strangers, so I need a way to treat a person I cannot see and my client does not know. I almost always make customized TFT algorithms. To date, this method has been 100 percent effective with this invisible population. With an earthbound spirit, I often skip the 9 Gamut treatment and the repetition of the algorithm. Once they get to a state of peace, we get them on their way through the doors of the pearly gates as soon as possible!

One can use other energy therapies to work with earthbound spirits, but most of them take longer. Diagnostic TFT has been my therapeutic lifeline.

TFT Meridian Treatment Points and Associated Emotions

Meridian	Treatment Location/Abbrev.	Positive Emotions*	Negative Emotions*
Lung	Base of the thumbnail, medial side (the outside of the thumb) **t** (thumb)	Tolerance Humility Modesty	Intolerance Disdain Scorn Contempt Prejudice
Large Intestine	Base of the index fingernail, medial side (closest to the thumb) **if** (index fingernail)	Self-worth	Guilt
Stomach	Just below the center of the eye in the indentation on the intraorbital ridge **e** (eye)	Contentment Tranquility	Fear Anxiety Disgust Bitterness Disappointment Greed Hunger Deprivation
Spleen/ Pancreas	Eight fingers' width under the armpit **a**	Security Faith in the future Confidence	Fear Anxiety
Heart	Base of the inside of the little fingernail **lf**	Love Forgiveness	Anger
Small Intestine	Outside edge of the palm where the heart line (the top line) intersects the edge of the hand **h**	Joy	Sadness Sorrow
Bladder	Beginning of the eyebrow **eb**	Peace Harmony	Trauma Restlessness Impatience Frustration
Kidney	Under the clavicle, right next to the sternum **c** (collarbone)	Calm Sexual assuredness	Fear Anxiety Sexual Indecision

TFT Meridian Treatment Points/Emotions, cont.

Meridian	Treatment Location/Abbrev.	Positive Emotions*	Negative Emotions*
Pericardium (the protective lining around the heart)	Base of the middle fingernail on the thumb side **mf**	Relaxation Generosity Renunciation of the past	Jealousy Regret Remorse Sexual Tension Stubbornness
Triple Warmer (also called Triple Heater and Thyroid)	Back of the hand between 4th and 5th metacarpals **G** (gamut spot)	Hope Lightness Elation	Depression Despair Heaviness Grief Hopelessness Despondency Loneliness
Gallbladder	Outer corner of the eyes, in the "pupil seam" where the bone above the eyes meets the bone below **oe** (outer eye)	Love Forgiveness Adoration	Rage Fury Wrath Frustration Indecision
Liver	Upper edge of the 8th rib, directly below the nipple **r** (rib)	Happiness Cheer	Unhappiness
Conception Vessel	In the depression between the lower lip and the chin **ul** (under lip)	Healthy Pride	Shame
Governing Vessel	Under the nose, right above the lips **un** (under nose)	Balanced Power Individuation Healthy Pride	Embarrassment Inferiority Powerlessness

*Based primarily on John Diamond's *Life Energy,* 1985.

Appendix F

Energy Psychology Treatment Modalities

Note: This appendix lists only the therapies that are most familiar to me. There are numerous other amazing energy treatment techniques.

Allergy Antidotes was created by Sandi Radomski, ND, LCSW, DCEP, and specializes in noninvasive treatment of physical and emotional reactions to food and other substances. Radomski and her colleague Paula Shaw also developed Imprint 24-7 labels to wear affirmations on the body. See www. allergyantidotes.com.

Be Set Free Fast (BSFF) was developed by clinical psychologist Larry Nims, PhD, one of the first professionals trained by Dr. Roger Callahan. BSFF simply and gently releases the subconscious unresolved emotional roots and self-limiting belief systems that perpetuate problems. See www. besetfreefast.com.

Bioenergetic Emotional Access Method (BEAM) was developed by Toronto physician Joan Beattie, MD. BEAM uses muscle testing to identify unprocessed trauma, the dysfunctional patterns associated with it, and the toxins embedded with this process. BEAM then peels away these layers, one by one, with a chakra-based procedure and vials imprinted with emotional/ toxin vibrational frequencies. See www.beamtherapy.org.

Dynamic Energetic Healing (DEH) was created by Mary Hammond, MA, LPC, DCEP; Howard Brockman, LCSW; and Nancy Gordon, LCSW. It integrated their learnings from various energy psychology trainers. Brockman published on coupling DEH with his shamanic work, and Hammond published on using the DEH protocol in her clinical practice. See www.dynamic energetichealing.com and www.onedynamicenergetichealing.org.

Earth Release is the work of Rev. Diana Burney, a certified hypnotherapist and an ordained minister who teaches courses on developing intuition. For information on the spiritual clearings she provides for people, dwellings, businesses, animals, and real estate worldwide, see www.earthrelease.com.

Educational Kinesiology, created by Paul Dennison, PhD, and his wife, Gail Dennison, is now known as Edu-K or Brain Gym. One of the pioneers of energy work, Dr. Dennison overcame his own learning challenges and became an internationally known educator. See www.braingym.org.

Emotional Freedom Techniques (EFT), developed by Gary Craig, uses a standard treatment to eliminate psychological reversals, then taps meridian points on the head and torso, top to bottom. For more information on EFT and a free download of the EFT manual, see www.emofree.com.

Energy Diagnostic and Treatment Methods (EDxTM) was developed by Fred Gallo, PhD. Dr. Gallo also developed a short global treatment called Negative Affect Erasing Method (NAEM) or Midline Energy Treatment (MET) that can be used to treat a wide range of psychological problems. A prolific author and the originator of the term "energy psychology," more information on Dr. Gallo is on the ACEP website at www.energypsych.org.

Evolving Thought Field Therapy (EvTFT) is the work of psychologists John H. Diepold Jr., PhD and Sheila S. Bender, PhD, and social worker Victoria Britt, MSW. Dr. Diepold developed a Touch and Breathe (TAB) alternative treatment approach for meridian-based psychotherapies. See www.tftworldwide.com.

Eye Movement Desensitization and Reprocessing (EMDR) was developed by Francine Shapiro, PhD, and uses eye movements or other forms of bilateral stimulation to help the system process information. For more information, see the EMDR Institute website at www.emdr.com.

Family Constellation Work, developed by German psychotherapist Bert Hellinger, teaches that the family as a whole has a soul. Actions of every member impact the whole family system, and leaving anyone out hurts the whole system. See www.hellinger.com.

Focusing, the work of Eugene T. Gendlin, PhD, provides direct access to bodily knowing by "listening" to a physical symptom long enough to interact with it. Staying with these physical clues opens up a wealth of information to use for change. See www.focusing.org.

Guided Self Healing (GSH), developed by Andrew Hahn, PsyD, uses a psychospiritual mind-body framework for healing and transformation. Muscle testing accesses the client's inner wisdom to remove energetic blocks to creating one's dreams and intentions. See www.guidedselfhealing.org.

The Healing Codes, originated by Alex Loyd, ND, PhD, use muscle testing both to find the origin of the stress involved in a problem and to identify a series of hand positions a client can use to activate healing within the body. Practitioners teach clients who get the Healing Codes package how to use these sequences and corresponding affirmations for self-help. See www. thehealingcodes.com.

Healing from the Body Level Up (HBLU), developed by Judith A. Swack, PhD, finds blockages to self-actualization using muscle testing to connect with a person's knowing at the deepest level of being. Then HBLU teaches people how to remove these interfering patterns at all levels: physical, emotional, mental, and spiritual. See www.jaswack.com.

Healing Touch was developed by Janet Mentgen, BSN, RN, HNC, CHTP/I, as a medically based energy therapy training program for nurses. Healing Touch practitioners use their hands in a heart-centered, intentional way to support physical, emotional, mental, and spiritual healing with noninvasive touch to clear, energize, and balance the energy centers and the human biofield. See www.healingtouch.net.

Inner Counselor, a system developed by Ann Nunley, MFA, PhD, and taught at Holos University, connects with "Inner Wisdom" to find the level of consciousness of the true healer that lies within each of us. See www. innercounselor.com for a free download of Nunley's Integration Chart and a discussion of how to use this whole systems approach to self-healing and integration. For Holos University, see www.innercounselor.com and www. holosuniversity.org.

Integrated Energy Therapy (IET), developed by Rev. Stevan Thayer, works with the energy of the angelic realm for healing. Easy to learn and practice, IET identifies areas on the cellular map of the body where trauma and negative emotions are stored and releases them by calling on an angelic ray to do the clearing. See www.LearnIET.com and www.CenterOfBeing.com.

Jaffe-Mellor Technique (JMT) was developed by Carolyn Jaffe, DAc, PhD, and Judith Mellor, RN, PhD. One of the many protocols JMT developed is called Directional Eye Movement Therapy, a technique that restores the flow of energy to scar tissue by testing muscle strength while holding twelve different eye positions and then using eye movements to restore strength to any positions that tested weak. See www.jmttechnique.com.

Lindwall Releasing Process, the work of Isa (1919–2007) and Yolanda Lindwall, is a simple process of releasing negative thoughts, emotions, and memories through affirmative statements of release and then using affirmations to instill positive qualities to replace the negative ones. The technique can be used alone or with a trained Releasing facilitator. See their website for more information at www.lindwallreleasing.org.

NeuroModulation Technique (NMT) is a proprietary form of energy medicine that modulates the nervous system. Developed by chiropractor Leslie Feinberg, NMT is also called "The Feinberg Technique." NMT built on the discoveries of Carolyn Jaffe and Judith Mellor, who developed JMT. Treating the mind like a computer, NMT uses muscle testing to identify unwanted "programs" of illness or outside interference, then reprograms the autonomic control system for proper functioning. NMT has dozens of protocols called "pathways" that outline and treat the parameters of specific problems, based on Dr. Feinberg's detailed understanding of how the mind and the body function. See www.neuromodulationtechnique.com.

Psychoenergetic Healing (PEH), the work of Martin F. Luthke, PhD, DCEP, and Linda Stein-Luthke, brings in the metaphysical realm by calling in Beings of Light and setting therapy inside sacred pyramids of light, anchored at the four corners and the apex by archangels. See www.u-r-light.org.

REMAP, developed by Steve B. Reed, LPC, LMSW, LMFT, DCEP, assesses with client self-report rather than muscle testing and uses all the points on a meridian for treatment. See www.remap.net.

Seemorg Matrix Work, recently renamed **Advanced Integrative Therapy** (AIT), was developed by Asha Clinton. AIT accesses unconscious material through muscle testing and then moves energy through the body's major energy centers (chakras) to eliminate the traumatic roots and residue of targeted problems. For more information on this in-depth approach, which has had success treating personality disorders, dissociative disorders, and obsessive-compulsive disorders, see www.seemorgmatrix.org.

Soul Detective protocols, developed by the author, work with earthbound spirits and past life trauma using the tools of energy psychology, the subject of this book. See www.souldetective.net.

Tao of Presence is a protocol developed by Mayer Kirkpatrick, LAc, based on the premise that the most important gift one can give to another person is Presence. This protocol includes body scanning for somatic clues and a blend of energy psychology methods to release negativity and to come fully into the present moment with one's whole being. Mayer can be contacted at mayer@wildblue.net.

Tapas Acupressure Technique (TAT) was originated by Tapas Fleming, an acupuncturist. TAT holds the hands on the front and back of the head in a specific configuration while focusing on a series of steps to desensitize trauma and bring the system back to balance. For more information and a free download of a self-help booklet on "How to do TAT," see www.tatlife.com.

The Grace Process (TGP), developed by Lori Leyden, PhD, is a transformative spiritual practice for healing our judgments, opening to forgiveness, and expanding our vision for personal and global healing. See www.thegraceprocess.com and www.magical-living.com, and www.create globalhealing.org.

Therapeutic Touch (TT), cofounded by Dolores Krieger and Dora Kunz, balances and promotes the flow of energy in the human energy field. Kunz used her natural ability to perceive blockages and disturbances in the rhythms in a patient's energy field to develop an understanding of the universal healing field from which both patients and healers can draw healing energies. See www.therapeutictouch.org.

Theta Healing dialogues directly with the unconditional love of the Creator for all that is. For more information and the extraordinary story of its developer, Vianna Stibal, see www.ThetaHealing.com.

Thought Energy Synchronization Therapies (TEST) were developed by Greg Nicosia, PhD, BCFE, DCEP. Nicosia trained in many pioneering psychotherapies, including biofeedback, EMDR, and Thought Field Therapy, and has expanded the range of effective application of energy psychology with his understanding of the quantum mechanics behind these healing modalities. See www.thoughtenergy.com.

Thought Field Therapy, now a generic description for meridian-based energy psychology, was originated by psychologist Roger Callahan, PhD. TFT gently taps on points on the meridian system to desensitize the negative emotions associated with a targeted problem and then to install the positive correlates. TFT is highly effective with trauma, phobias, and anxiety disorders. See appendix E and www.tftrx.com.

Whole Healing–Easily and Effectively (WHEE) is a hybrid of EFT and EMDR developed by Daniel J. Benor, MD, who presented a teleclass for ACEP on WHEE on February 20, 2007, available to ACEP members online (www.energypsych.org) in the Teleclass Library. See also Dr. Benor's website: www.wholistichealingresearch.com.

Glossary

Akashic Records: The histories of each lifetime every soul has ever experienced. These former lives for each soul are stacked, like cards in a deck, and can be "opened" and read intuitively.

Algorithm: A sequence of meridian points used to treat a specific issue. The sequence can be as short as one point or as long as fourteen points.

Angelic hierarchy: According to medieval Christian theologians, of the nine ranks of angels, only the bottom two levels interact with people on Earth. The highest level, the Seraphim, circle God's throne constantly, singing praises. The nine ranks of angelic choirs are:

Seraphim

Cherubim

Thrones

Dominions

Virtues

Powers

Principalities

Archangels

Angels

Archangel: Superior in rank to ordinary angels, scripture indicates that the primary duty of the archangels is carrying out God's will as it relates directly to humanity. In this role, they intervene regularly in the affairs of men and women.

Astrals: A common generic term for spirits not incarnate in a body.

Lower astrals: A place like a bar may attract lower astral earthbound spirits such as people who had been alcoholics. Mediums may also attract lower astrals by opening themselves to the spirit world without adequate spiritual protection. Some mediums take on the job of soul rescue as a fulfilling way to help humankind.

Lost astral: Another term for earthbound spirits.

Higher astrals: Spirits in heaven, our ancestors, and helping guides. The place people visit during near-death experiences is the higher astral plane. Often the soul visiting this plane does not want to return to the Earth plane because of the immense love that flows in the higher realms.

Aura: The aura includes all of the layers of the biofield. Specialized photography can capture images of the light of the aura emitted by the human energy system. Some people are able to see the aura in the form of emanations of colored light extending outward from the physical body.

Bardo: A place identified by Tibetan Buddhism where the soul goes between death and the next incarnation.

Beings of Light: Figures from the spiritual realm appearing to people to communicate comfort, guidance, and unconditional love. These figures may include angels, ascended masters, deceased loved ones, and perhaps even beings from other planets. People who have out-of-body experiences or near-death experiences frequently encounter these Beings of Light.

Biofield: A field of energy that surrounds and interpenetrates the physical body with a number of distinctive layers: physical, etheric, emotional, mental, intuitive, and spiritual. The size and shape of the biofield change with one's state of health. When vitality is strong, the biofield is larger. With illness, the biofield becomes smaller and unbalanced.

Chakra: A Sanskrit word meaning "wheel." These wheels of energy, also called energy centers, run along the midline of the body. The root chakra at the bottom and the crown chakra at the top have just one vortex of energy each. The five chakras between (sacral, solar plexus, heart, throat, and brow) have a vortex at both the front and the back of the chakra.

Crossing into the Light: The passageway after death through the veil between the worlds into a higher vibrational plane of existence. Often, our families, friends, pets, or spirit guides greet us in this higher plane.

Devic realm: A term referring to the plane of existence of the Devas, a Sanskrit term meaning "the shining ones," which include angels, fairies, and nature spirits. The Devic realm is the creative force behind all that manifests on the Earth plane. Those who incarnate from the Devic realm value love, peace, and harmony, and they respect and care for the environment.

Dowsing: An ancient craft used to obtain information not accessible through ordinary means. See appendix B.

Earthbound spirit: A discarnate person who has not yet crossed into the Light and remains bound to the gravitational field of the Earth, also called a wayward, a spirit-walker, a lost astral, or a ghost.

Earthbound spirit attachment: The attachment of an earthbound spirit to the energy field of a living person.

Etheric body: An energetic template determining the form of the physical body, the etheric body is the innermost layer of the human biofield. If life energy is blocked in any portion of this template, physical illness may result.

Feng shui: The ancient Chinese practice of placement and arrangement of space to achieve harmony with the environment.

Guardian angel: An angelic presence with us from birth through death, supporting us with guidance.

Human energy field: The interlocking octaves of energy surrounding and interpenetrating the physical body. Nonphysical layers of the biofield include the etheric body, the emotional body, the mental body, the intuitive body, and the spiritual body.

Inner child: 1) Part of the personality fixated at an early stage of development. 2) In dissociative identity disorder, trauma carried by the inner child splits from the core personality. These split-off parts, alternate personalities with younger ages, are commonly called "alters." 3) In normal development, psychiatrist Eric Berne's model of transactional analysis identifies three ego states: child, parent, and adult. The child ego state is the structure containing the inner child.

Karma: The idea, originating from Hindu belief, that both the good and the evil a person does in one lifetime will return, either in this life or in a later one.

Kundalini: The Sanskrit word for "snake" or "serpent power." According to Hindu texts, this latent form of spiritual energy lies coiled at the base of the spine. As spiritual practices such as yoga, prayer, and meditation awaken Kundalini, it flows upward through the chakras to its final goal of union with the Absolute.

Numinous: An adjective describing a sense of awe-inspiring wonder at sensing the presence of God or spiritual beings—a sense of "otherness" about the situation.

Past life: A previous incarnation of the soul essence.

Psychoenergetic reversal: A limiting belief that may be held either at the conscious or unconscious level that blocks a client from reaching a treatment goal, also called a "barrier to success." For example, a client may feel undeserving of healing or feel that reaching a goal is not safe.

Self-testing: Using kinesiology to test the strength of one's own selected indicator muscle. Self-testing can be helpful in determining the proper dosage of nutritional supplements, diagnosing oneself for problems, and surrogate testing for others when working over the telephone.

Soul Detective: A therapist using energy therapy to detect what is happening at the soul level, including assessing for the presence of earthbound spirit attachments, soul loss, past life trauma, and other nonphysical energetic disturbances.

Soul retrieval: Recovering the part of one's soul energy that has been locked in trauma. Traditionally, shamans have done this work, but many forms of energy therapy also retrieve soul loss.

Spiritual body: The multiple layers of nonphysical energy that connect the human to the Divine. Through our spiritual biofield, whose highest octaves reach to the ends of the Universe, we are all connected in the web of life.

Surrogate muscle testing: Muscle testing one person for someone else, as in testing a mother for her infant or a therapist self-testing for a client in a telephone session.

Third eye: The energy center related to the brow chakra identified in yoga as "the seat of the soul." Sometimes called "the Celestial Eye," this organ of perception located between and slightly above the physical eyes gathers psychic information from nonphysical realms.

Bibliography

Baldwin, W. (1995). *Spirit Releasement Therapy*. Terra Alta, WV: Headline Books.

Benziger, I. K., and A. Sohn. (1989). *The Art of Using Your Whole Brain*. Rockwall, TX: KBA Publishing.

Bischof, M. (1998). *Biophotons: The Light in our Cells*. Frankfurt, Germany: Zweitausendeins (available only in German).

Bolen, J. S. (1984). *Goddesses in Everywoman: Powerful Archetypes for Women*. New York: Harper & Row.

_____. (1989). *Gods in Everyman: Archetypes that Shape Men's Lives*. New York: Harper & Row.

Bowman, C. (1988). *Children's Past Lives: How Past Life Memories Affect Your Child*. New York: Bantam Books.

Braden, G. (2006). *Secrets of the Lost Mode of Prayer: The Hidden Power of Beauty, Blessings, Wisdom, and Hurt*. Carlsbad, CA: Hay House.

Brennan, B. A. (1987). *Hands of Light: A Guide to Healing Through the Human Energy Field*. New York: Bantam.

Callahan, R. (1985). *Five Minute Phobia Cure: Dr. Callahan's Treatment for Fears, Phobias, and Self-Sabotage*. Wilmington, DE: Enterprise.

Callahan, R., and R. Trubo. (2002). *Tapping the Healer Within: Using Thought Field Therapy to Instantly Conquer Your Fears, Anxieties, and Emotional Distress.* New York: McGraw-Hill.

Church, D. (1994). *Facing Death, Finding Love: The Healing Power of Grief and Loss in One Family's Life.* Lower Lake, CA: Aslan Publishing.

————. (2007). *The Genie in Your Genes: Epigenetic Medicine and the New Biology of Intention.* Fulton, CA: Elite Books.

Dawa-Samdup, K., and W. Y. Evans-Wentz. (2000). *The Tibetan Book of the Dead.* New York: Oxford University Press.

Dennison, P., and G. Dennison. (1982). *Brain Gym: Simple Activities for Whole Brain Learning.* Ventura, CA: Edu-Kinesthetics.

Diamond, J. (1979). *Your Body Doesn't Lie.* New York: Warner.

————. (1985). *Life Energy: Using the Meridians to Unlock the Hidden Power of Your Emotions.* St. Paul, MN: Paragon House.

Durlacher, J. V. (1997). *Freedom from Fear Forever: The Acu-Power Way to Overcoming Your Fear, Phobias, and Inner Problems.* Tempe, AZ: Van Ness Publishing.

Eden, D., with D. Feinstein. (1998). *Energy Medicine: Balance Your Body's Energies for Optimal Health, Joy, and Vitality.* New York: Jeremy P. Tarcher/Putnam.

Feinstein, D. (2004). *Energy Psychology Interactive: Rapid Interventions for Lasting Change.* Ashland, OR: Innersource.

Fiore, E. (1987). *The Unquiet Dead: A Psychologist Treats Spirit Possession.* Garden City, NY: Doubleday.

Franco, D. P. (2007). *The Dynamics of Our Sixth Sense: Psychic and Mediumistic Phenomena in the Light of Spiritism.* Bahia, Brazil: Pathway to Redemption Spiritist Center.

Gallo, F. (1998). *Energy Psychology: Explorations at the Interface of Energy, Cognition, Behavior, and Health.* Boca Raton, FL: CRC Press.

Gallo, F., and H. Vincenzi. (2000). *Energy Tapping.* Oakland, CA: New Harbinger Publications.

Gerber, R. (1988). *Vibrational Medicine: New Choices for Healing Ourselves.* Santa Fe, NM: Bear & Co.

Guggenheim, B., and J. Guggenheim. (1995). *Hello from Heaven!* Longwood, FL: ADC Project.

Hammond, M. (2008). *Living Your Soul's Purpose: Wellness and Passion with Energy Psychology and Energy Medicine.* Denver, CO: Outskirts Press.

Harner, M. (1990). *The Way of the Shaman.* San Francisco, CA: Harper & Row.

Hawkins, D. R. (1995). *Power Versus Force: An Anatomy of Consciousness, The Hidden Determinants of Human Behavior.* Sedona, AZ: Veritas.

Hellinger, B. (2001). *Love's Own Truths: Bonding and Balancing in Close Relationships.* Phoenix, AZ: Zeig, Tucker & Theisen.

Hill, G. L. (2005). *People Who Don't Know They're Dead.* Boston: Weiser.

Hover-Kramer, D. (2002). *Creative Energies: Integrative Energy Psychotherapy for Self-Expression and Healing.* New York: W. W. Norton.

Hover-Kramer, D., and M. Murphy. (2007, rev. ed.). *Creating Right Relationships: A Practical Guide to Ethics in Energy Therapies.* Cave Junction, OR: Behavioral Health Consultants.

Ingerman, S. (1991). *Soul Retrieval: Mending the Fragmented Self.* San Francisco, CA: HarperSanFrancisco.

Jung, C. G. (1989). *Memories, Dreams, Reflections.* New York: Vintage Books.

Karpinski, G. (1991). *Where Two Worlds Touch: Spiritual Rites of Passage.* New York: Ballantine Books.

———. (2001). *Barefoot on Holy Ground: Twelve Lessons in Spiritual Craftsmanship.* New York: Ballantine Wellspring.

Lambrou, P., and G. Pratt. (2000). *Instant Emotional Healing: Acupressure for the Emotions.* New York: Broadway Books.

Losey, M. B. (2007). *The Children of Now: Crystalline Children, Indigo Children, Star Kids, Angels on Earth, and the Phenomenon of Transitional Children.* Franklin Lakes, NJ: Career Press.

Luthke, M., and L. Stein-Luthke. (2001). *Beyond Psychotherapy: Introduction to Psychoenergetic Healing*. Chagrin Falls, OH: Expansion Publishing.

Milliren, T. (1997). *Ancient Mysteries of Healing Discovered*. New Florence, PA: Angel 99.

Moody, R. (2001). *Life After Life: Investigation of a Phenomenon—Survival of Bodily Death*. New York: HarperSanFrancisco.

Narby, J. (1999). *The Cosmic Serpent: DNA and the Origins of Knowledge*. New York: Tarcher.

Nelson, P. (2002). *Left for Dead: A Young Man's Search for Justice for the USS Indianapolis*. New York: Delacorte Press.

Newton, M. (1994). *Journey of Souls: Case Studies of Life Between Lives*. St. Paul, MN: Llewellyn.

———. (2000). *Destiny of Souls: New Case Studies of Life Between Lives*. Llewellyn.

Ring, K., and S. Cooper. (1999). *Mindsight: Near-Death and Out-of-Body Experiences in the Blind*. Palo Alto, CA: Institute of Transpersonal Psychology.

Ritchie, G. G. (1978). *Return from Tomorrow*. Waco, TX: Chosen Books.

Ritchie, G. G., and I. Stevenson. (1998). *Ordered to Return: My Life After Dying*. Charlottesville, VA: Hampton Roads.

Roberts, J., and R. F. Butts. (1994). *Seth Speaks: The Eternal Validity of the Soul*. San Rafael, CA: New World Library.

Siegel, B. (1986). *Love, Medicine, and Miracles: Lessons Learned About Self-Healing from a Surgeon's Experience with Exceptional Patients*. New York: Harper and Row.

———. (2003). *365 Prescriptions for the Soul: Daily Messages of Inspiration, Hope, and Love*. Novato, CA: New World Library.

———. (2006). *Love, Magic, and Mudpies: Raising Your Kids to Feel Loved, Be Kind, and Make a Difference*. New York: Rodale.

Snow, R. L. (1999). *Looking for Carroll Beckwith: The True Story of a Detective's Search for His Past Life*. Emmaus, PA: Daybreak Books.

Stein-Luthke, L., and M. Luthke. (1998). *Angels and Other Beings of Light: They are Here to Help You! A Discourse from the Ascended Master St. Germain*. Chagrin Falls, OH: Expansion Publishing.

Stibal, V. (2000). *Go Up and Work with God*. Idaho Falls, ID: Rolling Thunder.

———. (2006). *Theta Healing: Go Up and Seek God/Go Up and Work with God*, rev. and exp. Idaho Falls, ID: Rolling Thunder.

Stone, B. (1994). *Cancer as Initiation: Surviving the Fire*. Chicago: Open Court.

Webber, M. C., and W. D. Webber. (1994). *A Rustle of Angels: Stories About Angels in Real Life and Scripture*. Grand Rapids, MI: Zondervan.

Weiss, B. L. (1988). *Many Lives, Many Masters*. New York: Simon & Schuster.

———. (1993). *Through Time into Healing*. New York: Simon & Schuster.

Whisenant, W. F. (1994). *Psychological Kinesiology: Changing the Body's Beliefs*. Kailua, HI: Monarch Butterfly Productions.

Index

Brain-heart integration exercise, 287–289

C

chakra, 30, 83, 91, 155–157, 159, 182, 184, 194, 200, 204–206, 218, 223, 230–232, 240–241, 254, 266, 281, 303, 307, 311, 312, 313

Chiron, the wounded healer, 85, 99, 219

Christ, 74, 85, 88, 118, 122, 145, 169, 171, 187, 263

Clinical Kinesiology, 12, 291

collarbone breathing exercise, 285–286

Council of Souls (Soul Council), 115, 120, 126, 257

Cross Crawl exercise, 286–288

crossing into the Light, 33, 109, 131, 189, 194–198, 201, 203–204, 255–256, 259, 311

customized meridian tapping sequence, 20–21, 32–33, 39, 49, 59, 64, 66, 73, 76–78, 87, 97, 107, 109, 114, 120, 160–161, 164, 171, 177, 193, 214, 223–224, 235, 249, 251, 255, 266, 272, 297, 300

D

Devic realm, 65, 311

discarnate spirit (*see also* earthbound spirit), 1, 7–8, 13, 22, 26, 30, 63–65, 69, 178–179, 191, 195, 311

dissociation, dissociate, 12, 87–88, 106, 109, 126, 140, 222–223, 243, 307, 312,

dowsing, 12, 16, 58, 167, 275–279, 282, 311

dreams, nightmares, x–xi, 5, 15, 29, 30, 32, 35–38, 42–43, 45–46, 55, 161, 168, 173, 175, 221–223, 248, 317

Dynamic Energetic Healing (DEH), 304

E

Earth Release work, 230, 304

earthbound spirit, earthbound spirit attachment (*see also* discarnate spirit), x, 2, 7–9, 12–13, 17, 21–22, 25–26, 31, 33, 35, 37–38, 41, 45, 49, 51, 58, 63, 73–75, 83, 101, 107–108, 167–168, 173, 175–201, 203, 206, 213–215, 222, 226, 230, 250, 252, 255–257, 259, 293, 300, 307, 310, 311, 312

Educational Kinesiology, 20, 278, 304

Electromagnetic field (EMF), 26, 155, 156, 187, 276

K

L

M

N

O

P